Selections from

HELLENISTIC PHILOSOPHY

Selections from

HELLENISTIC PHILOSOPHY

Gordon H. Clark

BUTLER UNIVERSITY

 New York

APPLETON-CENTURY-CROFTS

DIVISION OF MEREDITH PUBLISHING COMPANY

694-1

LIBRARY OF CONGRESS CARD NUMBER:

40 – 31306

PRINTED IN THE UNITED STATES OF AMERICA

E-19350

Preface

THE PRESENT VOLUME undertakes to supply college courses
with source material in the Hellenistic age. Such material
for the Presocratics is found in Milton C. Nahm's *Selections from Early Greek Philosophy,* Fourth Edition.

The problems inherent in such an undertaking vary in
degree and in kind, and they have been met as they arose.

The first chapter is a condensation of Lucretius'
De Rerum Natura into one sixth of its original length.
Permission has been granted by, and grateful apprecia-
tion is addressed to, Basil Blackwell, Publisher, Oxford,
for the privilege of using the excellent translation of
Thomas Jackson.

To offer adequate selections from the Stoics was a
more difficult matter. The well-known translations in the
Loeb Classical Library might have been satisfactory for
some Stoic fragments had the translators been less willing to sacrifice the technical meaning of the original to
the literary ease of the translation.

For example, while one hesitates to criticize the editor
of the remarkable edition of *Aristotle: De Anima,* yet
the passage in Diogenes Laertius VII 50, reproduced in
Arnim II 55, Διαφέρει δὲ φαντασία καὶ φάντασμα, R. D. Hicks
translates, "There is a difference between the process and

the outcome of presentation." For this, I have preferred, because of the preceding paragraph in Arnim, the rendering, "There is a difference between representation and illusion." Again, in Diogenes Laertius VII 66, given in Arnim II 186, the three words, πρᾶγμα ὅμοιον ἀξιώματι, are turned into the impossible clause, "whether that to which these terms are applied be a thing or a judgment." In the next paragraph, however, the translator has felicitously rendered the same three words, slightly rearranged, by the phrase, "a quasi-proposition." This I have accepted.

From the same set of translations another example may be taken. In Sextus Empiricus, *Adv. Math.* VII 151, or Arnim II 90, R. G. Bury translates the phrase, τρία γὰρ εἶναί φασιν ἐκεῖνοι τὰ συζυγοῦντα ἀλλήλοις, as, "For the latter assert that there are three criteria." The word *criteria* does not occur in the text, and the paragraph goes on to show that not all three mental states but just one of them is the criterion. Hence I have translated it, "For they say that three things are joined together."

Unwilling to reproduce the faults of existing translations, the present volume offers the opinions of the Stoics in a new rendering. This procedure has the additional advantage that it permits the inclusion of material not hitherto done into English. The numbering of the selections refers to Arnim's *Stoicorum Veterum Fragmenta.*

The material from Plutarch and Philo, their chronological order inverted because Philo contributes to a new religious development, is taken from the Bohn Classical Library.

Hermes Trismegistus was translated in its entirety by the late William Romaine Newbold, Professor of Philosophy at the University of Pennsylvania until his death in

1926, though he never saw it through to publication. Since I was studying it with him at the time of his death, Mrs. Newbold most graciously gave me his copy with its interleaved translation and extensive notes. The four tractates here reproduced and the few notes attached are a belated and wholly inadequate indication of the work he accomplished on this mystic literature.

Mackenna's translation of Plotinus is practically the only one in English. While it often evinces a clear appreciation of Plotinus' meaning, its style—the awe-inspiring barbarisms better received by mystics than by more sober persons—and its occasional inaccuracies make a new translation desirable. One illustration may be found in IV vii 10, lines 18–19: ἀνάγκη θεῖον τὸ τοιοῦτον εἶναι, ἅτε θείων μετὸν αὐτῷ, διὰ συλλένειαν καὶ τὸ ὁμοούσιον. Mackenna has, "What possesses these [qualities of wisdom and virtue] must be divine by its very capacity of the divine, the token of kinship and identical substance." The excellent French translation of Bréhier, if less florid, is more accurate: "Un tel être doit être divin, puisqu'il a part aux choses divines, grâce à sa parenté et à sa communauté d'essence avec elles." The venture of the present volume in translating this sentence is, "Such a being is necessarily divine, inasmuch as the divine is with it because they belong to the same genus and are consubstantial." For further remarks on the translations of Bréhier and Mackenna, see *The New Scholasticism*, Vol. XII, No. 1, Jan. 1938. The translation offered here is more literal than either of the other two; its interpretation, like its phraseology, profits from both, but is thoroughly independent.

Contents

Selections from

HELLENISTIC PHILOSOPHY

EPICUREANISM

THE Hellenistic age is clearly marked off from the previous Hellenic period by significant events both in politics and in philosophy. The long period of seven hundred years which began with Homer, which saw the rise of nationalistic, independent city-states, which gave birth to great art and literature, which in its last three centuries developed the first true science and philosophy, and which finally in its decline eclipsed its own grandeur by producing Plato and Aristotle, came to an end with the latter's death and the extinction of independent, political life under Alexander. The era that followed, ending with the death of the gods under Constantine and their philosophic obsequies in A.D. 529, was of approximately the same duration. In politics it begins with the vigorous expansion of Rome and ends in the barbarian invasions. In philosophy, as the schools of Plato and Aristotle become less important, Epicureanism and Stoicism also evince the vigor of a new life; they then become popular and stagnate, until Plotinus (A.D. 205–270) by gathering together all the strands of the Greek tradition gives late antiquity a philosophic golden age. In the meantime there had come into the world a new religious force which finally ended the Greek schools. It is therefore erroneous to suppose, as is often done, that the years 306 B.C.–A.D. 529 are merely a time of decay. From the standpoint of Greek political history, to be sure, the Roman legions made such a judgment true; from the standpoint of pure Greek culture, the admixture of Roman civilization, and later of eastern religious ideas, made it plausible; but to compare, or, rather, to contrast every philosophic writer with Plato and Aristotle, and cry, "Decay," is such a harsh procedure that no period of seven or eight hundred years could on that basis be judged otherwise. Surely, decay, to be called such, ought not to speed so slowly. And it is but just to note that while we have complete volumes from Plato and Aristotle, many of the best philosophers of the Hellenistic age are known to us only by fragmentary quotations and polemic criticisms which fail to transmit their true worth.

There is another common misunderstanding of the Graeco-Roman period. This later age is frequently contrasted with the Pre-Socratic interest in science, and with the Platonic and Aristotelian interest in epistemology and metaphysics, as being exclusively occupied with ethics. Undoubtedly the Hellenistic age is dominated by an interest in ethics and religion, and Marcus Aurelius and some others are exclusively so occupied; but it is not true that the age produced no scientists or cosmologists. Rather, as in the cases of Aristarchus and Ptolemy, a science became so specialized that it is no longer to be regarded as philosophy, and yet it is a credit to the age. In medicine, too, there is the discovery that the nervous system centers in the brain and not in the heart; there are collected important observations on special diseases, as, for example, that malaria may cure syphilis; and Galen tried to work out a theory of induction. Within the field more strictly called philosophical, with the Epicureans and with the Stoics, it is not true that everything but

the restricted sphere of ethics was regarded as an unnecessary annoyance. While ethical interest was dominant—
owing perhaps to the popular diffusion of philosophic
discussion beyond the aristocratic isolation of the schools
—yet all the better thinkers quite well appreciated the
necessity of a unified system integrating all phases of
philosophic investigation.

If any school can be charged with a narrow ethical interest, it will be the Epicurean. The following pages will
show why. And yet, when one surveys the great amount
of scientific detail in Lucretius' *De Rerum Natura*—the
Stoics placed still more emphasis on logic and physics—
it will be seen that even for the Epicureans ethics, nar-
rowly understood, was not the whole thing. It was, however, the chief thing. Underlying all the teaching of Epicurus, who in the year 306 B.C. came to Athens and
founded the school which bore his name, are the practical or ethical propositions that the aim of philosophy is
to promote happiness, and its more arresting converse,
that all promoting of happiness is philosophy. How Epicurus understood this in detail is preserved for us in
Diogenes Laertius' (A.D. 225) *Lives and Opinions of Emi-
nent Philosophers,* Book X. This work includes three let-
ters from Epicurus' own hand and his *Principal Doctrines,* which are articles used for catechetical instruction
in the school; but the poem of Lucretius (94–55 B.C.), reduced to one sixth its size in the following selection, is
the most ample source of Epicureanism.

Since no one is likely to achieve happiness without
taking thought, some attention must be paid to logic—
or perhaps it would be less ambiguous to say epistemology, for there is no such thing as formal logic in the

Epicurean system. The epistemology required consists in showing how truth can be extracted from sensation. Because pleasure and pain are sensations, such a thoroughgoing hedonistic system as Epicureanism is virtually forced to base truth on sensation. And to a skepticism which in denying the possibility of truth makes a fixed rule of life impossible, the Epicureans reply that neither reason nor other sensations can overthrow the truth of a sensation. Reason cannot do so because it is founded on sensation. One sensation cannot overthrow the truth of another sensation because each relates to a different object. That which immediately affects the sense is not a book or a tree, but an image, which, thrown off from the surface of the book or tree, traverses the distance to the eye and enters it to produce the sensation. Since the objects of the outer world constantly emit images; since, too, these are modified by the medium through which they travel; no sensation can contradict another. Thus a firm basis for truth is established. From repeated sensations, by coincidence, analogy, similarity, and some admixture of reason,—not clearly explained—there arise notions or concepts, which as bases of classification are required for any further knowledge. Then come opinions or judgments, and so all knowledge.

The attainability of truth is necessary for a happy life, but beyond proving this point the study of logic is useless. Physics, however, is more closely related to the causes of pleasure and pain, and therefore requires more careful consideration. Yet even in physics there are many detailed questions which do not need definite solutions. The knowledge of the exact motions of the sun and the planets contributes nothing to our happiness; one may suggest several possible explanations of these phenomena, any one of which permits us to live a tranquil life; hence it is unnecessary to determine exactly which explanation is the true one. But while one need not choose from among the various theories that do not disturb our peace of mind, there is one world view which is the cause of more pain and evil than anything else this world boasts of. To the refutation of this view the study of physics must be vigorously directed.

The source of most, if not all, human ills is religion. Religion mainly consists in the belief that the gods reward and punish mankind; these punishments, foreshadowed in this life, are meted out in full severity in the life after death; hence religion begets the fear of death, which in turn makes a happy life impossible.

So serious is this matter that the truth cannot be made a matter of induction or demonstration; the problem can be met only by postulation and assumption. "At the start we must posit this principle, *viz.* nothing ever comes from nothing by divine power." To admit a controlling providence would be to destroy the unity of nature; if God governs the world, anything could arise from anything, and all orderly processes would be disrupted. As there is no creation, so too there is no annihilation; and from this Epicurus deduces the indestructibility of the atom.

Corresponding, therefore, to the negative postulate denying creation, there is the positive proposition that all phenomena are to be explained in terms of atoms and void. With an infinite number of atoms, of a limited number of shapes,—for if shapes were infinite, sizes would increase until there would be an atom large

enough to see [1]—in an infinite space, the present condition of the world is but one chance arrangement among
the infinite arrangements already realized. The system is
ateleological.

To justify ethics, however, and to preserve human responsibility, this ateleological system is not strictly mechanical. Man must be free from mechanical law, and
since he is composed only of atoms, atoms also must be
free. The very fact that there is a world, with its objects
compounded of atoms, rather than an army of discon-
nected atoms all falling separately in a straight downward direction, is owing to occasional, uncaused deviations of atoms from their straight paths. Such deviations
or declinations produce collisions and vortices among the
falling atoms, and these vortices grow into a world.
Similar deviations guarantee freedom for man. Previously
the argument was that providence must be denied to
maintain cosmic order; now cosmic order, or at least
universal causation, must be denied to give man liberty.

Developing a science based on these fundamental principles Epicurus attempted to remove the three greatest,
perhaps the three only, impediments to a happy life. The
first obstacle is pessimism, which can result only in an
unhappy consciousness. But freedom from mechanical
law, obtained by rejecting uniform causality, gives the
feeling that our choices and endeavors count, and that
life is worth living. "The wise man," Epicurus says in his
letter to Menoeceus, "does not deprecate life . . . the
thought of life is no offence to him. . . . We must remember that the future is neither wholly ours nor wholly
not ours, so that neither must we count upon it as

1. This peculiar reasoning is found in Lucretius II 478 ff.

quite certain to come nor despair of it as quite certain not to come." Some pain is inevitable, but our control of conditions is sufficient to rule out pessimism.

Second, by showing, as Lucretius does at length, that all phenomena can be explained without recourse to divine providence, the fear of the gods with its superstition and attendant inquietude is removed. It is under this heading that all the specifically scientific investigations must be placed. But while the ethical motive dominates, and while the extent to which investigation should be pursued is limited by its purpose, still the Epicureans did not regard it sufficient to assert atoms, deny providence, and let it go at that. They recognized that it was incumbent upon them to consider many particular phenomena and to explain each concretely without reference to theology. This involves more detail perhaps than the motive leads one to expect.

The third great obstacle to happiness, strictly related to the other two, namely the fear of death, is overcome by the same methods. Death can cause us the pain of fear now while we are living only if it will cause us pain in an afterlife. Obviously it is unreasonable to fear a future event which will not pain us when it happens. And a thorough study of psychology shows this to be the case. Man is nothing but a collection of atoms; their motions are sufficient to explain animation, sensation, and thought. To be sure man has a soul and a spirit but they are neither immaterial nor immortal. Consequently, when death comes the atoms disperse, and man as a sensitive being no longer exists to suffer either the wrath of the gods or any other unknown evil. "Exercise thyself in these and kindred precepts day and night, both by thyself and with him who is like unto thee; then never, either in waking or in dream, wilt thou be disturbed, but wilt live as a god among men. For man loses all semblance of mortality by living in the midst of immortal blessings."

EPICUREANISM

LUCRETIUS: ON THE NATURE OF THINGS [1]

Book One

I 1–10. Mother of the Aeneadae, delight of men and gods, life-giving Venus, who beneath the gliding constellations of the sky dost fill with life the ship-conveying sea, the corn-producing lands, since every kind of living thing conceived through thee springs up and sees the light of day; from thee, O goddess, thee, the winds take flight, from thee and thy approach the clouds of heav'n; for thee the levels of the ocean smile, and the calmed sky shines with a widespread light.

I 62–101. When human life lay ignominiously before men's eyes upon the ground, trodden beneath the heavy foot of Superstition, who revealed her head from heaven's tract and threatened mortals from above with dreadful mien, a man of Greece first dared to lift up mortal eyes against her and withstand her to her face. Him neither the traditions nor the lightnings of the gods could daunt, nor heaven's threatening thunder, but they spurred the more the eager manhood of his mind, so that he longed to be the first to break the close-set bars of Nature's gates. Therefore his living energy of mind prevailed; outside the flaming ramparts of the world he far advanced and traversed with his mind and understanding the immeasurable All; whence he triumphantly reports to us what can, what cannot, be created; on what principle, in short, each

1. Translated by Thomas Jackson and used with the permission of Basil Blackwell, Publisher.

thing has had its faculty defined, its boundary deep-fixed. Thus Superstition in her turn is overcome and trodden underfoot; to us his victory gives equality with heaven.

Yet this I fear in dealing with these matters, lest you haply may suspect that you are being taught the rudiments of impious reason and are walking in the way of wickedness. Whereas 'tis she, this Superstition, who too oft has been the mother of accursed and impious deeds; as when at Aulis the selected leaders of the Greeks, their first of men, stained shamefully the altar of the Trivian Maid with Iphianassa's blood. For, when the sacred fillet was put round her virgin tresses, spreading equally on both sides of her cheeks, and she beheld her father standing sorrowful before the altar, the attendants near him trying to conceal the knife, and all her fellow-countrymen in tears at sight of her, then, dumb with terror, sinking on her knees, she sought the ground. Nor could it profit her, poor girl, in such an hour that she had been the first to call the monarch by the name of father: lifted in men's hands, all-trembling she was carried to the altar, not that, when the customary sacrificial rite was ended, she might be escorted by the ringing bridal-song, but that, in wedlock's very season, she might guiltily (though guiltless) die, sad victim, slaughtered by a father's hand, in order that a happy and auspicious outlet might be granted to his fleet. Such wickedness could Superstition prompt.

I 146–173. This terror then and darkness of the mind must be dispersed, not by the sunbeams and bright shafts of day, but by the spectacle and plan of nature: and the principles thereof shall start for me with this, that nothing ever is begotten out of nought by power divine. Indeed fear holds all mortals in so tight a grasp, because they see that things are done in heav'n and earth, the cause of which they can in nowise see, and so believe that they are done by deity. And therefore, when we see that nothing can be born from nothing, we shall soon from that more clearly see what we are seeking, both the source from which each thing can be created and the way in which all things are done without the agency of gods.

For, if things came from nothing, every kind of thing

could then be born from all; none would need seed. First,
men could spring up from the sea, the scaly tribe from land,
and birds be hatched from out the sky: cattle and other flocks,
and all the races of wild-beasts, would populate tilled lands
and waste with undetermined offspring. The same fruits
would not stay upon their wonted trees, but would be changed:
all trees could bear all fruits. For, since each thing would have
no generative particles, how could there be for things a fixed
creatress? But, as it is, because the things are each created from
fixed seed, they are produced and go forth to the coasts of light
from that wherein their substance and their first-beginnings
are; and all things cannot be begotten out of all things for
this reason, that in each fixed thing a separate faculty resides.

I 215–220. Moreover, Nature breaks up everything again into
its particles and does not bring things down to nothing. For,
if each thing in all its parts were mortal, it would suddenly
be snatched from view and perish. For there would be no
need of any force to cause disunion in its parts and loosen
their connections.

I 334–345. There is then untouched space or empty void. For,
if it were not so, in nowise could things move; for that which
is the property of matter, to obstruct and hinder, would belong
to all things always; so that nothing would begin to give it
room. But, as it is, o'er seas and lands and through the heights
of heav'n we plainly see that many things are moved in many
ways, by various laws; which things, if void were not, would
not so much be robbed of restless motion as would never have
been born in any way at all, since matter, packed all round,
would be at rest.

I 358–369. Again, why do we see one thing exceed another
in its weight, although it has no larger size? For, if a ball of
wool has just as much of substance as a ball of lead, it ought
to hang as heavy, since it is the property of matter to press all
things downwards, whereas void remains of weightless nature.
Therefore a thing of equal size, but seen to be less heavy than
another, sure enough gives notice that more void is in it; on
the other hand, the heavier declares that it is more substance
and less void by far. So then, what I am with keen reason

seeking sure enough exists, mixed up with things; this I call void.

I 419-421. —all nature then, so far as it has being of itself, consists of two things; there is matter; there is void, in which the matter lies and moves in different directions.

I 445-448. Moreover, there is nothing which you could describe as severed from all matter and disjoined from void, forming a kind of third within the list of natures.

I 503-550. First, since there has been found to be a two-fold nature of two widely differing things, of matter, and of space in which each thing is carried on, each must exist both for and of itself, unmixed. For, wheresoever there is empty space, which I call void, there matter cannot be; again, wherever matter is, there empty void can by no means exist. The primal particles are therefore solid and exempt from void. Besides, since void is in begotten things, there must be solid matter round about it; nor can anything be demonstrated by true reason to contain and harbour void within its substance, if you do not grant that what imprisons it is solid. Further, it can be nothing but the union of matter which can keep enclosed the void of things. That matter therefore which consists of solid substance can last on for ever, when the rest of things pass into dissolution.

Once more, if there were no such thing as void, the All would then be solid; on the other hand, if there were not fixed particles to fill all places that they occupy, then all that is would be composed of void and empty space. And therefore, sure enough, matter has been alternately marked off from void, since there is neither utter fullness, nor yet utter vacancy. So then there are fixed particles, such as can separate void space from full. These can be neither broken up by blows dealt from without, nor penetrated and unwoven deep within, nor loosed by any other manner of assault, as I have shown to you already a short while ago. For without void nothing seems able to be crushed or broken or be split in two by cutting, nor to take in either moisture, permeating cold, or penetrating heat, by which three forces all things are destroyed. The more void too each thing contains, the more completely it gives way when these assail it. Therefore, if there are primal particles, as I have shown there are, exempt from void and solid, these must be eternal, then all things ere this had utterly returned to nothing, and whatever things we see had been reborn from nothing. But, since I have already shown that nothing can be born from nothing, and that what has been begotten cannot be recalled to nothing, first-beginnings must be of immortal substance, so that each thing may be broken up into them at its final hour, that there may be a store of matter for renewing things. The first-beginnings then are of a solid singleness, and in no other way can they have been preserved throughout the ages from a time now infinite in order to renew things.

I 565–576. Moreover, though the particles of matter are most solid, yet we can explain how all soft things become soft, such as air, earth, heat, and water; also by what force each thing is carried on, since void has once for all been mixed in things. But, if the first-beginnings, on the other hand, be soft, no explanation can be given of the means whereby strong flint and iron can be formed; for all their nature will entirely lack the principle of a foundation. The first-beginnings then are potent with a solid singleness, and by a combination of them more than usually dense all things can be close-packed and show a stalwart strength.

I 615–626. Unless there is a very smallest part, the smallest particles will each consist of parts unlimited, since half a half will always have a half and nothing will set bounds to such division. Between the sum of things, then, and the smallest thing what difference will there be? There will be none; for howsoever absolutely limitless the total sum may be, yet smallest particles will equally consist of parts unlimited. But, since true reason cries protestingly, denying that the mind can credit this, you must surrender and acknowledge that such particles exist as are endowed no more with any parts at all and have the very smallest nature.

I 959–983. Well then, the All is limited in no direction of its paths; for otherwise it must have had a furthest point. Moreover, it is clear that there can be no furthest point to anything,

unless there be beyond it something that may form its bound,
so that a point is seen further than which our nature of perception cannot follow. Now, since it must be granted that outside
the sum of things is nothing, then the sum can have no furthest point, and therefore lacks all bound and measure. Nor
does it matter in what quarter of it you may take your stand;
so surely, wheresoever one has placed himself, he finds the
All is just as infinite in all directions. Again, if for the moment
we assume that bounds are set to all existing space, suppose
a man runs forward to the furthest verge and from that last
position throws a flying dart; would you then say that, hurled
with stalwart strength, it will proceed in that direction whither
it is sent and fly far on, or do you think that something has the
power to check and stop it? For you must needs allow and
choose one of the two results. But either of them shuts off your
escape, compelling your admission that the All extends exempt
from bounds. For, whether there is something to prevent and
thwart the dart from going whither it was sent and reaching
its due goal, or whether it is carried on abroad, in either case
it has not left its bounds. In this way I will follow you, and,
wheresoever you shall fix the farthest verge, will ask what
happens in the next place to the dart. The consequence will
be that bound can nowhere find a footing, and the means of
flight will constantly enlarge the outlet of escape.
I 1021–1028. For certainly the first-beginnings did not by design arrange themselves sagaciously, each in its proper order,
and [assuredly they did] not [stipulate] what [motions they
should] severally [give]; but, being in great numbers and exchanging places through the All in many ways, since they are
stirred and vexed with blows from boundless space, while trying every kind of motion and of union they fall at length into
arrangements such as those by which this sum of things has
been created and exists.

BOOK TWO

II 1–19. 'Tis pleasant, while the winds are stirring up the
levels of the mighty sea, to look out from the shore upon the

great toil of another; not that any one's distress is sweet delight, but it is pleasant to behold from what misfortunes you yourself are free. 'Tis pleasant too to gaze, without partaking of the danger, upon war's great contests marshalled through the plains. But nought is sweeter than to dwell within the fair and lofty temples builded by the teaching of the wise; from which you may look down on other men and see them wandering to and fro and seeking, as they roam, the path of life; vying in intellect, contending in nobility of birth, and striving night and day with passing toil to rise up to the highest power and be the master of events. O wretched minds, O blinded hearts of men! How thick the darkness and how great the risks in which this span of life, whatever be its length, is spent! Can men not see that Nature cries out for no more than this, that from the body pain may somehow be withdrawn and held aloof, while in the mind she may enjoy sensations of delight, exempt from care and fear?

II 80–85. If you believe that first-beginnings can stand still, and by their pausing can beget for things new motions, you have lost your way and wander widely from true reason. For, since they roam through void, they all must needs be moved either by their own weight or haply by the impact of another. II 133–164. For first-beginnings are the first to move, and of themselves; and then those particles which are of small formation and are nearest, so to put it, to the powers of first-beginnings are impelled and set in motion by the unseen blows of these; and they in their turn stir up those which are a little larger. Thus from the first-beginnings motion mounts and by degrees emerges to our senses: so those particles move also which we can distinguish in the sunbeams, though we do not clearly see the blows that make them do so.

Now what velocity has been assigned to particles of matter, Memmius, you may in few words learn from this. When first the morning sprinkles with new light the earth, and various birds flit through the yielding air amid the pathless woods and fill the region round with liquid notes, how suddenly the rising sun is wont at such a time to clothe all things and flood them with his light is evident and manifest to all. But that heat and that light serene which he sends forth pass not through empty void; wherefore they are compelled to go more slowly, while they strike apart, as one might say, the waves of air. Nor do the several corpuscles of heat move one by one, but intertwined and coalesced: therefore they are both dragged back by each other to go more slowly. But those beginnings which are of a solid singleness, since they pass through the empty void, and nothing outside keeps them back, and they themselves, each single in the union of its parts, are borne with might and main to that goal only whither they have started, must be, sure enough, of passing speed and travel much more swiftly than the sunbeams, and in the same time in which the sun's bright rays swarm through the sky must traverse distance many times as great.

II 167–181. But some, opposing this and ignorant of matter, think that not without the sanction of the gods can Nature so conformably with human needs change the year's seasons and create the crops and do those other things as well which godlike Pleasure, guide of life, prompts men to take in hand, herself escorting them and coaxing them to propagate their tribes by Venus' ways, that mankind may not perish. But, when they represent the gods as having ordained all things for man's sake, they seem in all respects to wander very widely from true reason. For, even though I knew not what beginnings of things are, yet this, considering the dispositions of the sky alone, I should be bold to say as well as to assert on many other grounds, that our world's system was in nowise framed for us by power divine, so great is the defect with which it stands endowed.

II 216–260. This too upon this subject I am eager that you learn, that particles, while they are borne straight downwards by their own weights through the void, at quite uncertain times and in uncertain places push a little from their track, only to such extent as to enable you to say that movement has been changed. For, if they were not wont to swerve, all would fall downwards through the void profound like drops of rain,

and for the first-beginnings neither shocks nor blows would
have been born: thus Nature never would have formed a single thing.

But, if perchance someone believes that heavier particles, because they are more swiftly carried straight down through the
void, can from above fall on the lighter, thus begetting blows
such as are able to impart the generative motions, he strays
widely from the pathway of true reason. For whatsoever things
fall down through water and through loose-meshed air must
needs accelerate their falling in proportion to their weights,
because the water's substance and the subtle nature of the air
cannot retard each thing in equal measure, but give way more
quickly when the heavier overcomes them. But, on the other
hand, in no direction nor at any time has empty void the power
to withstand anything, but, as its nature seeks, continues to
give way: therefore all things, though of unequal weights,
must yet at equal speeds be carried through the quiet void.
The heavier particles will therefore never have the power to
fall upon the lighter from above, nor of themselves beget such
blows as give the various motions through which Nature carries on her work. Therefore, I say repeatedly, the particles must
swerve a little, yet not more than in the least degree, lest I appear to be assuming oblique motions and the truth refute that
doctrine. For this we see is clear and manifest, that weights,
as far as in them lies, cannot obliquely move when they fall
headlong from above, at least as far as you can see. But who
is there who can detect that nothing turns itself aside at all
from the unbent direction of its path?

Again, if every motion is connected always with another,
and a new one always rises in fixed order from an old, and if
the first-beginnings by their swerving do not form a kind of
principle of motion which may break through Fate's decrees,
that cause may not from time unending follow cause, whence
comes this free will o'er the earth to living things—whence
has this will, I say, been wrested from the fates, by which we
each walk onward as our pleasure leads, and likewise turn
aside our motions, neither at fixed times nor yet in fixed directions, but according as the mind itself has led?

II 284-293. Wherefore in seeds as well you needs must make
the same admission, that besides the blows and weights there
is another cause for motions, whence the power I have referred
to has been born within us, since we see that nothing can be
formed from nothing. For weight forbids the possibility of all
things being formed by blows, by some kind of external force.
But, that the mind itself is not held by an inward need in
doing all its acts, and is not, as though vanquished, forced to
bear and suffer it, this the slight swerving of the first-beginnings causes, but at no fixed time and in no fixed direction.

II 333-341. Now mark once more, and in the next place learn
the primal origins of all things, of what kinds they are, how
widely differing in form, and how they are diversified with
many kinds of shapes; not that but few of them are furnished
with like forms, but all are not in general the counterparts of
all. Nor is this strange; for, since there is so great a store of
them that there is neither any end nor sum, as I have shown,
all must not, sure enough, be furnished with a size and shape
of absolute equality and similarity to all.

II 398-413. Moreover, the liquidities of honey and of milk are
drawn out in the mouth with an agreeable sensation of the
tongue, but wormwood's nauseous nature and wild gentian
distort our mouths with an offensive taste; so that you may
with ease perceive that those things which can touch the senses
pleasantly consist of smooth and rounded particles, but, whatsoever things appear as rough or bitter, these are held together
intertwined by particles more hooked, and so are wont to tear
their way into our senses and to rend the body at their entering.

Lastly, all things that strike the senses by their touch as
good or bad are mutually opposed, because they are made up
of different atomic-shapes. Think not then, as perchance you
do, that the harsh roughness of the creaking saw consists of
elements as smooth as those of the melodious strains which
with his mobile fingers a musician wakes from strings and
gives them form.

II 422-443. For no shape whatsoever that is soothing to the
senses has been formed without some elemental smoothness;

and, again, whatever shape is painful or severe, this is not
found without some roughness in its substance. Moreover,
there are other particles which cannot rightly be considered
either smooth or altogether barbed with twisted points, but
must be fancied rather to have angles slightly jutting, so as
somehow more to tickle than to hurt the senses; such as lees
of tartar, for example, and the taste of elecampane. Once
more, that hot fire and cold frost are differently toothed and
differently prick the senses of the body, touch in each case
gives us proof. For touch—I call the holy powers divine to
witness—touch is what the body feels when something from
without makes its way in, or something born within it hurts
or gives it joy when going out of it on Venus' generative business, or when, from some shock, the seeds within the very
body make a turmoil and confound sensation by their mutual
disturbance; as would happen if yourself should now strike
any portion of your body with your hand and make experi-
ment. Wherefore the forms of first-beginnings needs must
widely differ, since they can produce diverse sensations.

II 478–499. And, now that I have shown this fact, I will go
on to link with it another, which may win belief from close
dependence on it, that the first-beginnings vary in a finite
scale of shapes. For, if it be not so, then, once again, some seeds
will have to be of boundless bulk of substance. For in the same
small single size of even any particle you please the shapes
have not the power to vary much from one another. Suppose,
for instance, that first-bodies are composed of three least parts,
or add a few more to them: obviously, when you shall have
experimented every way with all these portions of one particle, shifting the top and bottom and transposing right and
left, to find what contour of its total form the several arrangements give, if you shall haply wish to go on varying the shapes,
some other portions must be added; and from this it follows
that, if you shall wish perchance to give still further variations
to the shapes, the arrangement in like manner will require
still other parts: therefore increase of size accompanies new
shapes. And thus you cannot possibly believe that seeds have

infinite varieties of form, lest you force some to be of monstrous magnitude, a supposition which, as I have shown already, cannot be admitted.

II 522–528. And, now that I have shown this fact, I will go on to link it with another, which may win belief from close dependence on it, that the first-beginnings that are formed with shapes like one another are of number infinite. For, since the difference of forms is limited, those which are like each other must be limitless, or else the sum of matter must be limited; which I have proved is not so.

II 560–568. So, if once for your part you shall lay it down that certain first-beginnings are of finite number, then the diverse tides of matter will be bound to scatter and disperse them through all time, so that they never can be forced to enter into union, nor stay in union, nor grow in bulk. But plain fact shows that each of these things openly occurs; that things can both be born, and, when born, grow. Therefore 'tis plain that the first-particles in any kind of things you please are limitless, and from them all things are supplied.

II 730–738. Now mark, and grasp my words, which I have sought with pleasant toil, and do not think, as possibly you may, that those white things, which you see shining bright before your eyes, consist of white beginnings, or that black things are begotten from black seed, or that, when things are steeped in any other colour, this they wear because their particles are dyed with a like hue. For particles of matter have no colouring at all.

II 749–756. For every colour changes into all without exception, but such change the first-beginnings must in nowise make, since something must remain unchangeable, that all things be not utterly reduced to nothing. For, whatsoever thing is changed and quits its bounds, this is at once the death of what has been before. Therefore beware of dyeing seeds of things with colour, lest you see all things returning utterly to nothing.

II 795–798. Besides, since colours cannot have existence without light, and first-beginnings do not come forth into light, you may be sure they are not clad with any colour. For in blind darkness how can there be any kind of colour?

II 804–816. The peacock's tail, when filled with lavish light, changes its colours similarly as it turns about; and, since these are begotten by a certain stroke of light, you must believe and may be sure that they cannot be formed without it. And, since the pupil of the eye, when it is said to notice a white colour, receives a kind of blow, and then another kind when it perceives a black or other colour, and it matters nothing with what colour such things as you touch may chance to be endowed, but rather with what kind of shape they are provided, so you may be sure that first-beginnings have no need of colours, but give varying effects of touch from their distinctive forms.

II 842–846. But, lest perchance you think that first-beginnings are despoiled of colour only, know that they are wholly sundered too from cold and warmth and heat, that they are borne along devoid of sound and dry of sap, and from their substance throw no odour of their own.

II 865–882. Now all things that are seen to have sensation you must yet acknowledge are composed of first-beginnings that have none. The plain things, visible and known to us, do not refute and contradict this fact, but rather take us by the hand themselves and force us to believe that, as I say, all living things are born from particles without sensation. Indeed you may see living worms produced from noisome dung, when the damp earth is seized with rottenness after untimely rains, and all things else may likewise be perceived to change. Streams, leaves, and joyous pastures change themselves to cattle; cattle change themselves into our bodies; oft too from our bodies grow the wild-beasts' strength and bodies of winged birds. Therefore all foods are changed by nature into living bodies, and from them she fashions all the senses of things living, very much as she transforms dry logs to flames and turns them all to fire.

II 963–968. Again, since there is pain when, troubled by some force throughout the living flesh and limbs, the particles of matter throb in their abodes within, and genial pleasure follows when they go back to their place, you may be sure that first-beginnings cannot be assailed by any pain or gather any pleasure from themselves.

II 973–977. Again, if for the moment we must needs assign sensation to their first-beginnings that the several living things themselves may have it, what of those of which the human race is specially composed? Of course they both guffaw, convulsed with quivering mirth, and sprinkle with bedewing tears their cheeks and faces.

II 1052–1076. No longer must we deem it probable in any way, since space spreads, void and measureless, in all directions round, and seeds, in number numberless and of unfathomed sum, fly to and fro in many ways, stirred with eternal motion, that this single earth and heav'n alone has been created, and that those so many particles of matter out beyond are doing nought; especially since this world has been made by Nature, as the seeds themselves of things, in their spontaneous and fortuitous collisions, when they had in many ways, but idly, to no purpose or result, been brought together, at length coalesced—such seeds as suddenly combining, were to be for ever the beginnings of great things, of earth and sea and sky, and of the race of living things. Wherefore, I say repeatedly you must acknowledge that elsewhere are other aggregates of matter such as this which ether holds with greedy grasp.

Besides, when much material has been prepared, when space is there, and neither any thing nor any cause delays, things sure enough must needs be carried on and made. Well now, if the supply of seeds is so immense that all the lives of living beings cannot count them up, and if the self-same force of Nature still remains, such as can fling the seeds of things into their several places just as in this world they have been flung, you must acknowledge that in other parts of space are other earths and various tribes of men and races of wild-beasts.

II 1090–1095. Which things if you learn well, and hold them fast, Nature at once is seen, set free from haughty lords, to do all things spontaneously, by herself, aloof from gods. For tell me, holy deities, that spend in tranquil peace your placid span of life serene, which of you has the power to rule the sum of the immense?

BOOK THREE

III 94–105. I say, first, that the mind, which oft we call the understanding, that in which is placed the guidance and the government of life, is no whit less a portion of a man than hands or feet or eyes are portions of the total living thing. [Some say, however,] that the mind's sensation is not placed in a fixed part, but in a certain vital habit of the body, called in Greek a harmony, because it makes sensation the companion of life, although the mind is in no single part; just as we often say the body has good health, which yet is not a part of him who is in health. Thus then they do not station the sensation of the mind in a fixed part; in which they seem to me to wander far astray in different ways.

III 117–129. And now, that you may learn that soul as well as body is within the limbs and that 'tis not by harmony the frame is wont to feel, note principally this, that, when a great deal of the body is removed, yet often life still lingers in the limbs; whereas this self-same life, when a few particles of heat have fled and air has been sent forth abroad from out the mouth, at once deserts the veins and leaves the bones; enabling you to learn that not all particles have equal functions, and not all support well-being in a like degree, but those which are the seeds of air and heat are more concerned that life may linger in the frame. Heat then and vital air are actually in the body, and desert our limbs at death.

III 136–146. Now this I say, that mind and soul are held in union and together form a single nature, but ,the guiding power, which I call mind or understanding, is the chief, and lords it, so to speak, throughout the body. And this is situate and fixed in the mid region of the breast; for here throbs panting fear, and round these parts joy lays a soothing touch; here therefore is the mind or understanding. The other part, the soul, distributed throughout the body, moves obedient to the nod and prompting of the mind. The guiding power, alone and by itself, has self-discernment, it has self-enjoyment, when impressions do not stir the soul or body with it.

III 152–169. But, when the mind is moved by some intense fear, we see that all the soul has fellow-feeling 'mid the limbs, that sweats and pallor thus break out o'er all the body, that the speech is broken and the voice miscarries, that the eyes are misty, that there is a ringing in the ears, and that the legs give way: in fine we often notice men collapse from terror of the mind; whence anyone can learn with ease that soul is closely joined with mind, and, when the force of mind has struck it, it forthwith propels and strikes the body.

This doctrine also shows that mind and soul have a material nature. For, when you see them move the limbs, catch up the frame from sleep, transform the look, and guide and turn about the total man—none of which things we know can happen without touch, nor touch in its turn without substance— must you not admit that they consist of a material nature? Besides, you notice that the mind within our body suffers in like measure with the body and has fellow-feeling with it.

III 177–188. Now I will go on to expound to you in verse the kind of substance that the mind has and of what it is composed. Firstly, I say that it is very subtle and is formed of particles exceedingly minute. That this is so, you may by giving heed learn clearly from what follows. Nothing is seen to happen with such speed as that with which the mind suggests its happening, and even starts it. Mind then is stirred with greater speed than any of the things whose natures are in evidence before our eyes. But that which is so very swift is bound to be composed of seeds extremely round, exceedingly minute, so that with little prompting they can be impelled and moved.

III 208–220. The following fact too shows the nature of the mind, how fine its texture is, and in how small a space it would confine itself if it could be compressed together, that, as soon as the untroubled rest of death has got possession of a man, and when the mind and soul have gone away, you thereupon can notice nothing lessened from the total body in appearance or in weight: except the vital feeling and the heat, death makes all good. Therefore the total soul must needs consist of very little seeds, which are entwined with veins and flesh and sinews, seeing that, when all of it has now departed from the total body, yet the outer contour of the frame preserves itself intact, and not a jot of weight is wanting.

III 231–251. And yet we must not think this nature single. A kind of subtle exhalation leaves the dying, mixed with heat, and heat in turn draws with it air; nor is there any heat with which air too has not been mixed; for, since its nature is loose-meshed, it needs must be that many particles of air move through it. Therefore the nature of the mind is now found threefold; yet all these combined are not sufficient to create sensation, since the mind does not admit that any of them can create sensation-causing motions and the thoughts a man revolves within his mind. Therefore to these there must be also added a fourth nature. This is quite unprovided with a name, but than it there is nothing speedier or more subtle, or composed of smaller and of smoother elements. This first distributes the sensation-causing motions through the limbs; for it is first stirred up, being composed of small atomic-shapes; from it the heat and unseen power of exhalation get their motions, then the air; then everything is speeded up; the blood is shaken; all the flesh feels deeply; lastly to the bones and marrow there is given, maybe, pleasure, or, maybe, a contrary emotion.

III 323–326. This mind and soul, then, is contained by all the body, and itself is the custodian of the body and the cause of its well-being; for with common roots they cling together, and appear unable to be torn apart without destruction.

III 337–338. Besides, the body never is begotten by itself, nor grows up by itself, nor by itself is seen to last on after death.

III 350–353. Now to proceed; if anyone rejects the notion that the body has sensation, and believes that soul in its commixture with the total body undertakes that motion which I call sensation, he is fighting against truths and facts quite manifest.

III 359–369. To say, moreover, that the eyes are able to see nothing, but the mind looks out through them as through an open door, is hard to credit, inasmuch as their sensation leads

us in the opposite direction; for it draws and drives us to the eyes themselves, particularly since we often cannot look on shining things, because our eyes are hampered by their light. Which is not so with doors; for doors, through which we look ourselves, do not when opened suffer any pain. Moreover, if our eyes are the equivalents of doors, in that case it appears that, if the eyes are taken out, the mind must see things better, now that doors and even doorposts are removed. III 417–428. Now mark; that you may learn that unsubstantial minds and souls of living things are subject to both birth and death, I shall go on to fashion verses worthy your attention, sought-for long and found with pleasant toil. Be careful, you, to join them both under a single name, and, when for instance I proceed to speak of soul and show that it is mortal, then imagine that I speak of mind as well, since they are one in two, a conjoint thing. Firstly, since I have shown that it is subtle and consists of tiny atoms, being made of first-beginnings smaller far than those of water, mist, or smoke . . .
III 434–458. Now therefore, since you see that water flows away and passes off on all sides when the vessel holding it is broken, and since mist and smoke pass off into the air, believe that much more speedily the soul too is dispersed and perishes, and much more quickly is resolved into its primal particles, when once it is withdrawn and has departed from the body of a man. For, since the body, which is so to speak its vessel, cannot hold it in if shattered from some cause and made loose-meshed by blood abstracted from the veins, how can you think it can be held by any air? how can the air, more loose-meshed than our bodies, hold it in?

Besides, we feel that mind is born together with the body, grows up with it, and with it gets old. For, just as children totteringly walk with weak and tender body, so this is accomplished with slight intelligence of mind. Then, when the age has ripened and the strength become robust, the understanding too is greater and the force of mind increased. Later, when Time's great might has now impaired the body, and the limbs have dropped with blunted force, the intellect is crippled, there is babbling of the tongue and tottering of the mind; all things at once give way and fail. Therefore it follows that the whole soul too dissolves, like smoke, into the lofty air, since we perceive that with the body it is born, and with it grows, and, as I have just shown, sinks with it to decay, worn out by age.

III 558–565. Again, the living functions of the body and the mind are strong and have enjoyment of their life by being interknit; for mind alone without the body cannot furnish vital motions; neither, on the other hand, can body when devoid of mind, continue to exist and use sensations. Just as, of course, the eye, torn from its roots, can of itself distinguish nothing when disjoined from the whole body, so the soul and mind are seen to have no power by themselves.

III 624–633. Besides, if the soul's nature is immortal, and can have sensation, sundered from the body, then we must, I think, suppose it furnished with five senses; and in this way only can we picture to ourselves the souls below roaming in Acheron. And so the painters and the writers of past times have introduced souls thus equipped with senses. But by themselves souls can have neither eyes, nor nose, nor tongue, nor even hands, nor can the ears exist and have the sense of hearing by themselves (in soul apart from body).

III 657–678. Nay more, if, when a serpent's tongue vibrates, and when its tail is menacingly waving at the end of its long body, 'tis your fancy with a knife to cut both tail and body into many parts, you presently will notice all the severed portions separately writhing round their recent wounds, bespattering the ground with gore, and the front part attacking with its mouth the hinder quarters, so that, smitten with the burning anguish of the wound, it may allay it with a bite. Shall we then say that there are full-formed souls in all these little pieces? Why, on that principle 'twill follow that one living thing has had within its body many souls; and, since this cannot be, therefore that single soul has been divided into parts together with the body. Wherefore both soul and body must be reckoned mortal, inasmuch as each alike is severed into many parts.

Besides, if the soul's nature is immortal, and finds entrance to the body at our birth, why can we not remember bygone time as well as present? why do we retain no traces of past deeds? For, if the function of the mind is so completely changed that every reminiscence of things past has dropped away, that in my judgment is no longer very far removed from death. Wherefore you must acknowledge that the soul which previously lived has perished, and the soul which now is now has been created.

III 713–721. Besides, are seeds of soul left in a lifeless frame or not? For, if they are so left and so remain, the soul cannot be justly deemed immortal, since it has withdrawn diminished by the loss of parts. But, if in its withdrawal it has fled with members so entire that it has left no portions of itself within the frame, whence come the worms that carcases exude from the soon rancid flesh, and whence does such a swarm of bone-less, bloodless creatures fluctuate throughout the swollen limbs?

III 748–756. But, if mind were immortal and were wont to change its dwelling-place in bodies, living things would be of mingled habitudes; hounds of Hyrcanian breed would often flee from the attacks of antlered deer; the hawk would tremble at the coming of the dove and take flight through the air; men would lack reason and the savage tribes of wild-beasts would possess it. For, that which some men say, that the immortal soul is changed with change of body, is put forward by false reason. For what is changed dissolves, and therefore perishes.

III 830–842. Death then to us is nothing and concerns us not a whit, now that the mind is proven mortal. For, just as in time past we felt no trouble when the Carthaginians assembled from all sides to battle, when all things beneath the sky's high borders, shaken by war's throbbing tumult, shudderingly quaked, and it was doubtful to the sovereignty of which of the two nations all things human on both land and sea must fall, so, when we are no more, when there shall be a severance of soul and body, out of which we are conjoined in one, why

then of course to us, who will not then exist, nothing at all
will have the power to happen and arouse sensation, not if
land be mixed with sea and sea with sky.

III 919–951. When we are lulled in sleep, and mind and body
rest together, no one misses personality and life; for all we
care the sleep in such a case may be eternal, and no longing for
ourselves affects us. And yet the first-beginnings scattered
through our limbs are then by no means foaming far away
from the sensation-causing motions, when a man is snatched
from sleep and recollects himself. Death therefore must be
deemed to be much less to us than sleep—if less can be than
what we see is nothing—for a greater dissipation of the mass
of matter follows death, and no one wakes again whom once
life's cold cessation has befallen.

Again, if Nature unexpectedly lifted her voice and thus
in person chided anyone of us, "What ails you, mortal, so
exceedingly, that you indulge too much in sickly grief? Why
do you groan and weep at death? For, if the life now past and
gone was pleasant to you, and your blessings have not all, as
though they had been poured into a sieve, flowed through and
perished thanklessly, why not retire, O foolish one, from life's
feast like a well filled guest, and take resignedly the rest that
cannot be disturbed? But, if your joys have all been lost and
squandered, and if life is an offence to you, why seek to add
a longer span, that it again may come to a bad ending and all
thanklessly be lost? Why not prefer to make an end of life
and labour?" . . . what could we reply except that she directs a righteous charge and sets forth in her words a true
indictment?

III 978–983. Also, whatever torments have been said to be
deep down in Acheron, these, sure enough, are all with us
in life. No wretched Tantalus, as in the story, numbed with
groundless dread, fears the great rock impending from the
air; but rather during life the groundless fear of gods oppresses
mortals, and the fall they dread is such as chance may bring
to each.

III 995–1010. Also a Sisyphus we have in life before our eyes,
persisting in petitioning the people to confer on him the con-

sul's rods and cruel axes, and retiring from the contest always
beaten and dejected. To seek for rule which is delusive and is
never given, and in seeking ever to endure hard toil, this is to
push with might and main the rock uphill, which after all,
now at the very top, rolls down again and seeks with headlong
speed the levels of the plain. Again, to be for ever feeding
the ungrateful mind but ne'er to fill it full and satiate it with
good things (as the year's seasons do for us when they return
and bring their produce and their various charms, and yet life's
blessings never fill us full) this, in my judgment, is the story
told about the youthful Danaids; this is to pour the water in
the sieve, which can in nowise be filled full, for all one's pour-
ing.

Book Four

IV 33–45. Now I will essay to deal with what has intimate
connection with this subject, that there are what I call images
of things, which, just like membranes stripped from surfaces,
fly to and fro through air, which also, meeting us awake and
in our sleep, alarm our minds, when oft we see strange shapes
and images of persons dead, which often waken us alarmingly
when sunk in slumber; these I will explain, lest haply we believe that souls escape from Acheron and ghosts fly to and fro
among the living, or that something of us can be left behind at
death, when mind and body, perishing alike, have taken their
departure into their respective first-beginnings.
IV 72–80. For certainly we see that many things shed particles
in much abundance, and not only from their inner depths, as
I have said before, but often from their surfaces as well, and
even colour. For yellow, red, and violet awnings commonly
do this when, stretched across large theatres, they flap and
flutter, spread on poles and beams; and then they dye the
audience in the pit below and all the splendour of the stage
and Parian marble of the gods, compelling them to flutter in
their colours.
IV 87–109. There are then, you will now admit, fixed traces
of the forms of things, which fly about at large, endowed with

subtle texture, and, when separate and single, are invisible. Again, all smell, smoke, heat, and other suchlike properties flow off from things diffusely, since, while they are coming from the depths within whence they arise, along the winding roadway they are rent, and there are no straight outlets to their paths, whereby at their uprising they may hasten forth. But, when a subtle film of colour from the surface is thrown off, nothing can scatter it, because it stands in readiness, placed in the fore-front. Lastly, whatever likenesses appear to us in mirrors, water, and in all bright objects, these, since they are furnished with a semblance like to things, must needs consist of images sent off from things. There are then subtle forms and likenesses of things, which, though they singly are unable to be seen, yet, thrown back by repeated and continuous repulse, return a picture from a mirror's surface, and not otherwise do they seem able to be so preserved that shapes are given back so very like the several things.

IV 145–160. For surface after surface ever overflows from things, so that they throw it off, and, when this reaches other things, it passes through them, and especially through glass; but, when it comes to rugged rock or the solidity of wood, then it is straightway rent, so that it cannot give back any image. But, when things both compact and bright, like mirrors in particular, come in its way, neither of these things happens. For it can neither travel through them, as it does through glass, nor yet be rent; the smoothness of the mirrors takes care to ensure its safety. Therefore, it is that images flow back from them to us. And howsoever suddenly at any time you place each object opposite the mirror, images appear; whence you may learn that from the surfaces of things is an unceasing flow of subtle textures and of subtle shapes. And therefore in a moment many images are born, so that with reason is their birth called swift.

IV 216–217. Wherefore, I say repeatedly, you must admit that particles which strike the eyes and challenge vision are sent off. IV 230–236. Again, since any figure handled in the dark is recognized to be the same as we can see in daylight and clear brightness, touch and sight must needs be instigated by like cause. Now then, if what we feel and what attracts our notice in the dark is square, what square thing save its image will have power to fall upon our vision in the light? Wherefore the cause of vision plainly lies in images, nor without these could anything be seen.

IV 244–255. The image too enables us to see and causes us to recognize how far each thing is from us. For when it is despatched, at once it pushes and impels before it whatsoever air is situate between it and the eyes; thus all this air glides through our eyes and brushes, so to say, the pupils, and so passes through. Therefore it is that we can see how far off each thing is. The larger the amount of air thus driven on before it and the more drawn out the breeze with which our eyes are brushed, the farther off each thing is seen to be withdrawn. Of course these processes are carried on extremely swiftly, so that at the same time we perceive of what kind is a thing and how far distant.

IV 269–295. Now mark, and learn why images are seen beyond the mirror; for they certainly appear withdrawn far in. Just so with those things that are seen in their reality outside a house through doors, when these are opened and afford a prospect through them and enable many things outside it to be looked at from the house. For that sight too is caused by twin or twofold airs; for first an air is then discerned between us and the doors; then come the folding doors themselves with right wing and with left; later the eyes are brushed by outside light, and by a second air, and by those things beheld in their reality outside. And thus, when first the image of the mirror is sent forth, in coming to our eyes it thrusts and drives before it all the air that lies between it and our eyes, and makes us able to perceive all this ere we perceive the mirror. But, when we have perceived the mirror too, at once the image borne from us arrives thereat and is repulsed, and comes back to our eyes rolling and driving on another air before it, and it makes us notice this before we can be conscious of itself, and therefore seems to be so far withdrawn and there is no fitting cause for wonder to the things that give back vision from the surfaces of mirrors, since in each case the result is brought about by two-fold airs. Now, that the right side of our frame is seen in mirrors on the left is due to this, that, when the image, coming to the surface of the mirror, strikes against it, it is not turned round intact but dashed straight backwards.

IV 311–317. Nay more, all mirrors that have sides endowed with curvature like our sides send back images to us, right answering to right, either because the image is transferred from one side of the mirror to the other and, when twice repulsed, then flies to us, or else because, when it has reached the mirror, it wheels round, the curved shape of the mirror teaching it to turn about towards us.

IV 337–363. Further, we can behold from darkness things which are in light, because, when the black air of darkness, lying nearer, has stepped in beforehand and possessed the open eyes, there follows it at once the bright and lucid air, which purges them, as one might say, and scatters the black shadows of the former air; for it is many times more speedy, many times minuter and more powerful. As soon as it has opened up and filled with light the pathways of the eyes, which the black air had blocked before, at once those images of things that lie in light come after and incite the eyes to see. Contrariwise, we cannot from the light see things in darkness, since the denser air of darkness follows after, filling all the apertures and blocking up the pathways of the eyes, so that no things can throw their images upon them and incite them. Again, when from afar we look upon the square towers of a city, often they seem round, because each angle from the distance is beheld obtuse, or rather even is not seen at all; and so its blow is lost, nor does its stroke come gliding to our eyes; for, while the images are carried through much air, the air by numerous collisions blunts their stroke perforce. When every angle thus has simultaneously escaped the sense of sight, it is as though we see the stony structures rounded on a lathe; yet they appear not like things plainly, really round, but somewhat like them, as it were in shadow-form.

IV 469–506. Again, if anyone believes that nothing can be known, he knows not whether even that is knowable, since he admits that he knows nothing. Against one then so standing that his head is where his feet should be I will refrain from arguing. But, even though I grant that he knows that, I still would ask him this. Since he has never seen reality in things, how does he know what knowing and not knowing severally are? what has created knowledge of the true and of the false? what proof is there that doubtful facts differ from certainties? You will discover that the senses first created knowledge of the real, and that the senses cannot be refuted. For that which by its own authority can overcome falsehood with truth must be regarded as of special credit. Well, what ought to be deemed of higher credit than sensation? Shall reason, which springs wholly from the senses, have the power to contradict them, if it rises from a false sensation? For, if the senses are not true, all reason also becomes false. Will ears be able to find fault with eyes, or touch with ears? can touch again reprove, or nose confute, or eyes discredit touch? Not so, in my opinion. For to each sense its function has been set apart, to each its special force; and therefore there must be a separate sense for what is soft or cold or hot, and quite another to discern things' various colours and to see what things have colours joined with them. Taste likewise has its separate force; smell has its birth apart, and so has sound. So therefore of necessity one sense cannot confute another. Further, the senses cannot find fault with themselves, since equal faith must be assigned to them at all times. Therefore, what to the senses seems on each occasion true, is true. And, if our reason cannot ravel out the cause why those things which, when close at hand, were square, when seen far off, are round, yet it is better through the lack of reason to give faulty explanations of the several shapes than from our grasp to let plain facts escape on any side, and play false with our chiefest trust, and undermine all those foundations whereon life and welfare rest. For not alone would reason totally give way, but life itself too would at once collapse if you could not make up your mind to trust the senses.

IV 722–738. Now mark, and hear what things affect the mind,

and from a few words learn whence those things come that
come into the mind. First I say this, that many subtle images
of things are wandering in many ways in all directions round
about, which, when they meet each other in the air, with ease
unite, like cobwebs or gold leaf. For truly these are much more
subtle in their texture than the images that take possession of
the eyes and rouse the vision, since they penetrate the loose-
meshed body and excite the subtle nature of the mind within,
and rouse sensation. 'Tis thus that we see Centaurs and the
ill-assorted limbs of Scyllas, dogs with heads like those of
Cerberus, and images of those whom death has claimed, whose
bones the earth enfolds, since images of every kind are being
carried here and there, in part such as are formed spontaneously in the air itself, in part all those discharged from different things and those composed and formed of the atomic-
shapes of these.

IV 777–783. Now on this subject many questions rise, and
many things I must clear up if my desire is plainly to set forth
the facts. This question is particularly asked; how is it that,
because the inclination comes to anyone, his mind immediately thinks that very thing? Do images observe our will, and,
when we wish to see a thing, if sea, if land, if even heav'n is
what we would behold, does that thing's image run to meet
us?

IV 794–815. Because within a single point of time appreciable
by sensation, that is while a single sound is uttered, many
smaller times lie hidden, found by reason to be there, therefore in any point of time the images are all drawn up and
ready in their several places; such is their velocity and such
the store of things. In this way, when the previous image
perishes, and when another in another posture has been born
from it, the first one thereupon seems to have changed its
attitude. And, since they are so subtle, only those can be distinguished clearly by the mind which it exerts itself to see;
therefore all perish as superfluous excepting those for which
it has prepared itself. Accordingly it does prepare itself, and
hopes to see the consequence of every act; therefore it comes

to pass. Do you not see too that the eyes, when they essay to notice subtle things, strain and prepare themselves, and that, unless they did, there could not be a sharp discernment. Yet in the case of plain things also you may learn that, if you do not give them your attention, it is just as if they all the time were far removed and distant. Why is it strange then if the mind loses all other things save those in which it is itself engrossed?

IV 823–828. Now on this subject you must be extremely careful to escape this fault and anxiously to shun this error, of supposing that the bright lights of the eyes were made that we might see, and that the upper parts of thighs and calves, upheld by feet, have power to bend, that we may take long steps. IV 832–841. These and all other suchlike notions are preposterously based on perverse reason; inasmuch as nothing was begotten in our bodies that we might make use of it, but what has been begotten generates its use. Seeing did not exist before the eyes were born, nor use of words and speech before the tongue was formed; rather the tongue's birth long preceded discourse, ears were formed long ere a sound was heard, and all the other members, in my judgment, were in being ere there was a use for them; they cannot have grown, therefore, for the sake of being used.

IV 877–891. Now I will tell how we are able, when we wish, to walk, and how it has been given us to move our limbs in divers ways, and what the force is which is wont to push along this great and heavy burden of our body; do you grasp my words. I say, as I have said before, that images of walking first fall on and strike our minds. Then the desire to walk is formed; for no one takes in hand to do a single thing until the mind has predetermined what it wills. Because it predetermines it, an image of that act is formed. Then, when the mind so stirs itself that it desires to move or walk, at once it strikes the soul, which is disseminated in the limbs throughout the frame; and that is easy to be done, since it is held conjoined. Then in its turn this strikes the body; thus the whole mass by degrees is pushed along and moved.

Book Five

V 64–75. The order of my scheme has brought me to this point, that I must offer proof that the whole world consists of substance liable to birth and death; and I must show how yon great union of matter laid foundations for the land, the sea, the sky, the stars, and globes of sun and moon; further, what living things have come to birth upon the earth, as well as such as never have been born; how men began to use with one another varying speech by giving names to things; and how that terror of the gods crept into human breasts which still regards throughout the earth their temples, lakes, groves, altars, images as sacred.

V 92–96. First look at sea, earth, sky; their triple nature and three structures, Memmius, their three forms so unlike, their three so wondrous textures, will one single day give over to destruction, and the mass and fabric of the world, sustained for many years, will fall in ruin.

V 104–109. Perhaps the event itself will furnish credence to my words, and ere long you will see earthquakes break forth and all things violently shattered. But this may Fortune steer and turn far from us, and may reason rather than the very fact convince us of the possibility of all things giving way and falling to the depths with awful crash.

V 113–116. I will set forth for you many solaces in learned words, lest haply, held in superstition's curb, you may believe that land and sea, that sky and stars, that sun and moon are of divinely fashioned substance and must last for ever.

V 122–128. Yet those things are so very far from deity divine, so utterly unworthy of appearing in the number of the gods, that they may rather be imagined able to supply us with a notable example of remoteness from all vital motion and sensation. For certainly it cannot be supposed that the mind's nature and directing power can be allied with any substance whatsoever; just as trees cannot exist in ether.

V 144–173. These things then are not gifted with divine sensation, since they cannot breathe the breath of life.

This too you cannot possibly believe, that holy dwellings of the gods exist in any quarters of the world. For a god's subtle nature, far remote from our sensations, is with difficulty seen by the perception of the mind; and, since it has escaped the touch and impact of the hands, it can touch nothing that is tangible to us. For what cannot be touched itself has not the power to touch. Wherefore their dwellings too must be unlike to ours, as subtle as their bodies are. . . . Further, to say that they decided to construct the glorious world for man's sake, and that therefore it is meet to praise their laudable performance and believe that it will be eternal and immortal, and to say that it is wrong by any means at any time to try to shake from its abodes what by the ancient counsel of the gods was based on perpetuity for human kind, assailing it with argument and seeking to o'erthrow it from the bottom to the top; to say this and invent and add other such fictions is sheer folly. For what return could gratitude of ours confer on happy and immortal ones, that they should undertake to do aught for our sake? Or, when they had kept quiet hitherto, what new thing could have tempted them so late in time to wish to change their former life? For it is clear that he whom old things injure must rejoice in new; but they whom no ill had befallen in past time, while happily they spent their lives, what could have roused in them the love of change?

V 181–199. Moreover, whence was first implanted in the gods the pattern for begetting things and the idea, in particular, of human kind, so that they knew what they desired to do and saw it in their minds? or how was ever known to them the force of first-beginnings and what these could do by interchange of order, had not Nature of herself supplied the pattern of creative power? For first-beginnings, being numerous and stirred by blows in many ways from time now infinite, have been so wont to move, incited by their weights, to make all kinds of unions and try all possible creations by combining with each other, that it is not strange if they have also fallen into such arrangements and have come into such paths as those from which this sum of things is carried on at present by the process of renewal.

But, even if I did not know what first-beginnings are, yet this, considering the dispositions of the sky alone, I should be bold to say, as well as to assert on many other grounds, that Nature's scheme of things was certainly not framed for us by power divine, so great is the defect with which it stands endowed.

V 235–246. Firstly, since earth and water, air's light breath and heat, of which this sum of things is seen to be composed, are all of substance liable to birth and death, of such a substance all the world must be supposed to be. For certainly the things whose parts and members we perceive to be of substance that had birth and atoms that will die we see must be themselves without exception subject to both birth and death. Wherefore, when I see mighty parts and members of the world consumed and born again, I may be sure that heaven too and earth have had a birthday and will be destroyed.

V 324–350. Besides, if earth and sky have never had a birthday and have always been eternal, why have other poets too not sung of other themes before the Theban war and sack of Troy? Whither have countless deeds of men so often passed away, to be enshrined and cherished nowhere in eternal monuments of fame? The truth is, in my judgment, that the sum is new, the world is fresh, and not long since had its beginning. Therefore some arts are even now in stages of refinement, others only yet in process of development; many additions have but now been made to ships; musicians only lately brought forth tuneful sounds; lastly, this system and philosophy of things was recently discovered, and I now myself am found the very first and foremost to be able to express it in our native tongue. But, if perchance you think that all these things existed in time past, but that the tribes of men have perished under scorching heat, or that some mighty shaking of the world has laid towns low, or that devouring rivers from persistent rains have gone forth through the earth and blotted cities out, so much the more in every case must you give way and own that there will be destruction too of heav'n and earth. For, when things were assailed by such diseases and such risks, if a more baneful force had fallen on them, they would have gone to ruin and great downfall far and wide. And in no other way are we seen to be mortal, than because we suffer in our turn the self-same maladies as those whom Nature has removed from life.

V 416–431. Now, in what ways yon confluence of matter founded earth and heaven, the abysses of the sea, the orbits of the sun and moon, this next in order I will state. For certainly the first-beginnings did not by design arrange themselves sagaciously, each in its proper order, and assuredly they did not stipulate what motions they should severally give; but, being numerous and stirred by blows from time now infinite, since they are wont to move, incited by their weights, to make all kinds of unions and try all possible creations by combining with each other, so it is that, sent abroad through many ages, after making trial of all kinds of union and motion, those at length unite which, suddenly combining, oft become beginnings of great things, of earth and sea and sky, and of the tribes of living things.

V 534–544. Now, that the Earth may stay at rest in the mid region of the world, 'tis probable that by degrees her weight grows less and fades away, and that there is another nature underneath, joined with her from its birth, and closely tied to those aerial portions of the world in which it lives and is engrafted. Therefore it is no burden and does not depress the air, just as his own limbs have no weight for any man; the head is not a burden to the neck, nor are we conscious either that the body's weight all rests upon the feet. But all weights coming from without and laid upon us do us hurt, though oft much smaller.

V 564–584. The sun's disk cannot be much larger, nor its heat much less, than to our senses they appear to be. For, from whatever distance fire can throw its light and breathe its heat upon our limbs, that distance by this length of intervening space takes nothing from the flame's amount, nor is the fire made any smaller to the sight. And therefore, since the heat and light poured from the sun come to our senses and upon these quarters lay a soothing touch, the form and contour also of the sun must needs appear to be from earth just as they really are; nothing whatever can be added, great or small. Again, the moon, whether she, as she moves, illuminates the earth with borrowed light, or throws her own from her own substance—howsoever that may be—moves with no larger shape than she appears to have, seen by our eyes. For all things that we see far distant through much air seem blurred in form before they seem decreased in size. Since then the moon presents a clear form and fixed shape, she must be seen on high by us below precisely as she is defined by her contours and of the size she actually is.

V 592–655. In this too there is nothing strange, how yonder sun which is so little, can send out so great a light that it can fill and flood the sky and every land and sea, and steep all things in heat. For it may be that from that place one single copious fountain for the total world bubbles. . . .

It may be also that, although the sun's fire is of no great size, yet heat from it may take possession of the air with fervent glow, if air perchance is so amenable and apt that it can be inflamed by impacts of small heat, as sometimes from one spark we see a conflagration indiscriminately fall on standing corn or stubble. . . .

Nor is there any sure and single explanation of the way in which the sun, leaving his summer quarters, travels to the wintry turning-point of Capricorn, and, thence returning, bends his course to the midsummer goal of Cancer; also how the moon is seen to traverse in a month a space in travelling through which the sun takes up the period of a year. No single cause, I say, has been assigned to these events. For it seems very probable indeed that it may be as the revered opinion of Democritus propounds, and that, the nearer any constellation is to earth, the less the speed with which the whirling of the sky can bear it on; for the whirl's fierce devouring strength is lessened down below and fades away, and so the sun falls gradually back among the rearward constellations, since he is much lower than the glowing ones. He says too, that the moon falls more distant from the sky and nearer to the earth, the less has she the power to keep pace with the constellations. For she is lower than the sun; therefore, the more relaxed the whirl with which she now is borne, the more do all the constellations round about her overtake her and pass by. And so she seems more swiftly than the sun to come back to the several constellations, because they with greater speed go back to her. It may be too that out of quarters of the world athwart the sun's path double airs can flow alternately at a fixed time, of which one has the power to thrust him from the summer constellations right down to his wintry turning-point and cold rigidity, and one to drive him from the frost's cold shades back to the glowing constellations and the sultry quarters of the world. So with the moon, and with the stars that in great orbits roll great years along; we must suppose that these by means of double airs can travel from alternate quarters. Do you not see too that by means of diverse winds lower and upper clouds proceed in different directions? Why should it be less possible for yonder stars to travel through their great ethereal orbits, borne by currents contrary to one another?

But night comes on and covers earth with widespread darkness, either when the sun after his long career touches the farthest parts of heav'n and languidly breathes forth his fires, impaired by their long journey and enfeebled by much air, or else because the same force which has borne his disk above the earth compels him now to turn his course below it.

V 705–736. The moon may shine because the sun's rays strike her, and may daily turn her light in greater measure to our sight according as she draws away from the sun's disk, until she shines right opposite to him with light quite full, and at her rising, as she soars aloft, beholds his setting; then, reversing by degrees her course, in a like manner she must bury, so to say, her light, the nearer she now draws to him in gliding from a different direction through the circle of the zodiac; as they suppose who represent the moon as being like a ball and holding underneath the sun the tenor of her course. 'Tis also possible that she revolves with her own light, presenting various grades of brightness; for it may be that there is another body, which is carried gliding on beside her, getting in her path and thwarting her in every way, but which we cannot see, because it moves devoid of light. Or she may possibly revolve like a round ball half steeped in shining light, and, as she wheels her ball, present her varying phases, till she offers to the vision of our open eyes that half which is illumined, then, reversing by degrees her course, twists round and takes away the light-bestowing portion of her mass or ball. . . .

Again, 'tis hard to show by reason and to prove in words why a new moon cannot be born each day, in fixed succession of her shapes and phases, each moon being born and perishing each single day and in her stead and place another being reproduced, since many things can be created in succession just as fixed.

V 780–796. Now I return to the world's babyhood and the soft fields of earth; what they decided in their new fertility first to uplift into the coasts of light and to entrust to the uncertain winds.

In the beginning, round the hills and over all the plains the earth gave forth the race of grasses and their verdant lustre; flowery meadows gleamed with hues of green, and then was given to the various kinds of trees the great contention of unbridled growth through air. As feathers, hairs, and bristles are before all else formed on the frames of quadrupeds and bodies of winged birds, so then the new earth first bore grass and shrubs, and next produced the mortal tribes, arising numerous, in many ways, on various plans. For living things cannot have dropped from heav'n, nor can the creatures of the land have issued from the salty pools. It follows that with reason Earth has won the name of mother, since from earth all things have been created.

V 821–827. Wherefore, I say repeatedly, with reason Earth has won and holds the name of mother, inasmuch as she herself produced the human race, and brought forth at a time now nearly fixed all living things that run wild on great mountains far and wide, and with them all the varying forms of birds that fly in air. But, since she needs must have some end of bringing forth, she left off bearing, like a woman worn with long continuance of life.

V 925–930. But that race of mankind then in the fields was hardier far than now; as well it might be, since the hard earth had produced it; based on larger and more solid bones within, bound with strong sinews passing through the flesh, no easy prey to heat or cold or unaccustomed food or any bodily disease.

V 953–961. They knew not yet how to cook food with fire, nor how to use as dress the skins of which they robbed wild beasts, but dwelt in woods and mountain-caves and forests, and amid the bushes hid their squalid limbs, when forced to shun the lashing of the wind or rain. They could not keep in view the common good, and knew not how to make a mutual use of any laws or customs. Whatever booty chance exposed to each, each carried off, spontaneously taught for self alone to use his strength and live.

V 1007–1033. Then too the want of food enfeebled frames and gave them o'er to death, but now the surfeit of good things o'erwhelms. Men then unwittingly oft poured out poison for themselves; they now more skilfully distribute it to others.

Then, after they got huts and skins and fire, and man and woman yoked withdrew into one [home and] learned [the usages of wedlock] and saw offspring born from them, then first the human race began to soften. The use of fire had for its consequence that their chill bodies could not now so well endure the frost beneath heaven's canopy; Venus impaired their strength, and children's coaxings easily broke down the domineering temper of their parents. Then neighbours too began to make with one another leagues of friendship, wishing neither to inflict nor suffer harm, and also recommended children and the female sex to mercy, when with gestures and with stammering speech they signified that all men ought to have compassion on the weak. Yet concord could not altogether be begotten; but a great and goodly part observed with piety their covenants, or else mankind would even then have been cut off entirely, nor could propagation have prolonged the generations until now.

'Twas Nature forced them to pronounce the various sounds of speech, and usefulness wrung out the names of things, in much the same way as the very inability to speak is seen to draw on children to gesticulate, by causing them to point out with their fingers things that are before them. For every living thing is conscious how far it can use its special faculties.

V 1105-1119. And daily more and more the more intelligent and strong of understanding showed them how to change their former ways of life for new things and for fire. Then kings began to build their cities and set up their citadels, as places of defence and refuge for themselves, and portioned out their gifts of herds and fields, as each man's looks or strength or understanding claimed; for good looks were high-priced and strength was in repute. Afterwards wealth was found and gold discovered, and this easily took honour from the strong and the good-looking; for, however strong men are and howsoe'er endowed with comeliness, they follow for the most part in the train of the more wealthy. Yet, if one would but let true reason guide his life, great wealth consists in frugal living and contentment; for there never is a scarcity of little.

V 1161-1203. Now, why the worship of the gods has spread throughout great nations, filling cities with their altars, and has led to the establishment of solemn rites, which in great places and on great occasions flourish still, and from which even now such dread has been inspired in mortals that it rears new shrines of gods throughout the earth and prompts mankind to crowd them upon festal days—of this 'tis not so very hard to give account in words. For even then the mortal races used to see with wakeful minds, and still more in their sleep, the glorious forms of gods, of wondrous stature. To these then they assigned sensation, since they seemed to move their limbs and utter lofty words in keeping with their glorious forms and ample strength. And they ascribed to them eternal life, because their faces were unchangeably presented to them and their forms remained the same, and, quite apart from this, beause they thought that those endowed with strength so great could never lightly be o'ercome by any force. And they esteemed them far before themselves in bliss, because not one of them was troubled with the fear of death, likewise because in sleep they saw them doing many wondrous things, yet bringing no fatigue upon themselves by their exertions. Besides, they saw the map of heaven and the various seasons of the year revolve in a fixed order, but could not discover how that came to pass. And so they found a shelter for themselves in making over all things to the gods and in supposing all things to be governed by their nod. And in the sky they placed their stations and their dwellings, inasmuch as through the sky the night, the moon, are seen to roll, the moon, the night and the grave stars of night, the nightly roaming torches of the sky and flying flames, clouds, sun, rain, snow, wind, lightning, hail, and the quick roar and the loud roll of threats.

O hapless human race, when it attributed such acts to gods and deemed them capable of bitter wrath! What groanings did they then occasion for themselves! what pains for us! what tears for our descendants! It is no mark of piety to be beheld with veiled head often turning to a stone and drawing near to every altar, falling prostrate on the ground with outspread hands before the shrines of gods, besprinkling altars with much blood of beasts, and linking vows to vows, but rather to have power to gaze on all things with a quiet mind.

Book Six

VI 1–8. In days of old 'twas Athens of distinguished name that first to wretched men gave fruitful crops, enacted laws, and re-created life; and she first gave sweet solaces to life, when she brought forth a man revealed to be of such an intellect, who in old days poured all his words from truthful lips, whose former glory, spread abroad, even when he was dead, by his divine discoveries, now mounts to heaven.

VI 43–46. And, now that I have shown the quarters of the world to be but mortal, and the sky to be of substance liable to birth, and have unknit the greater part of whatsoever things go on therein and must go on, hear further what remains for me to tell.

VI 83–85. The plan and spectacle of heaven must be understood; storms and bright lightnings must be sung, what deeds they do and every cause that carries them along.

VI 96–131. Firstly, the reason why the blue of heav'n is shaken with the thunder is that, when the winds engage in battle, the ethereal clouds meet in collision as they fly aloft. For no sound issues from a cloudless quarter of the sky, but, wheresoever there are clouds of denser mass, from thence more often thunder comes with its loud roar. Again, clouds cannot be of substance so condensed as stones and logs, nor yet so subtle as are mists and flying smoke. For either they would have to fall, like stones, forced down by their dead weight, or else, like smoke, could not stand fast, nor hold cold snow and showers of hail within them. Clouds also give forth sound above the levels of the spreading firmament; as sometimes canvas, stretched above great theatres and tossed 'twixt poles and beams, give forth a rattling sound, and sometimes, rent by freakish breezes, waxes fierce and imitates the crackling sound of paper torn—for noise of that kind also you may hear in thunder—or as when with blows winds whirl and buffet through the air a hanging garment or a fluttering sheet of paper. Indeed at times the clouds cannot so much collide with hostile fronts as pass each other at the side in contrary directions, grazing one another draggingly, from whence that dry, long-drawn-out sound brushes our ears, until the clouds have issued from their straitened quarters.

VI 160–166. Likewise, it lightens, when by their collision clouds have struck from one another many seeds of fire, as when a stone strikes stone or iron; for then too a light leaps forth and scatters sparks of fire. But we receive the thunder in our ears after our eyes perceive the flash, because the things that stir the ears always arrive more tardily than those which stir the sight.

VI 535–547. Now mark, and understand the cause of earthquakes. First, bring yourself to think that, down below as well as on the surface, earth is full on every hand of windy caves, and carries in her bosom many lakes and many cavities and cliffs and broken rocks; also you must believe that many rivers, hidden underneath the surface of the earth are violently rolling boulders sunk beneath their waves. For very fact requires that earth be like herself in all her parts. These things then being placed below but in conjunction with her, earth above quakes, shaken by great downfalls, when the monstrous caves beneath are undermined by time; indeed whole mountains fall, and at the mighty shock earthquakes spread in a moment far and wide from thence in various directions.

VI 703–711. There are too some phenomena of which 'tis not enough to give a single cause, but several; yet of them all one only is the cause; just as, if you yourself should see some lifeless body of a man lying far off, it would be needful to enumerate all of death's causes to include the single cause of his. For you could not be sure that he had died from sword-thrust, cold, disease, or, haply, poison; yet we know that it is some one of these kinds which has befallen him. Likewise, in many other cases we can say the same.

VI 906–927. Now to proceed; I shall essay to show by which of Nature's laws it comes to pass that iron can be drawn by that stone which the Greeks call magnet by its native name, because it has its origin in the hereditary bounds of the Magnetes. This stone men wonder at; indeed it often forms a chain of rings depending from it; you may sometimes look on five or more, hanging in order, swaying in the fickle breeze; a chain in which one ring hangs from another, clinging underneath, and one after the other learns the force and fetters of the stone; in so continuous a stream its force prevails.

In things of this kind much is to be verified before you can explain the thing itself, and it must be approached by very long and winding paths; wherefore the more I claim attentive ears and mind.

Firstly, from all things whatsoever that we see there must be sent and scattered in perpetual flow such particles as strike the eyes and challenge vision. Scents also flow perpetually from certain things; as cold flows from the streams, heat from the sun, and spray, that eats away the walls about our shores, from the sea-waves; moreover, various sounds are ever flowing through the air.

VI 936–941. Now I repeat my statement, how loose-meshed of substance all things are; which is distinctly shown too in the first book of my poem. For verily, although the knowledge of this fact applies to many things, yet in regard to this especial matter which I am proceeding to discuss it must above all and directly be laid down that there is nothing evident to us save substance mixed with void.

VI 959–964. Moreover, whatsoever particles are thrown from things are not all furnished with the property of rousing like sensations, and are not adaptable to all things in the self-same way. Firstly, the Sun bakes and makes dry the ground, but ice he thaws, and with his rays constrains the snows, piled deep on the high hills, to melt away.

VI 979–987. There still remains a matter which appears worth mentioning, before I come to speak about the thing itself. Since many apertures have been assigned to various things, these apertures must be endowed with differing natures; each must have a path and nature of its own. Indeed in living beings there are various senses, each of which exclusively appropriates its special object to itself. For sound, we see, finds entrance into one sense, taste of flavours to another, smell of fumes into a third.

VI 998–1041. Wherefore, since these preliminaries have been all well stablished, grounded, and laid down by me—now to proceed—from them the explanation and full cause of the attraction of the iron will be easily set forth and rendered clear. Firstly, out of this stone must needs flow very many seeds or, let us say, an emanation, which disperses with its blows all air that lies between the iron and the stone. When this space is made empty and much room left vacant in between, at once the first-beginnings of the iron, gliding forward in conjunction, fall into the void; so that somehow the ring itself comes after and thus moves with all its substance. For nothing has its primal elements more interknit, or clings together with a closer complication than the nature and cold chill of stubborn iron. Therefore it is not strange—because it is drawn onward by its elements—that particles, arising in large numbers from the iron, cannot move into the empty space without their being followed by the ring itself: now this it does, and follows on until it now has reached the very stone and clings to it with ties invisible. The self-same process acts in all directions; wheresoever void is made, the neighbouring particles, whether crosswise or from above, are borne at once into the vacancy. For they indeed are driven on by blows from other quarters, and have no power of themselves to rise into the air. Moreover (for, to render it more feasible, this operation is assisted by the help of motion) when the air that lies before the ring has been made rarer and the space more emptied and evacuated, then at once what air soever lies behind propels and bears it forward, so to put it, from the rear. For circumjacent air for ever buffets things; but in a case like this it drives the iron forward, since the space is void on one side and can take it in. This air of which I speak, when it has subtly crept through many apertures into the iron's little parts, impels and pushes it, as wind drives ships and sails. Again, all things must needs have air inside them, since they are of loose-meshed substance and the air lies round about and close to all things. This air then, which is deeply hidden in the iron, is for ever tossed in restless motion; thus, no doubt, it beats upon the ring and stirs it from within; the ring of course is borne in that direction whither it has once already started in the effort it has made to reach the empty space.

THE STOICS

Zeno of Citium in Cyprus, not to be confused with Zeno the Eleatic, came to Athens about 320 B.C., studied chiefly with the Cynics, and established Stoicism at the same time that Epicurus was commencing his rival activity. Since the two schools are contemporaneous, the only reason for discussing the Stoics after rather than before the Epicureans is that the latter—perhaps because of their method of catechetical instruction, perhaps because of lack of initiative, perhaps because no improvements in their system were necessary—remain in detailed agreement with Epicurus himself; whereas the Stoics—perhaps because they were vigorous, original thinkers, perhaps because Stoicism appealed to a wide variety of temperaments, or perhaps because there were so many loose ends left over from their founders' philosophy—manifest constant change, if not improvement. This constant change makes the study of Stoicism more difficult than that of Epicureanism. And since the sources are in a much more fragmentary condition, one often wonders whether two Stoics merely disagreed on a certain point or whether there was a harmonization now lost.

A brief statement of the external history of the school is necessary. Zeno, as has been said, founded Stoicism shortly before 300 B.C. He had at first been pleased with the Cynics' insistence on a life of stern morality. The

Cyrenaics, to whom may fitly be given the device, "Eat, drink, and be merry, for tomorrow we die," had been teaching that the good life consists in enjoying the immediate sensual pleasures. The Cynics, on the contrary. taught and tried to practice a life of strict virtue. But their teaching was marred by a disregard of technical philosophy, which alone can provide a firm basis for practical principles; and their practice was perverted by an increasing emphasis on its negative side. In their revolt against luxurious licentiousness, instead of stressing the positive qualities of social life, they contemned all social custom and degenerated into beggary and bestiality. To avoid such a result Zeno saw that it was necessary to inaugurate a new movement in which personal virtue, social responsibility, and sound learning would be combined.

His successor, the noble poet Cleanthes, who presided over the Stoa from 264 to 232, exemplified personal virtue and social responsibility. But his scholarship was not equal to the task of continuing a philosophic school.

Hence it was fortunate for Stoicism that its next head, Chrysippus, was able, during a term of twenty-six years (232–206), to reorganize the movement, to increase the number of students and disciples, and by systematizing and defending Zeno's doctrines to place the school on a relatively stable intellectual foundation.

The sources of information for those who directed the Stoic movement after the time of Chrysippus are in a deplorable state. Not to be passed by without mention, however, are Panaetius of Rhodes (180–110?), who organized Stoicism in Rome and then returned to head the school at Athens, and Posidonius (130–50?), also of

Rhodes, who, emphasizing the religious aspect of Stoicism, influenced Philo of Alexandria.

Roman Stoicism, as it developed after this time, was characterized by three closely related factors: an increased proportion of ethical speculation over logic and physics, the popularization of philosophic themes among the educated classes, and the consequent breakdown of Stoic orthodoxy by the adoption of ideas from other schools. From this period many complete works have been preserved. Names worthy of mention are Cicero (106–43), Seneca (4 B.C.–A.D. 65), Epictetus (50–130), and the Emperor Marcus Aurelius (121–180).

It may be true that the Epicureans conceived of logic and physics merely as a means to the good life and nothing but a means, but this is not true of Stoicism.[1]

While the Stoics as well as the Epicureans were chiefly interested in living a good life, the reaction of Zeno to the Cynic position of virtue divorced from thought, and Chrysippus' recognition that a well-rounded system of philosophy is essential in sustaining a definite way of life, saved the Stoics, so long as they remained fairly orthodox, from that nervous and impatient temperament which prematurely applies each disjointed item of alleged knowledge to practical affairs and disregards everything that does not yield immediate results.

The Stoics, of course, wanted to use knowledge in practical matters; unlike the Epicureans they were will-

1. Zeller III 1, p. 52, writes, "selbst die Physik, . . . ist doch nach Chrysippus nur desshalb nothwendig, weil sie uns die mittel an die Hand gibt, um über die Güter und die Uebel, das, was wir thun und meiden sollen, zu unterscheiden." And he refers to Plutarch *Sto. Rep.* 9, 6. None the less it seems to be a mistaken opinion.

ing to engage in political activity; they did not recommend a life of pure contemplation. On the other hand, their conception of virtue was not restricted to honesty and temperance. When such a restriction is in force, science can contribute to morality only as a means to the more effective discharge of one's obligations. But for the Stoics, the study of physics, far from being merely a means to virtue, is itself a virtue. When they compare philosophy with an animal, representing logic as the bones and sinews, ethics as the flesh, and physics as the soul,[1] or again, when they compare it with an enclosed field, or a walled city rationally governed, they do not represent physics as a means to ethics, but rather they teach that both physics and ethics are indispensable phases of a virtuous life. The same is true of logic and dialectic also.[2]

Were these studies merely means, were they of no intrinsic value, one should expect always to find the order: logic, physics, ethics; whereas the fact is that physics often comes last, "for it is more divine, and requires more profound attention."[3] This last phrase is all the more convincing because it is quoted from Sextus Empiricus, who lived after the Roman Stoics had written with almost exclusive attention to ethics in its narrower sense.

Very obviously the Stoics were trying to maintain a sane view of life. The pure contemplation of an Aristotelian deity, the unvarnished licentiousness of the Cyrenaics, the Epicurean withdrawal from the obligations of family and state, the excellent aim but insufficient

1. S.V.F. II 38.
2. Diogenes Laertius VII 46 and 92.
3. S.V.F. II 44.

foundation of the Cynics, were all weighed and found
wanting. The good life is a life of logic, of physics, and
of ethics, all three.

As a substitute for a summary of the actual teaching
under these three divisions, which would be impossible
in the short space of a small introduction, an intimation
may be given of a few chief points which it would be
wise to examine in the source material.

In logic, the Stoics, while they did not duplicate the
comprehensiveness of Aristotle's studies, were much more
interested in form than the Epicureans were. Their detail includes an elaborate classification of judgments, an
examination of validity, an attempt at the sorites, and
many purely grammatical distinctions. However, for a
common reason, Stoic logic like that of Epicurus, is primarily epistemological. The common reason lies in the
previous history. In their examination of Pre-Socratic
philosophy, the Sophists, before the time of Plato, had
decided that truth was impossible. Plato and Aristotle,
undaunted by the physical problem of flux and stability,
undismayéd by the psychological puzzle of subjectivism,
concluded that the trouble lay in materialism, and that,
if the existence of immaterial Ideas or Forms were
granted, truth could be established. But not all the disciples of Socrates were willing to abandon Pre-Socratic
materialism without a more determined attempt to base
truth on sensation. Hence the logic of the Epicurean and
Stoic may be considered as a reaction against the Ideas
and Forms.

The Stoic solution to the problem centers in the theory
of the comprehensive representation. An ordinary representation is an image in the brain of the real object which

produces it. The image may be very accurate or it may be confused as in a dream. But how tell? If there is no criterion by which one may know which images accurately represent their objects, then all appearances are of equal value and Sophistic skepticism will be the result. To avoid this, the Stoics asserted that some representations are *comprehensive,* cannot be false, and cannot be mistaken for false images. This true image bears in itself the mark of its real source in such a way that no false image can counterfeit it. As the light of the sun enables us to see both the sense object before us and the sun itself, so the comprehensive representation reveals both its object and its own truth. Other images we may doubt and reject, but the comprehensive representation forces our assent. No further argument on this point is possible, for it is an appeal to an immediate experience which cannot be doubted.

Stoic physics may not treat of a great variety of particular problems, but it is interesting because of the originality with which it studies a few major topics. The systems of Plato and Aristotle, involving participation and formal causality, were basically systems of classification, that is, they emphasized the common element in single objects by which they could be grouped together. In reaction—not that Aristotle had ignored genesis—the Stoics returned to the inspiration of Heraclitus and considered mainly the history of each object, its evolution, and the forces it displays. But, in contrast with the Epicureans, they did not explain genesis and destruction in terms of atoms and void. They were materialists in the sense that they believed that nothing is real which does not occupy space; but, on the other hand, in place of the inertia which characterizes atoms there is a force which permeates all that exists so that each thing is a spontaneous being. If a descriptive title were needed, the system could be called dynamic vitalism.

Such emphasis was placed on the spatial and bodily nature of everything real, that, as it became evident that qualities must be real, the Stoics were willing to admit that qualities, for example the virtues, were corporeal. In fact, simple bodies are single qualities; and individuality, which for Aristotle was a negation and strictly unknowable, becomes a positive factor. Aristotle, of course, would have replied that the Stoics destroyed individuality and substituted infimae species.

The force which activates bodies is the spirit, corporeal as all else, and its mode of operation is called tension. But if a corporeal spirit permeates bodies in a system which is not atomistic, then it is possible for two bodies to be in the same place at the same time, and impenetrability must be denied. The Stoics, therefore, advanced the theory of "complete mixture." Such a view, which at first seems so peculiar, for it also denies the law of action and reaction, becomes a little more intelligible when it is recalled that the corporeal universe instead of being an aggregation of atoms is a continuum—the primeval fire of Heraclitus in its various modifications. To construct an illustration, which, though somewhat inaccurate, at least uses modern terminology, one may conceive of the world as a vast magnetic field or texture of fields. Each body, its center being a node of a particular degree of tension, extends indefinitely; and the absence of reaction may be considered as the inability of the medium to determine the intensity.

One of the particular problems involved in this world-view, interesting because typical of the Stoic approach, is the theory of space. The modern concept of space, however, unites two factors which the ancients kept distinct. First, there is that space which is full of body and is called place; then second there is an empty space or void. Aristotle, of course, denied the existence of void, but argued the necessity of place as the condition for the existence of bodies. As the interior surface of a vase is the place of the liquid it contains, so in general he defined the place of a body as the interior surface of its container. The Stoics disagreed and made the place of a body the interval between its extremities. In both cases there is an underlying reason for the definition. Aristotle, because his celestial mechanics requires each sphere to move the next lower by contact, makes an essential distinction between continuity and contact. In Stoicism, strict contact is impossible and the contents of the world form a continuum. Motion is explained, not mechanically, but rather by a biological analogy. Each particular thing develops as if from a seed, and hence the source of motion is internal rather than external. This accords with their theory of complete mixture. In fact, bodies are individualized only by their seeds, and these seeds are no more than fragments of divinity or particular degrees of tension in the universal reason. Hence, in the most ultimate sense, there is but one body and but one place. Another reason for holding that the world is a continuum, and therefore for excluding void from the world, is the necessity of a continuous medium between the eye and the most distant star if sight is to be possible.

The other aspect of the problem of space, namely the

void, now finds an unexpected solution. If the world be a continuum, one would at first expect a denial of void. But such is not the case. Within the world there is no void, but beyond it the void stretches infinitely. Since the world is conceived as a self-sufficient system, and since self-sufficiency excludes vagueness and indetermination, the world must have limits in space as well as limits in qualities. Order requires finitude. Then, one may well ask, why should there be any void at all? The first answer to this question is the common notion that it is absurd to proceed to an assumed end of space and not to be able to advance farther. The second answer is more peculiarly Stoic. The world is composed of fire. Its history is one of recurrent cycles. Briefly, all is fire at first, then things begin to emerge until the world becomes as it is now, and finally there will be a general conflagration in which all will again become fire. But in the conflagration the world expands, and therefore there must be a void beyond the present world-limits.

Beneath this simple statement of Stoic opinion lie hidden numerous perplexing puzzles and peculiar paradoxes. Further study of these would leave no doubt as to why questioning minds could not be satisfied with the ipse dixit of a founder. In fact, the fundamental difficulty in this world-view is that the Stoics, in attempting to rehabilitate materialism, involuntarily discovered its inherent impossibilities. To surmount these, they strained their conception of body until it approached the notion of spirit. Their polemic opponents were quick to take advantage of their embarrassment, and finally Plotinus used their failures in establishing his spiritualism.

In religion, while some of the later Stoics tended

toward a belief in a personal God, the earlier and standard position was that of pantheistic determinism. The
primeval fire or ultimate reason controls all existence.
Not only their physics, but a considerable portion of their
logical theory contributed to this view. An example may
be taken from Chrysippus. "If there is a motion without
a cause, not every proposition will be either true or false.
For that which does not have efficient causes is neither
true nor false. Every proposition, however, is either
true or false. Therefore there is no motion without a
cause." Although popular opinion is naturally averse to
determinism, it was exactly this phase of Stoicism which
won for its adherents a welcome that cultured Romans
denied to the Epicurean libertarians. For if the theory of
determinism be correct, the practices of divination—an
integral part of the popular religion—are scientifically
justifiable. The entrails of an animal, to be sure, do not
cause a future event, but since both are phases of one
system, the former are indicative of the latter. In harmony with this, no one would say because of this, the
Stoics conformed to common religious ritual and, further, took a serious interest in Roman government. Thus
on the whole they were more conservative than the Epicureans and made a much better impression on their
contemporaries in spite of their determinism.

The import of many of the statements relative to determinism is obscured by the suspicion that Cicero may
not have completely understood the Stoic position. However, no doubt can be cast on the Stoics' strong assertion
of moral accountability. Distinctions were drawn between
the doctrine of necessity, the doctrine of fate, and the
certainty of the future; responsibility was based on voli-

tion rather than on absolute freedom; and to this day the Stoic school enjoys the reputation of being the most virtuous of the ancient groups.

SPECIAL INDEX TO THE STOIC FRAGMENTS

Note: This table is taken from Von Arnim's *Stoicorum Veterum Fragmenta.*

THE STOICS

VOL. I. ZENO

2. ZENO'S OPINIONS

45. *Diogenes Laertius.* They assert that philosophic argument has three parts. One part of it concerns physics, another ethics, and the third logic. This division was first made by Zeno of Citium in his work *On Logic.*

46. *Diogenes Laertius.* But others place logic first, physics second, and ethics third, among whom is Zeno in his work *On Logic.* [Cf. Vol. II, 41–44]

A. Logic

49. *Stobaeus.* Zeno used to compare the tricks of the dialecticians with just measures which measure, not fire or some other noble thing, but husks and filth.

50. *Plutarch.* [Zeno] would solve sophisms and would require his disciples to understand dialectic because it was capable of doing this.

51. *Arrianus Epictetus.* The business of a philosopher is what Zeno says: to know the elements of argument, what type each of them is, how they harmonize with each other, and what their implications are.

Epistemology
(*Representation, Sensation, Criterion*)

52. *Cicero.* Arcesilas agreed with Zeno in considering the greatest power of the Sage to be the guarding against entanglement and the avoidance of error.

53. *Cicero.* He removed from the Sage and the virtuous man, error, rashness, ignorance, opinion, suspicion, and in a word everything foreign to a firm and constant assent.

54. *Cicero.* The Sage never opines, never regrets, never is mistaken, never changes his mind.—

Lactantius. Therefore if it is impossible to know anything, as Socrates taught, and nothing ought to be opined, as Zeno says, all philosophy is destroyed.—

Augustine. They accepted Zeno's position that nothing is more disgraceful than to opine.

Cf. *Stobaeus.* The Sage does not conceive anything weakly, but rather, surely and certainly; therefore also he does not opine . . . They believe that a rational person neither repents . . . nor is fickle, changeable, or perplexed.

55. *Cicero.* [Zeno] changed many things in that third part of philosophy, in which first he said some new things concerning the senses themselves, which he considered to be connected by some sort of impulse produced extrinsically, which he called representation (φαντασία) but which we call perception (*visum*).

59. *Cicero.* [Arcesilas] perhaps asked Zeno what would happen if the Sage could neither perceive anything nor have an opinion. I believe he replied that the Sage could never entertain an opinion because there was something which could be perceived. What is it then? Perceptions, no doubt. What sort of perception? Then he defined it as follows: It is an imitation, a seal, an impression from what exists just as it exists. Then it was asked further whether such a true perception was of the same type as a false perception. Here Zeno clearly saw that there was no perception which could be perceived if there could be one arising from that which exists, essentially similar to one arising from that which does not exist.

[*Arnim:* These passages prove that to Zeno are traced all the elements of the definition of comprehensive representation which are found in the Greek of Sext. *Adv. Math.* VII 248— to wit:]

A comprehensive representation is one which has been stamped and sealed by that which exists and just as it exists in such a way that it could not be produced by what does not exist.—

Augustine. But let us see what Zeno says. A perception can be grasped and perceived such as has no common characteristic with a false one.

60. *Cicero.* He [Zeno] did not place faith in every perception, but only in those which possess a peculiar mark of those things which are seen; but that perception when it was discerned by virtue of itself, he called *comprehensible*—will you permit this term? Yes indeed, said Atticus, for in what other way can you express καταληπτόν? But after it had been received and approved, he called it *comprehension,* resembling those things which are grasped (*prehenderentur*) by the hands—from which analogy he derived this noun, though no one had ever before used this word in this sense; and he also used many new words, for he was speaking of new things. But that which was grasped by sense he called a sensation (*sensum*), and if it was grasped so that it could not be destroyed by reason, he called it knowledge; otherwise he called it ignorance; from which also arises opinion, which is weak, and is common to what is false or unknown. But between knowledge and ignorance he placed that comprehension which I mentioned, and counted it neither as right nor wrong, but said that it alone was to be believed.

For this reason he placed faith in the senses also, because, as I said above, comprehension by the senses seemed to him to be true and trustworthy, not because it grasped everything in the object, but because it missed nothing which could affect it, and because nature had given it to us as a criterion of knowledge and principle from which afterward notions of things might be impressed on our minds from which not only principles, but some wider avenues of approach to rationality are discovered. But error, rashness, ignorance, opinion, and suspicion, and in a word everything foreign to a firm and consistent assent, he removed from virtue and wisdom.

61. *Cicero.* To these perceptions accepted by the senses he joins the assent of the mind, which he considers to be placed in us and voluntary.

65. *Stobaeus.* The "notions" of Zeno, they say, are neither things nor qualities, but are images of the soul like things and like qualities. The ancients called them ideas. For the ideas

belong among those things subsumed under the notions, as men and horses, to mention the more common of living beings and other things, of which they say there are ideas. But the Stoic philosophers say that ideas are unreal, and that we share in "notions," but that we only chance upon their modifications which they call "common nouns." [1]—

Aetius. Zeno's Stoics called the Ideas our notions.—

Diogenes Laertius. A notion is an image of reason, neither a real thing nor a quality, but like a real thing and like a quality, as an image of a horse arises when no horse is present.

66. *Cicero.* For Zeno denies that you know anything. How is that, you will ask, for we defend the proposition that even a fool grasps a great many things. But you deny that anyone except the Sage can *know* anything. And Zeno illustrated it by a gesture. For when he showed his hand with the fingers extended, he would say, perception is like this. Then when he closed his fingers a little, he would say, assent is like this. Then when he had completely closed his hand and made a fist, he would say that that was comprehension. And it is from this illustration that he derived for that mental state the name κατάληψις, which did not exist before. When, finally, he brought his left hand against his right fist and grasped it tightly, he would say that such was knowledge and no one but the Sage was capable of it.

68. *Stobaeus.* Knowledge is assured comprehension unchangeable by argument.—*ibid.* Ignorance is a changeable and weak assent.—

Sextus Empiricus. Knowledge is the assured and certain comprehension which cannot be set aside by argument.—

Diogenes Laertius. They say that knowledge itself is either assured comprehension or a habitude in the reception of representations, unchangeable by argument.

---

1. Arnim says: ultimum enuntiatum non intelligo. And Ludwig Stein, *Erkenntnistheorie*, p. 293, makes a similar confession. I suggest that the ἐννοήματα are the common notions which everyone has, and their modifications are the specific knowledges resulting from individual experience.

B. Physics

I. The Principles, etc.

85. *Diogenes Laertius.* They hold that there are two principles for the whole world, the active and the passive. The passive is unqualified reality or matter; the active is the reason in matter, or God. For God is an eternal reality fashioning each thing throughout all matter. Zeno of Citium asserts this teaching in his book, *On Reality.*—

Achilles Tatius. Zeno of Citium says the principles of the whole world are God and matter. The former is active, the latter passive, and from their combination the four elements arise.

86. *Chalcidius.* Many, however, distinguish between matter and reality, as Zeno and Chrysippus. Matter, they say, is that which underlies all those things which have qualities, but reality is the primary matter of all things, their most original basis, in its own nature without aspect or form. For example, copper, gold, iron, and other such things are the matter of whatever is made of them; but not their reality. But that which is the cause of the existence both of these things and others as well, that, they say, is substance.

87. *Stobaeus.* The primary matter of all things is reality, is all eternal, and neither increases nor decreases. Its parts, however, are not always arranged in the same way, but they are separated and are again conjoined. Throughout, this matter is arranged by the universal reason, which some call Fate, and which is similar to the seed in the womb.—

Chalcidius. The Stoics, of course, say that God is matter, or rather, a quality inseparable from matter, a god which permeates matter as semen permeates the genital organs.

88. *Chalcidius.* Next Zeno said that this reality is finite and that it is the single and common substance of all existing things. It is divisible and to a certain extent mutable. Parts of it can be changed, but not so destroyed that any existing thing is consumed into nothing. But, he thought, as in the case of

wax which serves as material for an innumerable diversity of figures, so there is neither form nor figure nor any inherent quality whatsoever in the basic matter of all things. Yet matter is always and inseparably conjoined to some quality. Since it is both without origin and without destruction, because it is neither produced from the non-existent nor subject to annihilation, it has never from all eternity lacked that spirit and vigor which moves it rationally, in its entirety at times, and at other times in part. This is the cause of the frequent and vehement turning of the universe. Further, this motivating spirit is not nature, but in truth, a rational soul, which, vivifying the sensitive world has provided it with that charm with which it is now adorned. So they call it a blessed living being and God.

89. *Stobaeus*. Zeno said that a cause is that through which; but that of which it is the cause is an accident. The cause is a body, that of which it is the cause is a predicate; and it is impossible for the cause to be present and that of which it is the cause not to occur. The significance of this statement is as follows. A cause is that through which anything occurs, for example through wisdom comes wise deliberation, and by the soul there is life, and through temperance there comes temperate living. For when there is temperance with respect to anything, it is impossible not to have temperate actions, or when there is a soul, not to have life, or wisdom, not wise results.

90. *Cicero*. [Zeno] disagreed with [the Peripatetics and Academicians] because he held that in no possible way could anything be affected by that which is destitute of body . . . nor could anything be incorporeal which either affected something else or was affected.

95. *Aetius*. Zeno and his disciples asserted that there was no empty space within the cosmos; but outside, it was boundless. They distinguish void, place, and space. The void is empty of body; place is that which is occupied by body, and space is that which is only partially occupied, as in the case of a cask of wine [half full].

II. The World, etc.

98. *Aristocles.* [Zeno] said the fundamental substance of all existing things is fire, in this following Heraclitus, and the principles of fire, he said, were matter and God, here following Plato. But he asserted that they both were bodies, an active and a passive, whereas [Plato] said that the primary active cause was incorporeal. Next, the whole cosmos at certain fated periods is dissolved by fire, and then again formed into a world. Now the primary fire is like a kind of seed, containing the "reasons" of all things and the causes of everything, past, present, and future. Now the union and sequence of these things is an inevitable and unavoidable fate, knowledge, truth, and law of existing things. And in this respect the affairs of the cosmos are arranged most excellently as in a well-governed city.

99. *Stobaeus.* From Zeno. Of all the things in the world constructed in their particularity, the parts have a motion towards the middle of the whole, and similarly towards the middle of the cosmos itself. Therefore it is correctly said that all parts of the world have a motion towards the middle of the cosmos, but most of all, the heavy parts. The same thing is the cause both of the fixation of the cosmos in the limitless void and likewise of the earth in the cosmos, settled about its center by an equilibrium of forces. A body is not in every case heavy, for air and fire are weightless; but even these somehow are stretched towards the middle of the whole sphere of the cosmos, but their composition has reference to its circumference, for by their nature these elements ascend, because they have no share in weight. In analogy with these things he says the cosmos itself has no weight because as a whole it is composed of elements some heavy, some weightless. He is satisfied that the whole earth in itself is heavy but in addition to this thesis he holds that because it has the middle position, and because bodies of this nature move toward the center, it remains in this position.

102. *Stobaeus.* Zeno expressly made this assertion. Of necessity this type of world formation out of reality by revolution must

occur whenever fire burns into water through air. Some of it sinks and becomes earth; of the rest some remains water; from the vapor air comes into being, and from some of the air fire is kindled, and "the mixture" arises by the change of the elements into one another,[1] when a body as a whole penetrates some other whole.—

Diogenes Laertius. God and Mind and Fate and Zeus are all one, and he is called by many other names. Existing in himself from the beginning he turns all reality into water through air. And as the seed is surrounded by the seminal fluid, so also he who is the seminal reason of the cosmos remains within the moisture and with ease fashions matter to his own purposes with reference to the production of the following stages. Then he first produced the four elements, fire, water, air and earth. Zeno discusses these things in his book *On the Whole.*

107. *Stobaeus.* It pleased Zeno, Cleanthes, and Chrysippus [to say] that it is possible for reality to change into a seed, fire, and again out of this to produce the arrangement of nature such as formerly existed.—

Eusebius. For it pleases the Stoic philosophers [to say] it is possible for all reality to change into fire as into a seed and again out of this to produce a world arrangement, such as previously existed. And Zeno, Cleanthes, and Chrysippus, the foremost and oldest of the school approve this belief.

109. *Tatianus.* Zeno declares that through the conflagration the same things reappear in the same relations, but I say that one must decline [to favor] Anytos and Meletos in their accusation, and Bousiris in his slaying of his guest, and Heracles in his suffering again.—

---

1. Arnim's notes are: μῖξιν seclusi, μῖξιν <καὶ> κρᾶσιν Diels|| γίνεσθαι—μεταβολῇ vix sana; nam κρᾶσις non potest fieri τῇ εἰς ἄλληλα μεταβολῇ. Fortasse ἐπιγίνεσθαι.

It would seem better to bracket κρᾶσιν or with Diels insert καί. The *vix sana* can be alleviated by considering the phrase as referring to the complete mixture. In this case μεταβολή should be understood as the generic term for motion, clumsily expressed perhaps, but elucidated by the following clause.

Nemesius. For Socrates and Plato and each of the men with them and their friends and fellow-citizens will exist again and they will argue the same things and meet with the same [friends] and follow the same pursuits, and every city and village and field will be restored in a like manner.

110. *Sextus.* But [Plato] sets forth virtually the same argument as Zeno. For even he says the All is most beautiful, a work executed according to nature, and in all probability a living being both intelligent and rational.

111. *Sextus.* And again Zeno says, the rational is better than the irrational. But nothing is better than the cosmos, therefore the cosmos is rational. And thus it participates in intelligence and life. For the intelligent is better than the non-intelligent, and the living than the non-living. But nothing is better than the cosmos. Therefore the cosmos is intelligent and animate.—

Cicero. That which uses reason is better than that which does not use reason. However nothing is better than the world; therefore the world uses reason.

112. *Cicero.* Furthermore he drew a conclusion by an analogy, as he often did, in this manner "If flutes playing musical tones grew on an olive tree, would you doubt that some knowledge of fluteplaying existed in the olive tree? If plane-trees bore flutes resounding melodiously, likewise naturally you would think that music existed in the plane-trees. Why therefore is the world not considered animate and intelligent when it produces from itself animate and wise beings?—

Cicero. Nothing which is without mind and reason can give birth from itself to an animate and rational being. The world however gives birth to animate and rational beings. Therefore the world is animate and rational.

114. *Cicero.* He [Zeno] also [argued] in this manner: "No part of anything devoid of sensation can be sentient. However, parts of the world are sentient; therefore, the world is not devoid of sensation."—

Sextus. Certainly that which contains the rational structures is itself completely rational. For it is not possible for the whole to be inferior to the parts.

V. *The Human Soul, etc.*

135. *Diogenes Laertius.* Zeno of Citium said the soul was warm breath. For by this we are alive and able to move.

137. *Chrysippus.* Death is a separation of soul from body. But nothing incorporeal separates itself from the corporeal; for nothing incorporeal touches the corporeal. But the soul both touches and separates itself from the body. Therefore the soul is a body.

VI. *Theology*

155. *Tertullian.* For see how Zeno also separates worldly matter from God, and says that he is diffused through it like honey through the cone.

159. *Tatianus.* And according to Zeno, God will be considered the author of evil, dwelling in sewers and in worms and in those acting lewdly.—

Sextus. And the Stoics extend spirit even through the putrid.

160. *Tertullian.* With your wise men also the Logos, that is the Word and Reason, is evidently the artificer of the universe. For Zeno denominates him the maker who has formed all things in an ordered arrangement, and he is called both Fate and God and the mind of Jupiter and the necessity of all things.

171. *Cicero.* Therefore Zeno defines nature thus: it is, he says, a skillful fire, proceeding methodically for the purpose of generation. For he holds that most of all the special work of an art is to create and generate, and that which in the works of our arts the hand accomplishes, nature accomplishes much more skillfully, nature, as I have said, the skillful fire, the teacher of the other arts.

172. *Cicero.* And by this theory all nature is skillful because it has as it were a certain method and plan which it follows. In fact the nature of the world itself, which encompasses and contains all things in its embrace, is declared by the same Zeno not only skillful but plainly a skilled workman, and a

provider taking care of the uses and advantages of all things. And as other natures are generated, developed and sustained by their own seeds, so the nature of the world has all the motions of will and impulses and desires that the Greeks call "urges." And it employs the actions consonant with these desires as we ourselves do who are affected by feelings and sensations. Since therefore the mind of the world is of such a nature, for this reason it can rightfully be called either prudence or providence, (for in Greek it is called "forethought,") and this nature provides most of all for, and is especially concerned with, these things, first that the world may be best fitted for permanent existence, then that it may lack nothing, but mainly that every adornment and excellent beauty may exist in it.

VOL. II. CHRYSIPPUS

Prolegomena. What is Philosophy?

38. . . . —*Diogenes Laertius*. And they compare philosophy with an animal, representing logic as the bones and sinews, ethics as the flesh, and physics as the soul. Or again, with an egg. The outside is logic, next [the white] is ethics, and the innermost part is physics. Or it is like an enclosed field. Its enclosing fence is logic, the fruit is ethics, and the earth and trees are physics. Or they compare philosophy with a walled city rationally governed.

42. *Plutarch*. Chrysippus thought it was necessary for the young students first to attend lectures on logic, second on ethics, and then on physics, and similarly at last to take up theology. Since he very frequently made these assertions, it will suffice to add a quotation from the fourth book on *Lives*. "First of all it seems to me, conformably to what was so correctly stated by the ancients, that there are three types of philosophic speculation, logic, ethics, and physics. Next it is necessary to arrange them by putting logic first, ethics second, and physics third. Now the final division of physics is theol-

ogy, therefore also they named the teaching of this subject the initiatory rites." [1]

44. *Sextus Empiricus.* The Stoics teach that we should begin with logic, continue with ethics, and place physics last. For first it is necessary to make the mind sure so that it will be an invincible guardian of the teachings. And dialectic serves to make the reason secure. Second we must subscribe to ethics to improve our character, for the study of ethics is without danger to one who has previously mastered logic. And finally we must proceed to physics, for it is more divine and requires more profound attention.

Logic

I. Epistemology

1. Representation

52. *Diogenes Laertius.* It pleased the Stoics to place first their theory of representation and sensation, because the criterion, by which the truth about things is known, is generically a representation, and because the theory of assent and of comprehension and thought, the presupposition of everything else, cannot be formulated without involving representation. For representation comes first, then articulate thought puts into words what representation has conveyed.

53. *Diogenes Laertius.* Representation is an impression on the soul, the name appropriately transferred from the imprint which a seal makes on wax. Representations are either comprehensive or non-comprehensive. The comprehensive representation, which they assert is the criterion of things, is that which is produced by a real object, resembles the object itself, and is sealed and stamped on the soul. The non-comprehensive representation either does not come from a real object, or if it does, it does not resemble the object. It is not well formed or distinct.

---

1. The order, logic, physics, ethics, is often given.

55. *Diogenes Laertius.* There is a difference between representation and illusion. For illusion is a fancy of the mind, such as occurs in sleep, but representation is an impression on the soul, that is, a qualitative change, as Chrysippus held in the second book of his *Psychology.* For one must not take the word "impression" in the sense of the impression of a seal, since one cannot hold that many imprints exist at the same spot at the same time.   60. We consider a representation to be that which comes from and resembles an object and has been stamped, imprinted, and sealed in the soul in such a fashion that it could not have come from an unreal object.   61. They say that some representations are sensible and others are not. The sensible representations are received through one or more sense organs, the others come through the mind as in the case with the incorporeals and other things received by the reason. Some sensible representations are from real objects and occur with a yielding and assent; but there are other representations which are appearances, only seeming to come from an object. Again, some representations are rational, others irrational. The rational belong to rational beings, the irrational to irrational animals. The rational representations are thoughts, but the irrational do not happen to have a name. Some also are the result of skill and others are not. For certainly a statue is regarded in one manner by a trained sculptor and in a different manner by an unskilled person.

56. *Sextus.* Since the Stoic theory remains, let us next discuss it also. These gentlemen, then, assert that the comprehensive representation is the criterion of truth. We shall understand this if we first learn what they think representation is and what its specific differences are. Now, they hold that a representation is an impression in the soul. But here differences of opinion commence. For Cleanthes understood "impression" as depressions and elevations just like the impressions made on wax by a signet. But Chrysippus considers such a view absurd. For first, he said, if the mind should simultaneously represent a triangle and quadrangle, this view would require the same body [i.e., the mind] at the same time to have in

itself the differing shapes of a triangle and a quadrangle or even a circle also, which is absurd. And if we should have a great many representations together, the soul also would have a multitude of shapes, which is worse than the previous case. But he conjectured that Zeno had used the word "impression" in the sense of "qualitative change," so that the definition should be: "Representation is a qualitative change of the soul," since it is no longer absurd that the same body at the same time, when we have many representations, should admit a multitude of qualitative changes. For just as the air, when many people are talking at once, admits in one place innumerable differences and contains many vibrations and qualitative changes, so also the ruling part of the soul somewhat analogously will suffer a variety of representations.

59. *Alexander Aphrodisias.* Therefore also they define representation as an impression in the soul, in fact an impression in the ruling part of the soul. Again they say that either the impression now coming into existence is a representation, or the one which previously began and still exists. But if it is the one now coming into existence they would be saying that actual representation is identical with sensation. For sensation is the beginning of the impression. But representations occur even apart from actual sensation. But if a representation is a previously generated impression which still exists, they would be saying that memory is representation.

63. *Sextus.* We must say that a representation is a certain affection of the living being, bringing into consciousness both itself and the other thing. For example, by looking at something, says Antiochus, we direct our sight in a certain manner, and do not continue it in the same condition as it was before looking. Now, by such a change we grasp two things, of which one is the change itself, i.e., the representation, and the second is that which induced the change, i.e., the thing seen. And similarly with the other senses. Therefore, just as light makes known both itself and all things in it, so also representation, since it controls a person's knowing, must, like light, both reveal itself and indicate that which clearly produced it.

69. *Sextus.* As to what this comprehensive representation is for which we are seeking, those who define it say: that one coming from a real object, etc. Then again, since everything which is learned definitively is learned from things known, when we inquire as to what a real object is, they turn around and say that a real object is that which produces a comprehensive representation.

2. Sensation

71. *Diogenes Laertius.* By sensation the Stoics mean the spirit which stretches from the center of the soul to the senses, and also comprehension by the senses, and also the apparatus of the sense organs, which apparatus some people lack. Furthermore, the activity itself is called sensation.

74. *Porphyry.* The Stoics do not place sensation in representation alone but make its essence depend on assent. For sensation is assent to a sensible representation, the assent being in conformity with desire.

78. *Aetius.* The Stoics assert that sensations are true, but representations are sometimes true and sometimes false.

80. *Sextus.* When such difficulties are met with in this matter the dogmatists are accustomed to say that the external, underlying, sensible object is neither a whole nor a part, but it is we who add the predicate of whole or part to it. For whole is a term of relation, since a whole is considered such with reference to the parts. And the parts are also relative, for they are considered parts with reference to the whole. But relations exist in our recollection and our recollection is in us. Accordingly the whole and the part are in us, and the external, underlying sensible object is neither a whole nor a part, but it is the thing of which we predicate our recollection.

3. Notions

83. *Aetius.* The Stoics say: When a man is born, the ruling part of the soul is like a sheet of paper suitable for writing. On this he writes off each single thought.—That which comes through the senses is the first thing written down. For those who perceive something, like white, have a memory which

comes from it. And when many similar memories have arisen, then we say people have experience, for experience is the manifold of similar representations.—But of thoughts, some arise naturally in the aforementioned ways without technical skill, while others come by our teaching and conscious effort. These latter are called thoughts only (ἔννοια) but the others are also termed preconceptions.—Now reason, because of which we are called rational, is said to have received all its preconceptions by the time a child is seven years old. And a notion (ἐννόημα) is an image of the mind of a rational living being, for when the image strikes a rational soul, then it is called a notion, taking its name from the mind.[1]—Therefore all those which strike irrational animals are images only, but those which we or the gods have are both images, generically, and notions, specifically.

85. *Sextus.* They attempt to relieve the situation by examples. [Namely, that the incorporeals neither produce anything nor give us representations, but it is we who frame representations with respect to them.] For, they say, just as a wrestling coach or drill sergeant sometimes takes the hands of the boy and teaches him rhythm by putting him through certain motions, and as at other times, standing away from the boy, the trainer goes through the rhythm as an example for the boy to imitate, so also some things represented make their mark as if by touching and coming into contact with the ruling part of the soul, for example, white, black, and, in general, body; but other things have such a nature that while the ruling part of the soul has representations which refer to them, yet the representations were not made by them, for example, meaning,[2] which is incorporeal.

88. *Sextus.* All thinking comes from sensation or not without sensation, and either from experience or not without experience. Therefore we shall not find the so-called false representations, as those of sleep or of insanity, to be separated from the knowledge we obtain by sensation and experience.—And in general nothing is to be found in reflection which one has not

1. A pun in Greek.
2. More accurately: the fact of being predicated.

learned in experience. For it will be grasped either by similarity to things which appear in experience, or by exaggera-
tion, or diminution, or composition.

4. Comprehension

90. *Sextus*. For they [The Stoics] say that three things are
joined together, *viz*. knowledge, opinion, and comprehension
which stands between them. Knowledge is a comprehension
which is sure, certain and unchangeable by argument, whereas
opinion is a weak and false assent. Comprehension which
stands between them is assent to a comprehensive representation. Now, a comprehensive representation, according to
them, is one that is true in such a way that it cannot become
false. They say also that knowledge occurs only in wise men,
opinion occurs only in foolish minds, but comprehension is
common to both and is the criterion of truth.

96. *Sextus*. Again the Stoics, with reference to goods which
concern the soul, say that the virtues are certain arts. For an
art, they say, is a system of organized comprehensions, and
comprehension arises in the ruling part of the soul. But it is
incomprehensible how a deposit of comprehensions, so numerous as to become an art, could arise in the ruling part of
the soul when they assert the soul to be air. For since the
[air or] spirit is fluid and is said to be moved as a whole
with each impression, each successive impression will erase
the one before it.

6. The Criterion

107. *Sextus*. Now it is possible to subdivide this rational
criterion by saying that one thing is the criterion in the sense
of agent, another in the sense of instrument, and the third
as application or temporary use. The agent is the man, the
instrument is sensation, and the third is the application of
the representation. The man by whom the judgment is made
is similar to a craftsman or to one who weighs and measures;
sensation and mind resemble the scales or the yardstick, by
means of which the elements of the judgment are clarified;
and the application of representation, in accordance with

which the man is moved to make a judgment, resembles the temporary use of the aforementioned instruments.

108. *Origen.* [Celsus] teaches something very similar to the Stoics, who destroy intelligible realities when they assert that whatever is grasped is grasped by the senses, and all comprehension is attached to sensation.

115. *Cicero.* Now let us discuss briefly assent and approbation, which the Greeks call συγκατάθεσις.—For when we were explaining the power of the senses it was made clear that many things are comprehended and perceived by the senses, and this could not occur without assent. Further, since the chief difference between the animate and inanimate is that the animate can do something (for a living being which could do nothing at all is inconceivable) either it must be denied sensation, or else assent, which is in our power, must be allowed to it. . . . These considerations also follow: Without assent there can be neither memory, concepts, nor arts. And most important of all, though some things may be in our power, nothing is in the power of the man who never assents to anything. Where then will virtue be, if nothing is in our power?

116. *Cicero.* Moreover it is also clear that there must be set down a principle which wisdom, when it begins to do anything, may follow, and this principle must be adapted to nature. For otherwise, desire, (for so we translate ὁρμή) by which we are impelled to act and by which we desire what is seen, could not function. But that which initiates this function must first be seen and believed, which could not be the case if that which is seen cannot be distinguished from what is false. But how can the mind be moved to desire, if what is seen is not perceived to be adapted to or alien to nature?

Furthermore, if it does not occur to the mind what one's duty is, a man will never do anything at all, he will never be impelled toward anything, he will never be moved. But if a man is ever to do anything at all, then it is necessary that what occurs to him seem true.

117. *Cicero.* Most of all the knowledge of virtue proves that many things can be perceived and comprehended. In these

matters alone do we say that knowledge exists. And we believe that knowledge is not just any grasping of a thing, but it is a stable and unchangeable grasp—in fact it is wisdom, the art of living, which derives its stability of itself. But if this stability cannot be perceived or known, I ask from what source is it derived and in what manner?

118. *Sextus.* But the dogmatists in their refutation regularly question the method by which the skeptic proves there is no criterion. For he argues with the aid of a criterion or without. If he does not use a criterion, he cannot be trusted; but if he has a criterion he will be overturned, and in saying there is no criterion he will admit accepting a criterion in order to banish it.

And again, when we [Skeptics] argue, "If there is a criterion, either it is or is not judged by a superior criterion," and then draw one of two conclusions, *viz;* an infinite regress or the absurdity that there is something which is a criterion of itself, they return the reply that it is not absurd to consider something as its own criterion. For the straight line is the norm both of itself and of other lines, and the balance measures the equality of the weights in the pans and of itself as well, and light reveals objects not only but itself also. Thus the criterion can be established as a criterion of itself and of other things too.

II. Dialectic

132. *Sextus.* Some, particularly the Stoics, think that truth differs from the true in three ways, in being, composition, and power; in being, in so far as truth is a body, whereas the true is incorporeal. And quite plausibly so, they say, for the true is a proposition and a proposition is meaningful and meaning is incorporeal. On the other hand truth is a body in so far as it is regarded as knowledge declaratory of all true things, and all knowledge is a state of the ruling part of the soul, just as the fist is considered as a state of the hand. The ruling part of the soul is body according to them, and thus truth is generically corporeal. And [they differ] in composition inso-

far as the true is conceived as something uniform and simple in its nature—whereas truth, being composed of knowledge, is on the contrary conceived as a system and articulation of many parts.—And they differ from each other in power, since the true is not altogether dependent on knowledge (for even the fool, and the child, and the insane person sometimes say something true, but do not have knowledge of the true) but truth is considered to require knowledge. Hence, also he who possesses this is wise (for he had knowledge of true things) and never speaks falsely, even if he says something false, because he says it not from an evil but from a kindly disposition.—Thus also the wise man, that is, he who has the knowledge of the true, sometimes says what is false but never speaks falsely because his mind does not assent to the false.—Speaking that which is false differs greatly from speaking falsely in that the former arises from a kindly mind but lying from an evil mind.

A. Things Signified: Sound

141. *Gellius.* The Stoics claim that sound is a body and they say it is air vibrating.

144. *Galen.* Sound, speech, and voice are not the same thing. Sound is the result of the sound-organs; and speech of the speech-organs, which are first the tongue, and then the nose, the lips, and the teeth. But the sound organs are the larynx and the muscles which move it, and the nerves which bring the power to them from the brain. But it was not everything properly perceptible by hearing which the ancients called voice, nor was it that only which issues from the mouth, a description which includes crying, whistling, wailing, coughing, and all such things; but it was only the sound produced by human beings by which communication with one another is possible that they called voice.

152. *Gellius.* Chrysippus says that every word is naturally ambiguous, since by the same word two or more things can be meant. However, Diodorus, whose surname was Cronos, says that no word is ambiguous, nor does anyone speak or

think ambiguously, nor ought anything seem to be said other than what he who speaks thinks he is saying.

B. *Things Signified: Meaning* [1]

166. *Sextus*. There was also [among the dogmatists] another disagreement, for some located truth and falsity in the thing signified, others in the sound, and others in the process of thought. The Stoics accepted the first opinion, asserting that there are three things joined together, the thing signified, the sign, and the existing object. The sign is the sound, for example the word "Dio." The thing signified is the matter itself which is indicated by the sound and which we grasp as it coexists with our thought, but which the barbarians, although they hear the sound, do not understand. And the existing object is the external thing, as Dio himself. Of these three, two are bodies, the voice and the existing object, and one is incorporeal, the matter signified or the meaning, and it is this that is true or false. Not every meaning, however, is true or false, for some are incomplete and others are complete. An illustration of the complete is what they call a proposition, which indeed they define in the statement: a proposition is that which is either true or false.

167. *Sextus*. Every meaning must be spoken, since this is how it got its name. . . . For to speak, as the Stoics themselves say, is to utter the sound significant of the thing thought.

168. *Ammonius*. By these arguments Aristotle teaches what the things principally and immediately signified by sounds are, and these are thoughts [νοήματα]. Through these as means we signify things; and it is not necessary to consider anything else as a mean between the thought and the thing, as the Stoics do, who assume what they name the meaning.

170. *Sextus*. Accordingly, the body is not taught [i.e. is not

1. Sometimes translated *the expressible;* the fact that an object is designated by a given term. Contrary to the title chosen by Arnim, meaning is not one of the things signified. Cf. Bréhier, *La Théorie des Incorporels,* p. 15.

the content of teaching], especially in the Stoic theory. For the things taught are meanings, and meanings are not bodies.

2. Incomplete Meanings

181. *Diogenes Laertius.* They say that meaning is that which is suggested in conformity with a rational representation. And some meanings, say the Stoics, are complete, while others are incomplete. The latter are those whose utterance is unfinished, for example, "writes." For we ask in addition, who? The complete are those whose utterance is finished, as, "Socrates writes."

4. Propositions

198. *Simplicius.* With respect to contradictories relating to the future, the Stoics think the same things as they do in the other cases. For they regard future contradictory pairs and their parts just as the contradictories of the present and the past. For a thing must be either true or not, if it must be either true or false. And surely one must determine future contradictories in the same way. If there will be a sea fight to-morrow, it is true to say so; if there will not be a fight, it is false to say there will be. Either it will be or it will not be; therefore one part of the contradiction is true and the other part false.

201. *Diogenes Laertius.* A probable proposition is that which leads to assent, for example, "if anything gave birth to something, the former is the mother of the latter." But it is false, because the bird is not the mother of an egg. Again, some propositions are possible, others impossible; and some are necessary, others not necessary. A possible proposition is one capable of being true, if nothing external prevents it from being true, as "Diocles is alive." A proposition is impossible if it is not capable of being true, as, "the earth flies." The necessary proposition is that one which is both true and is not capable of being false, or, if capable, is prevented from being false by external circumstances, as, "Virtue is profitable." Not necessary is that which is true although it can be false even when no external circumstance interferes, as, "Dio is walking

about." A reasonable proposition is one which has more occasions of being true [than false] as, "I shall be alive tomorrow." And there are other varieties of propositions. . . .
202. *Plutarch.* How can the theory of possible propositions
avoid being inconsistent with the theory of fate? For if a possible proposition is not defined as one which is or will be true,
as Diodorus says, "but everything capable of coming to pass
is possible even if it do not come to pass" there will be many
things possible which are not according to fate. Accordingly
either fate destroys the unconquered, invincible, victorious
power of all things or, if fate is as Chrysippus thinks, what
is capable of coming to pass is often to be classed as impossible.

6. Signs

221. *Sextus.* But perhaps it will be necessary to consider
cursorily the view that satisfies them, the view that the sign
is a proposition and therefore intelligible. Thus, in describing
it they say that a sign is an antecedent proposition in a valid
inference, indicative of the conclusion. But they say there
are many different bases for judging of the validity of an inference, and one of them . . . shall be described. Every inference either begins with a true statement and concludes
with a true statement, or it goes from false to false, or from
true to false, or from false to true. An illustration of the true
premise and true conclusion is: "if there are gods, the world
is governed by the gods' providence." An inference from a
false premise to a false conclusion is: "if the earth flies, the
earth has wings." From false to true: "if the earth flies, the
earth exists." From true to false: "if this man is moving, he
is walking," when as a matter of fact he is not walking though
he is moving. Of these four types of inference . . . the first
three, they say, are valid . . . and the other one only is invalid, the one which begins with a true premise and has a
false conclusion. Since all this is so, one must seek the sign,
they say, not in this invalid but in the valid inference, for it is
called a proposition which is the antecedent of a valid inference. However there was not one valid inference; there were
three, the one which begins with a true premise and has a

true conclusion, the false premise and false conclusion, and the false premise and true conclusion. Therefore one must investigate whether the sign is to be sought in all the valid inferences, or in some, or in one. Accordingly if the sign must be true itself and indicative of truth, it will reside neither in the combination of false premise and false conclusion, nor in the false premise and true conclusion. It can therefore only be found in the combination of true premise and true conclusion, because it exists and the thing it signifies must also exist with it. Therefore whenever one says that the sign is an antecedent proposition of a valid inference, it will be necessary to understand that it is the antecedent only in the inference which has a true premise and true conclusion. Nor is it true that every antecedent proposition in a valid inference of the true-true type is a sign. For example take such an inference as: "if it is day, it is light," The premise is the true statement, "it is day" and the conclusion is the true statement, "it is light." But the antecedent does not have in itself anything which is a sign of the conclusion. For it is not the fact that "it is day" which reveals that "it is light," but the conclusion, "it is light" is grasped by its own perspicuity just as much as the premise is perceived in virtue of itself. The sign, therefore, . . . must be of such a nature as to reveal the conclusion. Take for example the premise in such inferences as these: "If this woman has milk in her breasts, she has conceived," and "if this man spits through his windpipe, he has an ulcer of the lung." For this inference is valid, since it is of the true-true type . . . and besides, the first proposition is indicative of the second, for, by attending to the former we grasp the latter.

Further, they say that the sign, since it is present, must be the sign of something present. For some are utterly deceived and hope that even something present may be the sign of something past, as in the inference: "if this man has a scar, he has had a wound." For if he has a scar it is present, for it is obvious, but to have had a wound is past, for it is no longer a wound; they also hope that something present may be a sign of something future, as that included in such an inference as this: "If this man is wounded in the heart, he will die." For they say the wound in the heart already exists, while the death is future. But those who say such things do not know that while things past and things future are different, the sign and the thing signified, even in these cases, are both present. For in the former inference . . . the wound has already occurred and is past but that this man had a wound is a present proposition, though spoken of something past. And in the inference, "if this man is wounded in the heart, he will die," the death is yet to come, but the proposition, "this man will die," though spoken of the future, is present, because it is true now. Consequently, the sign is a proposition, a premise in a valid inference whose premise and conclusion are both true, indicative of the conclusion, and is always a present sign of a present object.

9. Solution of Sophisms

283. *Epictetus.* The Master Argument seems to have been propounded on some such basis as this: These three propositions are mutually incompatible, *viz:* Everything past is necessarily true; and, an impossible proposition does not follow from a possible proposition; and, a proposition which neither is nor will be true is none the less possible. Diodorus, grasping this incompatibility, used the plausibility of the first two to prove that nothing is possible which is not now true or will be. But some maintain another pair, *viz:* something which neither is nor will be true is none the less possible, and, an impossible does not follow from a possible. But in this case not everything past is necessarily true. The followers of Cleanthes hold this position and Antipater vigorously supports them. But others accept the other two, *viz:* what neither is nor will be true is possible, and, everything past is necessarily true. But in this case an impossible follows from a possible. But the three propositions cannot be all accepted, because they are mutually incompatible.

Physics

I. Basic Physical Theory

1. The Two Principles: Matter and Cause

299. *Diogenes Laertius.* They say that elements differ from principles. For the latter are ungenerated and indestructible, while the elements are destroyed by the [final] conflagration. The principles are corporeal [1] but formless; the elements have form.

300. *Diogenes Laertius.* They believe that there are two principles in the universe, the agent and the patient. The patient is unqualified reality, *viz.* matter, and the agent is the reason inherent in the matter, *viz.* God. For he is eternal and, present throughout matter, is the artificer of each thing. Zeno of Citium set down this doctrine in his book *On Reality,* Cleanthes in *On Atoms,* and Chrysippus toward the end of his first book *On Physics.*

303. *Seneca.* Our Stoics, as you know, say that two things exist in nature from which all things are produced, cause and matter; matter lies inert, a thing ready for all things, never inclined to motion unless some one moves it; but cause, which is reason, informs matter and turns it wherever it wishes and produces from it various works. Therefore, there ought to be a source from which anything is made, and that by which it is made; the latter is cause, the former is matter.

310. *Alexander Aphrodisias.* At the very beginning of the discussion, in their assertion of two principles of all things, matter and God, of which one is the maker and one the patient, we might reasonably accuse them of saying that God is mixed with matter, extending through all of it, arranging, forming, and making the cosmos in this way. For if God is

---

1. The text Von Arnim uses reads ἀσωμάτους instead of σώματα as in B P F. The preceding context, included below as II 300, shows that the principles are matter and God. They are therefore corporeal, but formless as contrasted with the elements we perceive. Cf. II 408, Galen.

a body, as they say, being an intelligible and eternal spirit, and if matter is a body, then, in the first place there will be a body extending through a body, and second, this spirit will be either some one of the four simple bodies, which they also call elements, or a compound of them, as even they somewhere state—for they conceive spirit to derive its reality from air and fire—or, if it should be anything else, their divine body will be some fifth reality, asserted without demonstration or defense by those who object to a person who asserts this by proper proofs, on the basis that he is asserting a paradox.

3. Causes

338. *Aetius.* The Stoics defined the first cause as movable.

340. *Aetius.* The Stoics thought all causes were corporeal, for they are spirits.

341. *Sextus.* The Stoics said that every cause is a body and is a cause to a body of something incorporeal; for example, the scalpel is a body and to the flesh, which also is a body, it is the cause of the incorporeal predicate of being cut; and again, fire is a body and to wood, which is also a body, it is the cause of the incorporeal predicate of being burned.

344. *Clemens Alexandrinus.* That is properly called cause which is capable of effecting anything actively. Since we say that steel is capable of cutting not only when it is in the act of cutting, but also when it is not cutting, it follows that the capability of causing means two things, that which is already acting, and that which has not yet, but is capable of action.

6. Qualities

376. *Plotinus.* For them qualities must be different from their substrata, and they admit it. For [otherwise] they would not count them as the second category. . . . But if they should say that the qualities are qualified matter, then in the first place the [seminal] reasons must be material, and instead of producing a composite by being in matter, they will be composed of form and matter before the composite which they

produce. Therefore they will be neither forms nor reasons. But if they should say that the reasons are nothing but matter in a certain state, they will obviously have to call qualities "certain states," and classify them under the fourth category. But if there is some other classification, what is its distinguishing characteristic? Or is it not rather evident that the "certain state" is here hypostatized?

380. *Plutarch*. Again they say reality and matter are the subjects of the qualities, and this they practically make a matter of definition. On the other hand they make the qualities realities and bodies. And all this is very perplexing. For if the qualities have their own reality by which they are and are called bodies, they do not need any other reality, for they have a reality of their own. But if what these men call reality and matter is the only subject common to the qualities, obviously the qualities participate in body but they are not bodies [or realities]. For the subject and recipient must differ from those things which it receives and of which it is the subject. But they only see half. For they call matter unqualified and yet do not wish to call quality immaterial. . . . Some of them put forward an argument that they call reality unqualified not because it is devoid of all quality, but because it has all the qualities. But this is nonsense.

397. *Philo*. Chrysippus, therefore, the most celebrated of his school, in his book *On Increase* makes some marvellous assertions; after making an introduction to the effect that two peculiar qualities cannot attach to the same reality, he says: "Let us assume for the sake of argument that there is one man perfectly sound and another minus a foot. Call the sound man Dio and the cripple Theo, and then cut off one of Dio's feet. When one seeks which of the two is destroyed [logically] it is more proper to say Theo."

But this is the reply of a paradox-monger rather than of a lover of truth. For how can Theo, who was not mutilated, be taken away, while Dio, who had a foot cut off, remains unharmed?

"Very appropriately," he says, "for Dio, whose foot was

cut off, has fallen into Theo's classification of imperfect reality, and two peculiar qualities cannot attach to the same subject. Accordingly Dio necessarily remains, but Theo vanishes."

10. Spirit, Tension, and Habit

440. *Galen*. How it is necessary to reduce the argument to absurdity, when we assume that every existent object requires a conjoining cause, I shall forthwith discuss. As to this conjoining cause, whatever it is, for the disciples of Herophilus do not admit knowing it, do they consider it to be composed of existing objects or of non-existing objects? For if it is one of the non-existing objects, I am astonished at the wisdom of the men, if they also say each existent object requires something of the non-existent. But if they assert that the conjunctive cause is one of the existent objects, let them remember that they said every existent object requires a conjunctive cause in order to exist. For thus it will follow that the cause itself, in order to exist, will require another cause, and this one still another, and so on to infinity. But if they reply that some existent objects require another cause in order to exist, while others are self-existent, then let them know in the first place, that they no longer maintain their original proposition . . . and in the second place, they need a much stronger argument why some require a cause and others do not, or even what the characteristics of these two types of existing objects are. For neither the many disciples of Herophilus nor the younger Stoics give any demonstration at all of the proposition that spirit and fire hold together both themselves and other things while water and earth require something else to hold them together. For in immediate experience one would say that whatever is hard, resisting, and dense holds itself together, while the smooth, soft, and yielding requires another thing as conjunctive cause. Not only do these men think it unnecessary to give any reason why their hypothesis should be accepted, they did not even sense the internal contradiction of their position. For of all things the finest, and softest, and most yielding are fire and air, and these they make the causes of hardness and resistance in earth, as if it were possible for

one thing to give another a power or nature or activity or quality, which it itself did not have. For it is perfectly plain not only that nothing is held together by fire, but rather that all things are destroyed by fire.

442. *Alexander Aphrodisias.* In reply to these arguments, if the spirit has come into being of fire and air and permeates all bodies by being mixed with them all and if the existence of each body depends on it, how could there still be any simple body? And how, if a compound is posterior to simple things, could fire and air exist, from the mixture of which the spirit comes into being, when no body can exist without spirit? For if the generation of spirit comes from these and if none of these can exist without spirit, then none of them can exist before the generation of spirit, nor would spirit come into being since the things from which it is produced would not exist. And how could anyone say that there is something hot in the actually cold? And what is its simultaneous tendency toward contraries, by which it holds together the things that are in it, being, as they say, a spirit moving at the same time from itself and to itself, and by what form of change does it come into being?

443. *Plotinus.* And this world will be destroyed if anyone entrusts to a body the task of holding it together, giving the rank and name of soul to air and wind which are the least stable of all bodies. . . . Even they [the Stoics], led by the truth, admit that something prior to and better than bodies, a form of soul, must exist, for they assume an intelligent wind [spirit] and an intellectual fire; as if the better portion among existing things could not exist without fire and spirit and had to seek a place to reside! . . . But if they assume that life and soul are nothing beyond this wind, what is the meaning of their overworked phrase "a certain state," to which they retreat when forced to admit another active nature besides bodies? If, accordingly, not every wind is a soul, because there are thousands of inanimate breezes, but only, as they say, the spirit in a certain state, then this "certain state" and condition either is something existent or nothing. If it is nothing, there will be the wind only and the "certain state" will be but

a name. And thus it will follow for them that nothing exists but matter; soul and God . . . are all names, while matter alone exists.

458. *Philo*. Mind . . . has many powers, the power of habit, the power of engendering, the power of life, the rational power, the power of comprehension, and thousands of others, differing both in genus and species. Now habit is common also to inanimate objects, as stones and wood, and the things in us which resemble stones, our bones, of course, participate in it. Nature extends as far as plants. And the things in us which resemble plants, our nails and hair [also have a nature]. For nature is a habit already in motion; but soul is a nature which has acquired representation and spontaneity. This is common to the irrational animals also. And our mind has something analogous to an irrational soul. The power of comprehension, however, is peculiar to mind, and the rational power is perhaps common also to the more divine natures, but peculiar, among mortal beings, to man. This power is two-fold; by one phase of it we are rational and participate in mind, while by the other we reason discursively.

11. On Mixture: Body Penetrates Body

472. *Philo*. Now mechanical mixture is thought to occur with dry things, while chemical mixture requires fluids. Accordingly, mechanical mixture is an unarranged juxtaposition of different bodies, as when anyone makes a pile of barley, wheat, and pulse, and any other grain that might be put in the same pile. Chemical mixture is not just juxtaposition, but the mutual apposition, throughout the whole, of dissimilar parts penetrating each other, although their qualities can be distinguished by some device or other, as they say happens with wine and water. For these two things when united produce a chemical mixture, but none the less the mixture can be resolved again into the qualities of which it was made. For with a sponge dipped in oil water is taken up while the wine remains. Perhaps the fact that sponges are produced by water explains why they naturally absorb from the mixture the water which is akin to it, while the foreign substance, wine,

is left behind. Fusion is the destruction of the original qualities which are placed opposite each other in all the parts and the production of a single different quality, as happens in the case of the medical fourfold remedy. For wax, tallow, pitch, and resin, I believe, produce this combination. But when compounded it is impossible to distinguish again its component qualities. Each of them has vanished, and the destruction of all of them produces another, single, peculiar, property.

V. The Human Soul

1. The Substance of the Soul

773. *Nemesius.* The theory of the soul is much disputed by nearly all the ancients. For Democritus, and Epicurus, and the whole school of Stoic philosophers assert that the soul is a body. But even these who assert that the soul is a body disagree as to what it really is; for the Stoics say it is a spirit hot and fiery.

744. *Diogenes Laertius.* They believe that nature is a fire endowed with skill, occupied in generating things. It is a firelike, artistic spirit. And soul is a perceptive nature. It is the spirit which is born in us. Therefore it is a body and endures after death, although it is corruptible. But the soul of the whole world is incorruptible, of which the souls in living beings are parts.

2. Soul is Corporeal

790. *Nemesius.* Chrysippus said, "Death is the separation of the soul from the body; now, nothing incorporeal can be separated from a body—for an incorporeal cannot be fastened on to a body, and the soul is fastened on to and separated from the body. Consequently, the soul is a body."

799. *Plotinus.* Again, if the soul were a body and penetrated everything, it would be mixed in the same way that the mixture of other bodies occurs. But if the mixture of bodies prevents any of the constituents from existing in actuality, then neither would the soul exist in actuality in the bodies, but

potentially only, thus losing its essence. For example, if sweet and bitter are mixed, there is no sweet; and so we would have no soul. If the soul is a body and forms a complete mixture, so that wherever the one is, there the other is also, and each of them has the same mass and occupies the whole, and the addition of the one produces no increase in size, then nothing will remain undivided. For mixture is not the alternation of large parts, for this they would call juxtaposition, but mixture is the pervading, by the body introduced, of all the other body to its smallest part. And this is impossible, because the less becomes equal to the greater. Nevertheless, if it pervades all, it divides in every part.

5. The Soul is not Immortal

809. *Arius Didymus*. They say the soul can be generated and destroyed. It will not be destroyed immediately upon quitting the body, but remains itself for some time. The souls of the virtuous continue until the resolution of all things into fire, the souls of fools endure for an undetermined time. They say souls endure in such a way that we remain as souls separated from our bodies, changing into a lesser reality, that of the soul. But the souls of unintelligent and irrational animals are destroyed with their bodies.

811. *Diogenes Laertius*. Cleanthes held that all souls continued to exist until the conflagration, but Chrysippus asserted this of the souls of the wise only.

812. *Sextus Empiricus*. For it is not allowable to suppose that souls are borne downwards. For, since they are of fine particles, and no less fiery than gaseous [spiritual], they soar rather to the upper regions. When set free from their bodies they do not, as Epicurus said, disperse as smoke does, but they remain themselves. For even previously the body did not govern them, but they were the causes of the body's remaining together, and prior to that [they were the causes] of their own [holding together]. Having been removed from the sun, they dwell in the region below the moon where, because of the purity of the air, they continue to exist for a long time, and they use for their proper food the exhalations which rise from

the earth, as the other stars also do, and in this region there is nothing to dissolve them. Accordingly, if souls continue to exist, they are the same as the daemons; and if daemons exist, one must also assert that gods exist.

7. The Chief Part of the Soul

836. *Aetius.* The Stoics say that the highest part of the soul is the ἡγεμονικόν [the dominant or ruling part]. It produces representation, assent, sensation, and spontaneity; and they call it rational. Aside from the ruling part, there are seven parts which are born of the soul and are stretched through the body like the tentacles of a polypus are twined. Five of the seven parts of the soul are the senses: sight, smell, hearing, taste, and touch. Of these, sight is a spirit stretching from the ruling part to the eyes, [and similarly in the other four cases]. Of the remaining two, one is the seminal principle, which also is itself a spirit stretching from the ruling part to the testicles; and the other, called by Zeno "vocality," which they also call voice, is a spirit stretching from the ruling part to the pharynx, tongue, and the appropriate organs. The ruling part itself, like the sun in the cosmos, dwells in the brain.[1]

837. *Diogenes Laertius.* The chief part of the soul is the ἡγεμονικόν, in which representation and spontaneity arise, and whence speech is sent forth. Its seat is in the heart.[1]

VI. On Fate

1. Definitions of Fate

912. *Plutarch.* Conversely, the first and most important point seems to be that nothing happens without a cause, but by preceding causes; and second, that this world is arranged by nature, a world animate and sympathetic with itself; third, (the testimonies on these points seem to be greater) [2] divination, honored by all men, truly belonging to God, and the content-

---

1. Both Philo and Galen report a difference of opinion on this subject.
2. Arnim: seclusi lectoris notam, quae in margine inrepsit.

ment of the wise with whatever happens because all things happen by fate; and fourth, the well-known principle that every proposition is either true or false.

916. *Theodoretus*. And Chrysippus, the Stoic, says that that which is necessitated does not differ from that which is fated. For fate is an ordered, continuous, eternal motion.

917. *Aetius*. The Stoics say that fate is a series of causes; that is, an order and conjunction which cannot be violated.

926. *Justin Martyr*. The Stoics asserted that all things happen by fate. . . . It is the nature of everyone who has been born to be capable of vice and virtue. For no one would be praiseworthy if he did not have the power to turn to both. Men everywhere in philosophizing and in making laws according to right reason have demonstrated this fact by urging the doing of some things and the avoidance of others. Even the Stoic philosophers in their theory of ethics strongly honor the same things, so that it is clear they have not made good progress in their views on principles and incorporeals. For they will say either that human actions occur by fate, or that God is nothing else than the things which are always turning, changing, and being resolved, and so they will appear to have had a grasp only on things corruptible. The result is that God himself will come into being in every evil through the parts and through the whole, or else there is neither vice nor virtue, which is contrary to every sound notion, argument, and mind.

3. A Single Force Moving Everything

934. *Plotinus*. Does a single soul penetrating the universe execute everything, so that everything as a part of this soul is moved as the world directs? If the causes derive from it, there must exist that continuity and interrelation of everything which follows, which is called fate. To illustrate, a plant has its principle in the roots, which from there penetrates to all its parts; and with respect to action, passion, and mutual interrelation, it has one government, a sort of fate for the plant, as one might say.

935. *Plutarch*. For not once or twice, but everywhere, and especially in all the books on physics, he has written that there

are many hinderances and obstacles to particular natures and motions, but none to the nature of the whole.

937. *Plutarch.* For first, in the first book *On Physics,* he pictures the eternal motion as a mixed drink turning and agitating in every direction the things which come into being. He said, "the governance of the whole so disposes that by it we are necessarily whatever we happen to be, whether contrary to our proper nature we are sick or incapacitated, or whether we are grammarians or savants." And again a little later, "by this argument we shall draw the same conclusion with respect to our virtue also, and vice, and the whole range of skills and their lack, as I said." And a little later, removing all ambiguity, "For nothing, not even the least particle, can be otherwise than in accordance with the common nature and its reason." But that the common nature and the common reason of nature is fate, providence, and Zeus, is not unknown even to the antipodes, for they talk about these matters everywhere. And he approves the dictum of Homer,

"The counsel of Zeus is complete,"

who thus referred to fate and the nature of the whole, by which everything is arranged. . . . Chrysippus gives vice complete boldness, because it is done not only of necessity and by fate, but also by the reason of God and in accordance with the best nature. And these things are seen again in the following quotation. "Since the common nature pervades all things, everything that comes into being in any way whatsoever, whether in the whole or in any one of its parts, must come into being by that nature and its reason in an uninterrupted sequence. For there is nothing external to hinder the administration, nor can any part be moved or be given habits otherwise than according to the common nature." What, then, are the habits and motions of the parts? Obviously vices and diseases are habits, as miserliness, voluptuousness, pride, cowardice, injustice; and motions are adulteries, thefts, treasons, murders, and parricides. Chrysippus thinks that none of these, whether great or small, is contrary to the reason, law, justice, or providence of Zeus.

5. *An Infinite Series of Causes*

946. *Plotinus.* Some, when they come to the principle of the universe, deduce all things from it and say that it pervades everything as a cause, not only as the moving cause, but as the producing cause of each thing. This they posit as the highest cause and fate. It produces the universe, not only the other things that come into being, but even our thoughts proceed from its motions, just as the various moving parts of an animal do not depend each on itself, but on the dominant part of the animal's soul. And others . . . hold to a mutual interconnection of causes in a descending series, and assert that the consequents always follow the antecedents, that the consequents lead back to those by which they came into being and without which they could not have come into being, and that the later are subject to the earlier. Those who make these assertions are obviously introducing fate in a different manner. These people are correctly subdivided into two groups: for some make everything depend on one principle, and others do not.

949. *Alexander Aphrodisias.* It is absurd to say that causes regress to infinity and that there is neither a first nor a last in the series and linkings of causes. . . . By this argument even science would be impossible, if indeed science is chiefly the knowledge of first causes, and for them there is no first among causes. Not every violation of law is destructive of the sphere in which it occurs . . . and if such a thing occurred in the world, that would not absolutely ruin the well-being of the world anymore than some chance recklessness of the slaves ruins the well-being of the household and of the master.

950. *Cicero.* Let us return to the sophisms of Chrysippus. And first let us reply to him on the interconnection of things. . . . We see how greatly climates differ from place to place, some are healthful, some pestilential; in some, people become phlegmatic and, so to speak, diffuse; in others dry and arid. And there are many other climates which differ in many ways from place to place. At Athens the air is rare, which is supposed to make the Athenians acute; at Thebes it is misty and so the Thebans are stupid and sturdy. However, that rare air

does not cause one to study under Arcesilaus, and another under Theophrastus. Nor does the mist make a Theban seek victory in the Nemean games rather than in the Isthmian. A greater lack of connection: what in the nature of the place can make me walk in the portico of Pompey rather than in the field of Mars? And with you rather than with some one else? And on the Ides rather than on the Kalends? So, therefore, as the nature of the place has an effect on some things and has no effect on others, so there may be an influence of the stars on some things, if you wish, but certainly not on all.

951. *Cicero.* But since there are differences in the natures of men, so that some like sweet things and other bitter; some are lewd, some are hot-headed, or cruel, or proud, and others detest such vices . . . since, therefore, he says, there are such differences in human nature, what wonder is it that these differences are the results of different causes? In thus arguing he does not see the point at issue, nor in what a cause consists. If different people have different inclinations on account of natural, antecedent causes, still it does not on that account follow that the causes of our wills and desires are natural and antecedent. For if this were so, nothing would be in our power. Now indeed we admit that it is not in our power to be brilliant or stupid, strong or weak. But he who thinks it follows from this that we do not voluntarily sit or walk, does not see what follows what. For although by antecedent causes men may be born ingenious or slow, strong or weak, yet it does not follow that their sitting, walking, or doing anything is defined and constituted by principal causes.

6. Every Proposition is True or False

952. *Cicero.* Chrysippus concludes as follows: If there is a motion without a cause not every proposition, which the dialecticians call ἀξίωμα, is either true or false; for whatever does not have efficient causes is neither true nor false. However, every proposition is either true or false. Therefore, there is no motion without a cause. And if this is so, everything that happens, happens by antecedent causes. And if this is so, everything happens by fate. Therefore, whatever happens, happens by

fate. . . . And therefore, Chrysippus uses all his powers to prove that every ἀξίωμα is either true or false. For, as Epicurus fears that if this be conceded, it is conceded that everything happens by fate, . . . so Chrysippus fears that if he cannot prove every proposition to be true or false, he will not be able to hold that all things happen by fate and by the eternal causes of future events.

7. The Confatal (The Lazy Argument)

956. *Cicero.* This argument is refuted by Chrysippus. For some things, he says, are simple, and some are complex. A simple event is: Socrates shall die on that day. Here, whether he does anything or not, the day of his death is fixed. But if it is fated that Oedipus shall be born to Laius, one cannot say "whether Laius has been with a woman or not;" for this is a complex fact and *confatal*. He calls it this because it is fated both that Laius will be with his wife and that thus Oedipus will be begotten. Likewise, if it should be said, "Milo will contend in the Olympic games," and someone adds, "therefore he will contend whether he has an opponent or not," he is mistaken; for the notion "will contend" is complex because there can be no competition without an opponent. All such captious arguments can be refuted in the same way. "Whether you apply to a physician or not, you will be healed," is captious; for it is as much fated that you shall go to a physician as that you shall recover. These things, as I have said, he calls confatal.

8. Fate and Possibility

959. *Alexander Aphrodisias.* To say that fate does not rule out the possible and feasible in everything that happens because what nothing prevents from happening is possible even if it does not happen; "and [to say] contrary effects among things which occur by fate are not prevented from happening, therefore even things which do not happen are none the less possible;" and that our ignorance of what prevents them supplies a proof of the fact that they are not prevented from happening, at any rate if the things which may prevent are real, for whatever is a cause of contraries' happening in the sphere of fate,

the same things are causes of their not happening also, if indeed, as they say, contrary effects are impossible under identical conditions, but because it is not known to us what they are, therefore they say their occurrence is not prevented—to say such things as these is to talk like a child.

961. *Alexander Aphrodisias.* Similarly one may say also, the proposition "there will be a naval battle tomorrow" can be true, but cannot be also necessary. For the necessary is always true, and this will no longer remain true after the battle occurs. But if this is not necessary, neither does the thing signified by the proposition, there will be a battle, occur of necessity. But if it is to be, though not of necessity (for that there will be a battle is true but not necessary) it is obviously possible. And if possible, the possible is not ruled out by the fact that everything occurs by fate.

10. Fate and Free Will

974. *Cicero.* It seems to me that the ancient philosophers were of two opinions, one group holding that fate so controls everything that it exerts the force of necessity, . . . the other group holding that the voluntary motions of the soul occur without any influence of fate. Chrysippus, however, wished to hold a middle course like an honorary arbiter, but he rather attaches himself to those who believed that the motions of the soul are free from necessity. But by the expressions he uses, he falls back into the same difficulties so that unwillingly he affirms the necessity of fate. Let us see, therefore, how this affects assent. Those ancient philosophers, for whom everything occurs by fate, say that assent is produced by force and necessity. The others, however, who disagree, free assent from fate and assert that if fate rules assent, necessity cannot be avoided. . . . But Chrysippus, since he both rejects necessity and does not wish anything to happen without preceding causes, distinguishes two kinds of causes, so that he may escape necessity and retain fate. "For," he says, "perfect and principal causes are one thing, auxiliary and proximate causes are another. For which reason, when we say everything happens by fate and antecedent causes, we do not mean perfect and principal causes, but aux-

iliary and proximate." And so, the position I argued above, he opposes as follows: "If everything happens by fate, of course it follows that everything happens by preceding causes, but they are not principal and perfect; they are auxiliary and proximate. And if these are not in our power, it does not follow that our appetites are not in our power. But this would follow if we should say everything happens by perfect and principal causes, so that when these causes are not in our power, our appetites are not in our power. For which reason those who so introduce fate as to join necessity with it, must accept that conclusion; but those who do not say that antecedent causes must be perfect and principal escape that conclusion." For as to saying that assent occurs by preceding causes, he thinks it easily explained. For although assent cannot occur without a sense stimulus, yet, since sensation has a proximate and not a principal cause, it has the explanation, as Chrysippus desired, which we gave above; not that something can happen without any external force— for assent requires sense stimulation—but it comes back to his illustration of the cylinder and the top, which cannot begin to move unless an impulse be given them. But when that happens, the top spins and the cylinder revolves according to their own natures. "As therefore," he says, "he who pushes the cylinder gives it a principle of motion, but does not give it a motion of revolution, so an object strikes our sense and as it were stamps its image in the soul, but the assent is in our power, which, as has been said in the case of the cylinder, while put in motion from without, moves for the rest by its own force and nature. But if anything happened without an antecedent cause, it would be false to say that everything happens by fate; but if it is likely that for everything which happens a cause precedes, what reason can be given why we should not admit that everything occurs by fate? Provided it is understood what is the distinction and dissimilarity between causes." . . . For Chrysippus, while admitting that the proximate and adjacent cause of assent is found in sensation, does not concede it to be the necessary cause of giving assent; with the result that if everything occurs by fate, everything occurs by antecedent and necessary causes.

975. *Hippolytus.* These men [Chrysippus and Zeno] maintain the universal rule of fate by using the following illustration. Suppose a dog to be tied to a wagon. If he wishes to follow, the wagon pulls him and he follows, so that his own power and necessity unite. But if he does not wish to follow, he will be compelled to anyhow. The same is the case with mankind also. Even if they do not wish to follow, they will be absolutely forced to enter into the fated event.

988. *Origen.* Of things that are in motion some have the cause of their motion in themselves, others are moved only from without. Things which can be carried, such as wood and stones, and all matter which is held together by habit alone, are moved only from without. For the present we shall remove from the discussion the proposition that the flux of bodies is motion, since there is no need of it for the present purpose. But plants and animals, and in general whatever is held together by nature and soul, and they include metals in this class, have in themselves the cause of their motion. In addition to these, fire also is self-moved, and perhaps fountains. Of things which have the cause of their motion in themselves, some, they say, are moved out of themselves, and others from themselves. The former are the inanimate objects, the latter are living beings. For living beings are moved from themselves by an image which arises and calls forth spontaneity. And further, in some of these cases, the imaginative nature moves the faculty of spontaneity in an orderly manner, as the image of spinning arises in a spider and the urge follows until spinning results. For its imaginative nature in an orderly way calls the insect to this activity and nothing else beyond the faculty of imagination is believed to belong to the animal. In the bee the same process leads to the production of wax. The rational animal, however, in addition to his imaginative nature has reason also which judges the images, rejecting some and accepting others that he may be led by them. Wherefore since in the nature of reason there are occasions for contemplating the noble and the shameful, by taking advantage of which and contemplating the noble and the shameful, we choose the noble and refuse the shameful. We are to be praised if we give our-

selves over to the practice of the noble; we are blameworthy if
we do the reverse. We must not, however, be ignorant that the
greater part of the nature assigned to all things varies among
animals in greater and lesser degrees, with the result that, so
to speak, the ability in hunting dogs and war horses somehow
approaches rationality. Now to come under the influence of
some external thing which produces in us an image of this or
that sort is admittedly not in our power [to avoid]. But to
determine to use this occurrence in one way or another is the
function of nothing else than the reason within us, which, in
spite of the occasion, strengthens us in our efforts towards
what is noble and fitting, or turns us to the contrary. But if
anyone say that this external thing itself is such that it is impossible to look at it resolutely when it occurs, let him understand his own affections and motions and discover whether
there is not an approval, assent, or inclination of the dominant
part of the soul toward some individual object because of these
specious arguments. For example, the woman who has appeared to a man that has decided to be continent and to refrain
from intercourse, and who urges him to act contrary to his
decision, is not the complete cause of his setting aside his resolution. For since he is quite satisfied with the excitation and
luxury of the pleasure, and since he is unwilling to look at it
resolutely and confirm his decision, he commits the excess.
Take another man in the same situation, though with more
learning and discipline: the excitations and incitements occur,
but his reason, which has been strengthened to a greater degree, trained with care, and confirmed in its views on noble
action, or at least near to confirmation, drives back the incite-
ment and removes the desire.

990. *Origen.* [following immediately upon the preceding]
Since this is the case, it is neither true nor prudent to lay the
blame on external things and escape the accusation ourselves
by making ourselves appear like wood and stones which are
drawn along by the things that move them. This is the
argument of one who wishes to counterfeit the notion of self-
determination. For if we were to ask such a one what self-
determination is, he would say that it consists in the absence,

while one is purposing a certain line of action, of external causes inciting to the contrary. And again, it is stupid to blame the mere instrument when disciplinary reason can take hold of the most intemperate and savage, and, if they would follow its impulse, change them so that the turn and transformation for the better is very great; in fact it often happens that the most intemperate become better than the men who by nature never had seemed to be such, and the most savage are changed to such a state of gentleness that those who never had been savage seem to be savage by comparison—so great has been their change toward gentleness. And we see other men most stable and dignified being driven by compromise with evil manners from their respectable character, so that they turn to licentiousness, often beginning their wickedness in middle age and falling into disorderliness after youth, which is the natural time of instability, has passed. Accordingly, the argument proves that external things are not in our power, but to use them in one way or another is our own business, for we have received critical reason to examine how we ought to meet these things from the outside.

993. *Plutarch*. If, on the one hand, representations do not arise by fate, [how can fate be the cause] of assent? If, on the other hand, [fate] produces representations which lead to assent, and assent is said to occur by fate, does not fate oppose itself by producing frequently and in important matters representations which divert the mind in contrary directions? They say men make mistakes by choosing one alternative and not suspending judgment. [For example] if men yield to what is obscure, they stumble; if to what is false, they are deceived; and if, as usual, to non-comprehensive representations they are subject to mere opinion. And yet one of the three following propositions must be true: either not every representation is the work of fate, or every reception of a representation and every assent is correct, or else fate itself is not blameless. For I do not know how fate can be without reproach when it produces representations such that, not the resisting or the opposing of them, but the following and yielding to them is blameworthy.

PLUTARCH

When Stoicism became the predominant philosophic movement, the Academy founded by Plato and the Peripatetic school of Aristotle did not forthwith cease to exist. Though in eclipse the Academy in particular continued its activity and finally regained sufficient vigor seriously to challenge the Stoic system.

The Old Academy, by which is meant the Academy from Plato's death to 268 B.C., made no essential change in Platonic teaching. Speusippus, head of the Academy from 348 to 339; and Xenocrates (339-315) showed tendencies toward metamathematical speculation; Polemo and Crantor were more interested in ethics; they all felt the need of systematizing the results of Plato's free investigation; and the changes they introduced were at worst those of a rigid, artificial schematism, rather than a substitution of non-Platonic principles.

The New Academy may be said to have been founded by Arcesilaus, who presided over the school from 268 to 241. The Academy was called *new* because Arcesilaus, with little enthusiasm for dogmatism, re-established dialectic and argued against the Stoic criterion of truth. In attacking the possibility of a psychological test of truth, such as the comprehensive representation of the Stoics, he advocated suspension of judgment. And thus a type of skepticism was introduced into the school of Plato.

This skepticism continued until about 100 B.C. It may

be argued that Arcesilaus was not a skeptic in the technical sense. Plato in the *Theaetetus* had disposed of psychological criteria of truth, and Arcesilaus may be going no further. He was not opposing the general possibility of truth, perhaps, but was engaged in a polemic against Stoic empiricism.

It is more difficult, however, to defend Carneades against the charge of technical skepticism. Head of the Academy from 156 to 129, he denied that a criterion of truth could be found either in sense or in reason. Sextus Empiricus, *Adv. Math.* VIII 159, reports that his arguments apply not only to the Stoics but to all his predecessors. Briefly, he taught that there is absolutely no criterion of truth; and if there were, it would necessarily be psychological, testifying both to the object which produced it and to itself as well; but since there is no state of consciousness that cannot be deceptive, a criterion in sensation is impossible. No more can a criterion be found in reason, for reason is derived from sensory elements in consciousness and cannot of itself furnish a test of truth.

On the other hand complete suspension of judgment would render impossible the activities of daily life. Unless one held to some opinion as to what was better, how could one decide whether to doze in the sun or drive in a chariot race? Arcesilaus had previously posited the *reasonable* as the norm of action; Carneades argued that while nothing is certain, many things are *clear*. If, then, life must forego the certainties of dogmatism, skepticism must co-operate by admitting a theory of probability.

Whether this is strict skepticism, and how far it deviates from Plato's own views, became a subject of controversy between two later scholarchs. Philo (110–85) began, and Antiochus (85–69) continued, a trend away from skepticism toward eclectic dogmatism. The latter taught that Arcesilaus and the New Academy had denied the doctrines of Plato; that Plato, Aristotle, and Zeno were in essential philosophic agreement; and that he, Antiochus, was restoring true Platonism to the Academy. Philo, on the other hand, claimed that the previous skepticism was merely an attack on Stoicism, and that the Academy had never deviated from the pure doctrines of Plato. It may not be possible completely to settle this controversy. However, in support of Philo's less plausible opinion of the school's orthodoxy, one may note that the resumption of dialectic by Arcesilaus is a return to Plato himself after the relative sterility of Xenocrates. In the second place, it is improbable, in view of the Neo-Pythagorean literature and Plutarch's interest in Plato, that the oral tradition had completely died out. And finally, if Antiochus can be called Platonic with his extreme eclectic proclivities, Carneades ought charitably to be granted the same honor in spite of his extreme views in the opposite direction.

The next development leading on to Plutarch is the resuscitation of Pythagoreanism. The exact date is not known. During the fourth century, that is, during Plato's lifetime, the old Pythagorean school, as a school, is lost from view. Orphic Pythagorean mysteries continued to exercise some religious influence, and their asceticism and vegetarianism provided a standard gag for comedy.

In Italy the memory of Pythagoras was kept alive and from the mystery cults writings attributed to Pythagoras began to appear. There is a story that Petillius in 180 B.C.

dug up the skeleton and the books of Numa. Since Numa is made out to be a disciple of Pythagoras, this seems to be an attempt to introduce Pythagoreanism into Roman religion. Unfortunately the Roman Senate had the books burned, and while one may be sure they were religious, there is no certainty that they were Pythagorean.

There is no doubt, however, that Pythagoreanism had become active by 100 B.C. About this time Alexander Polyhistorius reports the doctrines with which he came in contact. For three centuries following this the literature multiplied, as did also the details of the teaching; and it is to the credit of Diogenes Laertius that he disregarded the later developments to preserve what was probably the earliest source he knew.

According to Alexander the Pythagoreans taught that the unit or monad is the principle of all things. From the monad comes the indeterminate dyad, which serves as matter. These two then give rise to numbers and geometrical figures, and from solid figures sensible bodies are produced. Earth, air, fire, and water, each of which can change into any other, combine to form a spherical, intelligent, geocentric universe. Since the heat of the sun, moon, and stars is the source and substance of life, they are to be regarded as gods. Because gods and men belong to the same genus, God exercises providence over man. The soul of man is divided into passion, intelligence,—both of which animals also enjoy—and reason, which is not shared by the lower animals. The seat of the soul extends from the heart to the brain—passion in the heart and intelligence and reason in the brain. Reason is immortal, the rest of man perishes. Hermes, since he

guides the souls after death, is called the steward of
souls. Pure souls are taken to the uppermost region, but
impure souls are bound by the Furies in unbreakable
bonds. The souls of those who have died, now properly
designated as demons or heroes, fill the atmosphere and
bring men dreams and premonitions. To enjoy a happy
future life one must be careful to purify himself by
virtuous living, baptism, avoidance of all deaths and
births, abstinence from the flesh of animals that have
died and from eggs and beans, and to perform all the
mystic rites.

Since what Alexander reports contains elements from
Stoicism, it is not the old Pythagoreanism but a Neo-
Pythagorean school to which he bears witness. The absence from Alexander's account of later elements, such
as the incomprehensibility of God, and the rigid opposition between the corporeal and the incorporeal, indicates that this represents the beginning of the development. The journey of the soul after death and the
demons are included, but the asceticism is less pro-
nounced than it became later, because he forbids neither
marriage nor the eating of meat.

The first Neo-Pythagorean whose name is known was
P. Nigidius Figulus, a Roman, Cicero's friend, who died
in 45 B.C. Cicero refers to him as the renovator of Pythagorean philosophy. From the reign of Augustus another
name is preserved, that of Sotion, who defended vegetarianism by basing it on the theory of the transmigration of souls. Other authors wrote under the name of
Pythagoras himself or of some early member of the
school, frequently that of Archytas, but what each author added of original thought cannot be determined.

Neo-Pythagoreanism, like all the other schools of this period with the exception of the Epicureans, was strongly eclectic. The number theory and the religious asceticism develop out of the old Pythagoreanism, but some of their tenets are derived from Stoicism, more from the Peripatetics, while the greatest number are Platonic.

A philosophy is called eclectic if its several propositions are taken from various other systems and combined without sufficient attention to consistency. On the contrary, when a philosopher adopts promising material from different systems and organizes it by some pervasive, dominating principle, he is no longer called eclectic; he is an original thinker and a genius. Eclecticism occurs when men grow tired of careful and detailed thinking, when schools lose their early orthodoxy, and when accurate distinctions are deprecated as hairsplitting. For example, it should be obvious that only a weak mind can assert the essential identity of Platonism, Aristotelianism, and Stoicism. And on any age in which this phenomenon occurs, history will pronounce the judgment that it represents a trough and not a crest.

A decline, however, is sometimes followed by a rise; and it may be not only more charitable but also more accurate to regard Neo-Pythagoreanism and the Platonism of Plutarch as a preparation for Neo-Platonism.

None the less Neo-Pythagoreanism was eclectic and its members, while adhering to a core of doctrine, wandered in many directions.

The unit and the dyad, identified as form and matter, were the basic principles; but some taught that the unit was the moving cause or God, the Platonic demiurge; while others, in some anticipation of Plotinus, placed the One above any moving cause. Again, Platonic-Aristotelian transcendence and Stoic immanence were rather mixed than harmonized. In one author God is superior to all thought, reason, and being, and would be degraded by contact with matter; in another, God is identified with the heat of the sun or is regarded as an omnipresent, immanent spirit.

Plato, late in life, connected the Ideas with a number-theory. Numbers and mathematics had always been congenial studies for the Pythagoreans, and with the stimulus from Plato it is not surprising that an increasing emphasis was placed upon these topics. But although serious attention was paid to mathematics, the ulterior interest lay in metamathematics. The Neo-Pythagoreans claimed that the old school by using numbers as symbols had concealed its true views; now the new school will explain the esoteric doctrine to anyone who will first study the symbolism.

For example, one is God, reason, good, and harmony; it may be called Apollo or Atlas; but in so far as One is the source of all, it is also matter, darkness, chaos, or Tartarus. Because of this double aspect, the one is odd-even and male-female. Two or duality is the principle of dissimilarity, opposition, and change; but because twice two equals two plus two, it is the principle of similarity as well. It is matter, nature, Isis, Artemis, Demeter, and Aphrodite. Since the chief musical relationship is the octave, which consists of the relation of one to two, two is the source of all musical chords. To be brief, three is the first real number, for it has a beginning, a middle, and end; hence it is the number of completion and perfection. And so on.

In this system of thought, the numbers, unlike Plato's Ideas, were not independent entities which God used as a model for this world. At this point the Neo-Pythagoreans made an innovation, adopted or more likely independently thought out by Philo Judaeus, which was not only accepted by Neo-Platonism, but without which Platonism could never have been so well received of the Christian theologians. Monotheism was so strong in Philo, and in paganism monism had developed to such a degree, that the picture in the *Timaeus* of a world of Ideas above the demiurge was inacceptable. Hence the Ideas or numbers, as the case may be, are derived from God—more explicitly they are the thoughts of God, the contents of his mind, and so unity is preserved.

Another part of the *Timaeus* also received serious attention. On the surface the *Timaeus* seems to teach that the world came into existence at a definite point of time in the finite past. Before the world's first moment, the matter out of which it was formed had been in chaotic motion. This interpretation of Plato, Aristotle had accepted in order to attack it; Plutarch later accepted it in order to defend it. But Xenocrates, most of the Platonists, and all the Neo-Platonists considered Plato's language a pedagogical device, putting into terms of time what is really a matter of logical relationship. The Neo-Pythagoreans generally followed this latter view; Ocellus early argued that the universe is unbegotten and imperishable, and by 50 B.C. this was recognized as the standard Neo-Pythagorean view. By an everlasting universe they did not mean a cycle of worlds such as is found in Stoicism, but rather the permanence of pres-

ent conditions. Involved in this is the notion that men
have always inhabited this planet, from which follows,
in the historical situation, the Aristotelian theory of the
fixity of species. They likewise preserve the Aristotelian
division between the supra-lunar and sub-lunar regions.

In anthropology the Neo-Pythagoreans were Platonic
and opposed Stoic materialism. The soul, as Xenocrates
had said, is a self-moving number, and like God is
incorporeal. The transmigration of souls, however, is
treated as a myth; it has a practical value in encourag-
ing people to avoid an evil life, but there is no literal
truth to it. On the other hand, the doctrine of demons,
derived from old Orphic and Pythagorean thought,
grows in importance. After men die, their souls wander
in the region between the earth and the moon, and it
is through these disembodied souls or demons that God
to a large extent exercises his providential administration of the world.

The Hellenistic age as a whole was chiefly interested
in ethics. The Epicureans neglected logic because they
thought it did not contribute to a good life; the Stoics
emphasized physics because they held it to be of practical importance. Similarly, the Neo-Pythagoreans and
the Academy desired a good life now and blessedness
hereafter. Beginners in philosophy may be delighted with
the subtleties of dialectic and the learned investigations
of physics, but the serious, and more advanced student,
seeks greatness of character. Mankind is sick, and philosophy, properly understood, is the medicine. The aim
of the good life, the aim of religion, Plato had defined
in the *Theaetetus* as likeness to God. Plutarch (A.D. 50-
120), a representative man of his time, carries on this

ethical and religious task with fervor. Although more widely known for his *Lives,* he also wrote an important group of ethical and religious essays. All schools, perhaps with the exception of Epicureanism, contributed to form his views. From Stoicism, which he attacked in general, he accepted some points in particular; even skepticism had its influence, in that mysticism and dependence on revelation are often the counterparts of distrust in reason. Plato, however, is the chief source of his thought, and so he may be properly described as an eclectic Platonist. Of course, he is not always consistent.

Philosophy as medicine to sick mankind: ethics as a way of becoming like God: and it is obvious that philosophy to be properly understood requires completion by theology. Since man's relation to God is thus fundamental, one must first obtain a correct concept of God.

Plutarch's concept of God comes chiefly from Plato and the Neo-Pythagoreans. God is true Being, the eternal nature; he is unitary and includes no plurality. To identify him with the world, as the Stoics do, is scarcely distinguishable from atheism. Immutable and transcendent, God has no direct contact with the world, and while we may know *that* he is, we cannot know *what* he is. But of all God's attributes, the chief one is his goodness. His transcendency is not to be understood as excluding a providential ordering of the world for the best. Whatever else be said, God is good.

But if God is good, then Plato was correct when he said that God is not the cause of everything in the world. He cannot be the cause of evil, and therefore, to explain the world, one must posit with God an independent,

evil principle. Not only in the *Republic* did Plato assert
that God is the cause of comparatively few things; in
the *Laws,* as Plutarch interprets it, Plato argued for
the existence of an evil world-soul. Such a dualistic explanation of the world is all the more plausible, and
the genius of Plato is signally supported, because the
more or less successful endeavors of previous philosophers and the unconscious wisdom of mankind preserved
under the mythical forms of eastern religions point in
this direction. When the old Pythagoreans constructed
their table of opposites with the One and Dyad at its
head, when the various religions spoke of Ahriman,
Typho, or Hades, they used different names, but they
all bore witness to an independent, evil principle.

A large segment of Plutarch's philosophy is given in
his essay *De animae procreatione in Timaeo,* and nowhere else does he more clearly show his attachment to
the text of Plato. In the *Timaeus* Plato had described
how the demiurge mixed the Same, the Other, and the
Essence, rolled the mixture out like dough, cut it into
two strips, and formed the celestial equator and the
ecliptic. Thus a good world-soul was formed to impose
order on the pre-existing chaos. With this description
goes a piece of number-theory that has suffered many
varieties of exegesis. To this paragraph in Plato Plutarch
devoted the entire essay, in which he preserves for us,
not only his own interesting views, but also a valuable
fund of information on the history of the Academy. The
De animae procreatione opens with the admission that
its explanation of the mysterious passage is at variance
with that of most Platonists from Xenocrates on down.
After offering some worth-while criticisms of his pred-

ecessors, Plutarch introduces his own views by demand-
ing what is the horror of a temporal creation. Does not
the refutation of atheism depend on it? God, he says,
is the author of nature, although he did not create the
material out of which he fashioned the world. This chaotic material contained body, motion, and an irrational
soul. The matter or body in motion is not itself the principle of evil. Matter should be considered as completely
neutral or even as having a slight tendency toward the
good. Plato definitely states that matter has no power
at all and compares it with the odorless base which the
manufacturers of perfume must use to produce an unmixed fragrance. Obviously a passive matter cannot put
the world in reverse, as *Politicus* expresses it, nor can
evil have arisen from a neutral source any more than it
can have arisen from the good or God.

Therefore, the principle of evil is a soul, the irrational
soul which is definitely alluded to in the *Laws,* and
which must be identified with the necessity in the *Timaeus* that requires persuasion to follow rational, scientific law.

By making the irrational soul a good world-soul, God
imposed numerical relations on the chaotic motions of
matter and reduced it to order. This action of God by
which the world was formed took place at a given moment. Xenocrates' interpretation that the world is eternal is impossible, because if the world had no literal
beginning, soul would not be prior to body, nor would
God be prior to the world.

The more the transcendency of God is emphasized,
and the more he must be separated from a world in
which evil forms a part, the more is it necessary to posit

mediators between God and man. Hence Plutarch includes in his system lesser gods and demons. To be sure
he speaks of God as being not merely an artist separated
from his work, but also as pervading the universe in the
form of the world-soul. The more usual and the more
consistent view, however, is that of demon-mediators.
And by means of these Plutarch is able to implement
his sympathy with the popular religions of all nations.
The normal abode of the demons is at the boundary
between the sub-lunar and supra-lunar regions. Through
them God sends premonitions and revelations to men.
By means of the demons, Plutarch, with a desire to
defend the doctrine of providence, attempted to follow
a middle path between Epicureanism and Stoicism. The
former philosophy destroys providence altogether, while
the latter transmutes it into a fatalism that rules out
freedom, makes evil necessary, and with great impiety
calls God its source.

The demons, or at least some of them, were once
men. Men now living on this earth are not merely compounded of soul and body as popular opinion holds.
Man is tripartite, composed of body, soul, and reason.
When a man dies, his soul, still combined with his
reason, journeys to the moon, there to be a demon. But
the reason is as superior to the soul as the soul to the
body. Accordingly in the moon there occurs a second
death by which the reason is loosed from the soul, and
leaving the soul in the moon, the reason returns to its
source and home, the sun.

PLUTARCH

MORAL AND THEOSOPHICAL ESSAYS

On Isis and Osiris

I. All good things, O Clea, it behoves persons that have sense to solicit from the gods. But more especially now that we are in quest of the knowledge of themselves (so far as such knowledge is attainable by man), so we pray to obtain the same from them with their own consent: inasmuch as there is nothing more important for a man to receive, or more noble for a god to grant, than Truth. For all other things which people require, the Deity who gives them doth not possess, nor use for his own purposes. For the Godhead is not blessed by reason of his silver and gold, nor yet almighty through his thunders and lightnings, but on account of knowledge and in- telligence.[1]

* * * * *

XLV. From all which, it is not unreasonable to conclude that no one singly says what is right, and that all collectively do so; for it is neither *drought,* nor *wind,* nor the *sea,* nor *darkness,* but generally every hurtful and mischievous part that earth contains, which belongs to Typhon. For we must not place the principles of the all in lifeless bodies, as do Democritus and Epicurus; nor yet assume as modeller of un- created matter, one Reason and one Providence, like the Stoics, that prevails over and subdues all things; for it is impossible that anything at all, whether bad or good, should exist, where God is cause of nothing. For the harmony of the universe is reciprocal, like that of a lyre or bow, according to Heraclitus, and according to Euripides:—

1. Here follows the myth of Isis and Osiris with its variations, an attempt to identify the gods of different religions, and several naturalistic explanations of the myth.—Ed.

> "Evil and good cannot occur apart;
> There is a mixture to make all go well."

Consequently this is a most ancient notion that comes down from theologians and lawgivers to poets and philosophers, which has its origin unattributed, but the belief therein strong and not to be effaced, not consisting in words and reports, but in ceremonies and sacrifices, of Barbarians and Greeks alike, and diffused in many places, that neither is the Universe without mind, without reason, and without guidance, and tossed about at random, nor yet is there One Reason that rules and directs all things as it were, by a rudder and by guiding reins, but there are many such directors, and made up out of good and bad; or rather, to speak generally, inasmuch as Nature produces nothing unmixed here below, it is not one Dispenser that like a retail dealer mixes together things for us out of two vessels and distributes the same, but it is from *two opposite Principles* and *two antagonistic Powers;* the one guiding us to the right hand and along the straight road, the other upsetting and rebuffing us, that Life becomes of a mixed nature; and also the Universe (if not the whole, yet that which surrounds Earth, and lies below the Moon), it made inconsistent with itself, and variable and susceptible of frequent changes. For if nothing can happen without cause, and good cannot furnish cause for evil, it follows that the nature of Evil, as of Good, must have an origin and principle of its own.

XLVI. And this is the opinion of most men, and those the wisest, for they believe, some that there are Two Gods, as it were of opposite trades—one the creator of good, the other of bad things; others call the better one "God," the other "Daemon," as did Zoroaster the Magian, who, they record, lived 5,000 years before the Trojan War. He therefore calls the former "Oromazes," the latter "Arimanios;" and furthermore explains that of all the objects of sense, the one most resembles *Light,* the other *Darkness,* and *Ignorance;* and that Mithras is between the two, for which reason the Persians call Mithras the "Mediator," and he [Zoroaster] taught them to offer sacrifice of vows and thanksgiving to the one, of deprecation and mourning to the other. For they bruise a certain herb called "omoine" in a mortar and invoke Hades and Darkness, and mixing it with the blood of a wolf they have sacrificed, they carry away and throw it into a place where the Sun never comes, for of plants they believe some to belong to the Good God, others to the evil Daemon; and similarly of animals, dogs, birds, and land hedgehogs belong to the Good, but to the Bad One water rats, for which reason they hold happy men that have killed the greatest number of such things.

XLVII. They too, nevertheless, tell many fabulous stories concerning their gods—for example, the following: that Oromazes sprang out of the purest Light, but Arimanios out of Darkness; they wage war upon each other. Oromazes created six gods, the first of Goodwill, the second of Truth, the third of Order, of the rest one of Wisdom, one of Wealth, one of Pleasure in things beautiful. The other God created, as it were, opponents to these deities, equal in number. Then Oromazes, having augmented himself threefold, severed from the Sun as much space as the Sun is distant from Earth, and adorned the heavens with stars; and one star he appointed before all for guard and lookout, namely Sirius. And having created four-and-twenty other gods, he shut them up in an egg; but those made by Arimanios, being as many as they, pierced the egg that had been laid, and so the bad things were mixed up with the good. But a time appointed by fate is coming, in which Arimanios having brought on famine and pestilence must needs be destroyed by the same and utterly vanish; when the earth becoming plain and level there shall be one life and one government of men, all happy and of one language. Theopompus says that, according to the Magi, one of the Gods shall conquer, the other be conquered, alternately for 3,000 years; for another 3,000 years they shall fight, war, and undo one the works of the other; but in the end Hades shall fall, and men shall be happy, neither requiring food nor constructing shelter: whilst the God who hath contrived all this is quiet and resting himself for a time, for that God may well slumber, but not long, like as a man reposing for a moderate space. The religious system of the Magi is of the aforesaid character.

XLVIII. The Chaldeans hold that the gods belong to the planets, of whom two they call "doers of good," two "makers of evil;" the other three they describe as intermediate and neutral. But the notions of the Greeks are, I suppose, plain enough to every one, for they make the good part that of the Olympian Jove, that of the hostile deity they give to Hades; and they fable that *Harmony* was the child of Venus and Mars, father, lord, and ruler of all things; and say that Homer, when he prays that

"Perish Contention, both from gods and men,"

forgets that he is cursing the origin of all things, inasmuch as they derive their origin from contention and antipathy, and the Sun will not overpass his appointed limits, otherwise:

"The avenging tongue of Law would find him out,"

and Empedocles calls the Beneficent Principle "Love" and "Friendship," and frequently too, Harmony, "with glowing face," but the Evil Principle he styles

"Contentiousness accurst, and blood-stained War."

Now the Pythagoreans characterize these Principles by several names: the Good One, as the "One," the "Definite," the "Abiding," the "Straight," the "Exceeding," the "Square," the "Equal," the "Right-handed," the "Bright;" the Bad One as the "Two," the "Indefinite," the "Unstable," the "Crooked," the "Sufficient," the "Unequally-sided" (parallelogram), the "Unequal," the "Left-handed," the "Dark"—inasmuch as these are supposed the final causes of existence—Anaxagoras defines them as "Mind," and the "Infinite;" Aristotle, the one as "Form," the other as "Deprival." Plato, as it were mystifying and veiling the matter, denominates in many places one of the opposing Principles as "The Same;" the second, as "The Other;" but in his "Laws," being now grown older, he no longer speaks in riddles and symbolically, but names them directly. "Not by one soul," says he, "was the universe set in motion, but by several, perhaps, at all events, by not less than *Two;* whereof the one is beneficent, the other antagonistic to this, and the creator of opposite effects: and there is room for a *Third Principle* to exist, one intermediate between the Two, which is neither destitute of soul, nor of reason, nor of impulse from within (as some suppose), but subordinate to those Two Principles, ever seeking after the Better One, and desiring and following after it," as the part of the treatise which follows will show, for he adopts into this system chiefly the religious notions of the Egyptians.

XLIX. For the origin and constitution of this world are mixed, being formed out of opposite principles—not, however, of equal force with each other, but the superiority belonging to the Better One. But it is impossible that the Bad One should be entirely destroyed, as it is largely implanted in the body, largely in the soul of the all, and always contending against the Better One. Now in the soul, *Mind, Reason,* the best masters and guides, are *Osiris;* but in Earth and Water, Winds and Stars, that which is ordered, permanent, and healthy, in seasons, temperament, and revolutions, are the issue of *Osiris,* and the image of him made visible. But Typhon is the part of the soul that is subject to the passions, Titan-like, unreasonable, and impulsive; but of the body (he is) the part that is unsound, subject to disease, and liable to disturbance by bad seasons and inclement weather, by the concealments of the Sun, and the disappearances of the Moon—such as deviations from its course, vanishings, and whirlwinds.

* * * * *

LXVII. But those theorists engender horrible and impious notions, who apply the names of deities to natural productions and to things that be without sense, without life, and necessarily consumed by men in want of and making use of them. For these things themselves it is impossible to conceive as gods (for we cannot conceive God as an inanimate thing, subject to man), but from these productions we have drawn the inference that they who created them, and bestow, and dispense them to us constantly and sufficiently, are gods—not different gods amongst different people, nor Barbarian or Grecian, of the South or of the North—but like as the Sun, Moon, Sky, Earth, Sea, are the common property of all men, but yet are called by different names by different nations; in the same manner, as one reason regulates all things, and one Providence directs, and subordinate Powers are appointed over all things, yet different honours and titles are by custom assigned to them amongst different peoples: and these have established, and do employ, *symbols,* some obscure, some more intelligible, in order to lead the understanding into things divine. And this not without danger: for some having entirely missed their meaning, have slid into *superstition;* whilst others shunning every superstition like a quagmire, have unknowingly fallen into *Atheism* [1] as down a precipice.

ON THE CESSATION OF ORACLES

XXXIX. When all the rest joined in this demand, I, after a short pause, continued: In truth, Ammonius, by an odd coincidence, 'twas yourself that supplied the starting-point and introduction to those discourses of mine. For whether daemons be spirits separated from the body, or never united to one, according to you and the divine Hesiod, being

"Pure dwellers upon earth, keepers of mortals,"

why shall we deprive souls in the body of that power by which the daemons are naturally enabled to foreknow and foretell future events? For that any new power or faculty is superadded to souls after they have left the body, which they did not previously possess, is by no means probable: but that they possess, indeed, those powers originally, but have them in inferior degree, whilst united with the body, some being imperceptible and latent, others feeble and obscure, in a similar way to things seen through a mist, or in moving water, inactive, and slow, and standing in need of much curing, and recovery of what is their own, and removal and clearing away of what obscures them—all this is probable enough. For just as the Sun doth not

1. Respectable antiquity considered Epicureans, Christians, and Atheists equally absurd.—Ed.

become bright, when he bursts through the clouds, but *is* so perpetually, yet he appears to us, when in a mist, dull and obscure, in like manner the soul doth not *acquire* the prophetic power, when it passes out of the body, as out of a cloud, but possesses it even now, though it is dimmed by its mixture and confusion with the body. We ought not to wonder or disbelieve this, when we observe, if nothing else, the faculty of the Soul which is the converse of Foreknowledge, that is what we call the *Memory:* how great an operation it doth perform in preserving and storing up things gone by, or rather, things that are! For of things past, none is or subsists, but all things are born and die together—both actions, and words, and passions—whilst Time, like a mighty river, sweeps them by, one by one; but this faculty of the Soul, laying hold upon them, I know not how, invests things not present with visible form and existence! For, truly, the oracle given to the Thessalians respecting Anna, promises

"To the deaf hearing, to the blind their sight."

But the Memory is to us the hearing of deaf actions, and the seeing of blind. No wonder, then, as I have said, if that which holds tight the things that be no more, should anticipate many of those that do not yet exist; for *these* belong more peculiarly to it, and for these it has a natural sympathy, inasmuch as it stretches itself out, and pushes forward towards the Future, but disengages itself from things that be past and come to an end, except so far as the remembering of them goes.

XL. Souls therefore possessing this faculty inherent in their nature, though obscured, and hardly showing itself, do nevertheless put forth blossom, and recover this power—in dreams often, on the point of death, some few—either that the body becomes purified, or assumes a new temperament on these occasions, or else that the reasoning and thinking parts of the soul are unbound and released from the irrational and visionary condition of the Present, and turn towards the Future. For it is not so, as Euripides says:

"He's the best prophet that can guess the best,"

But such a one is a man that has his wits about him, and follows the intelligent part of his soul as it guides him on his way, with a show of probability. For the prophetic part, like a tablet unwritten on, senseless, and indefinite of itself, but capable of receiving visionary impressions and forebodings, grasps the Future without any consideration, at the moment when it is first departing out of the Present. It makes the same escape from the Present by means of the temperament and condition of the body when in a state of change, which we call *inspiration*. Now the body doth frequently of its own accord acquire this predisposition; and the earth sends forth springs of water productive of various effects upon mankind—some being productive of delirium, and disease, and death; and others that are good, benignant, and salubrious, as they prove by experience to such as frequent them. But the prophetic stream or blast is the most godlike and most holy, whether it be taken in with air or drawn from the liquid fountain; for when it unites itself with the body it engenders in the soul a temperament altogether unusual and strange, the peculiar nature of which it is difficult to explain clearly, although history in many places affords us means for a conjecture. That by means of its heat and diffusion it opens certain passages suited to admit impressions of the Future is probable enough, just as when wine gets up into the head it brings about other effects, and unlocks words stored up in memory and forgotten. Also the Bacchic frenzy and madness itself possesses much of the prophetic spirit, when the soul, becoming heated and full of fire, shakes off the caution that human prudence lays upon it, and thereby frequently turns aside and puts forth the fire of inspiration.

On the Apparent Face in the Orb of the Moon

II. "For you see at once how absurd is the explanation that the apparent figure in the moon is merely an affection of the sight, which is dazzled by the brightness, by reason of its own weakness; . . . it takes no notice that this effect should rather take place in regard to the Sun, which strikes upon the eye

both sharp and forcibly; whence Empedocles hath described
the difference between the two, not inelegantly,

"'The shrill-voiced sun, the softly whispering moon,'

designating in this way the attractive, cheerful, and inoffensive
character of the latter luminary. Afterwards, giving the reason
why dim and weak eyes discern no difference of form *in* the
moon, but her orb strikes upon them as smooth and completely
filled up, whilst those that have sharp and strong sight make
out better, and distinguish the lineaments of the Face, and
seize upon the difference more clearly. For the contrary ought
to be the case, if that appearance were produced from the eye's
being overcome; because where the sense affected was weaker,
the stronger would be the impression produced. But the in-
equality [of the surface] refutes this explanation, for the sight
does not rest upon a continuous and confused shadow. . . .
For in reality the shaded parts, as they go round, creep under
the bright ones, and are in turn cut away and compressed, and
in a word, are interwoven one with the other. . . ."

III. And upon Apollonius taking up the conversation, and
asking what was the opinion of Clearchus: "It better suits,"
replied I, "any other person than yourself to be ignorant of the
story, inasmuch as it proceeds from the very focus of geometry: for the fellow says that the so-called face is only reflected
images and appearances of the great sea [the ocean] that are
shown upon the moon; for that her external circumference
when concave [1] is naturally adapted to catch the reflections rising up from various quarters, whilst the full moon is of all mirrors, in point of polish and of brilliancy the most beautiful and
the most clear. For just as you suppose that the rainbow, when
the light is reflected against the sun, is impressed upon the
clouds that have received gradually a watery smoothness and
surface, in the same way, that writer says, the external sea [our
ocean] is reflected on the moon, not indeed from the place it
occupies, but from where the reflection of the air has made the
image of it, that is to say, its surface and reflection. And Agesi-
anax, in another place, has said:—

1. When the moon takes the form of a crescent.—Tr.

" 'Or some great wave of ocean, rising steep,
Shows like an image on the blazing mirror.' "

IV. Apollonius then was amused, and exclaimed: "How
original and entirely new is the construction of this theory—it
bespeaks a man possessed of audacity as well as wit! But in
what way is it open to objection?" "In the first place," I replied, "because the nature of the outer sea is one and the same,
a uniform and unbroken expanse of water; whereas the appearance of the dark parts in the moon is not one and the same,
but shows as it were projecting tongues of land, because the
bright part diversifies and defines the dark; so that from each
of these being separated, and having a boundary of its own,
the projections of the bright parts upon the darkened, assuming the form of elevations and depressions, arrange in a most
natural manner the features that appear around the eyes and
lips; so that we must either suppose there are several outer seas
intersected by tongues of land and continents, which supposition is both absurd and false, or else there being but one it is
not reasonable that the image of it should be reflected diversified in this way." . . .

VI. . . . "Only," replied Lucius laughing, "do not bring an
action for impiety against us, just as Cleanthes thought it right
that the Greeks collectively should impeach Aristagoras the
Stoic, of impiety, for overthrowing the altar of earth, because
the fellow attempted to account for visible phenomena by supposing that the sky remains fixed, and that the earth rolls
round down an oblique circle, turning at the same time upon
its own axis. We, however, say nothing out of our own heads;
whilst they who suppose the moon an earth, how do they turn
things upside down, any more than you do who place the earth
here in the air, although it be, by far, bigger than the moon, as
mathematicians calculate her magnitude during her eclipses,
and by the length of time consumed in her passage through the
shadow? For the shadow of the earth is projected of lesser size
by the illuminating body being the larger; and that the upper
part of the shadow itself is fine and narrow, was not unknown,
as he says, to Homer also, for he entitles night 'swift,' by rea-

son of the *pointed* form of the shadow. But by this philosopher
the moon is convicted on the strength of her eclipses, and gets
off with hardly three of her own (apparent) magnitudes, for
consider to how many moons the earth is equal, if it projects a
shadow, which, at the shortest, is thrice the diameter of the
moon. But yet you are afraid for the moon, lest she should
tumble down; but as for the earth, Eschylus perhaps has reas-
sured you, like Atlas,

> " 'He stands, the pillar of the sky and earth,
> Propping a load not easy for the arms;'

that is, if there flows under the moon only thin air, not com-
petent to support a solid body; whilst the earth, according to
Pindar, 'adamantine-shod columns keep in on every side.' And
for this reason Pharnaces himself is under no apprehension of
the earth's falling, whereas he compassionates such as lie
under the roadway of the moon, namely, the Ethiopians and
people of Taprobane, lest so vast a weight should drop upon
them; and yet, a safeguard to the moon against falling down
is her motion, and the rapidity of her gyration, just as objects
placed in slings have a hindrance from falling out in the circular whirling. For the natural tendency acts upon each object, unless it be diverted by some extraneous force. Consequently, her own weight does not act upon the moon, because
by means of her rapid rotation its downward tendency is
neutralized; there were rather cause to wonder at her not
remaining stationary, like the earth, and not rolling out of
her place. As it is, the moon has the greatest reason for not
being carried in our direction; but the earth, as being destitute
of other motion, it was natural should remain fixed through
the force of gravity alone, because it is heavier than the moon,
not by the same proportion as it is the larger of the two,
but in still greater degree inasmuch as the latter is all the
lighter through heat and burning up of her substance. And,
in fine, the moon, from what you say, if she be *fire*, naturally
stands in need of earth and matter, in which she walks, and
clings to, and keeps together, and fans the flame of her force.
Now fire cannot be imagined as being maintained without

fuel, but earth, you assert, remains fixed without either foundation or root." "Certainly so," replied Pharnaces, "because it occupies its proper and natural place, as being itself the centre, for this is the place around which all weights gravitate and rest, and are carried and tend together from all parts; whereas the whole upper region, even though it should receive some earthy substance forcibly thrown up, immediately excludes it—better say, discharges it, to be carried downwards in the way its own natural tendency directs."

VII. In return for this, I wishing to obtain a little respite for Lucius whilst refreshing his memory, called to Theon: "Who was it, Theon," said I, "of the tragic writers that remarks of physicians that

" 'With bitter drugs they purge the bitter bile?' "

and on his answering, "Sophocles," "This privilege must be granted to them," said I, "whether we will or no; but we must not listen to philosophers when they choose to defend absurdities by other absurdities, and in fighting for the monstrosities of their doctrines invent others yet more strange and wonderful, just as these men bring in the 'gravitation to the centre'— a notion, what amount of extravagance does it not involve? Do not they make out earth to be a sphere, though it contains such depths and heights and inequalities of surface? Do not they make the Antipodes live like caterpillars or lizards, turned upside down, clinging to the earth? And they represent ourselves as not walking erect to stand firm upon it, but wavering away all on one side, like so many drunken men! Don't they pretend that masses of a thousand talents weight falling through the depths of earth, when they arrive at the centre are arrested, though there be nothing to encounter or support them? and that if, carried along by their velocity, they shoot past the centre, they are turned back again and retrace their course spontaneously? . . .

VIII. "Of such and such great absurdities not a walletful, but rather a whole juggler's stock and shopful, have these men strapped upon their backs and drag after them, and yet they say others are idle chatterers for placing the moon, being

an earth, up aloft, not where the centre is. And yet truly, if
every ponderous thing does tend towards the same point, and
presses with all its particles upon its own centre—earth will
claim for herself all ponderous things, not so much because
earth is the centre of the universe, as because they are particles
of herself; and the fact of things gravitating downwards will
be a proof, not of the centripetal force towards earth, but of
affinity and sympathy, as it were, with earth, in particles once
separated from her, and now flying back to her again. . . .
I do not see why the philosopher who forces all earthy and
ponderous particles into one and the same place, and makes
them out portions of one and the same body, does not concede
the same natural tendency to such as are without weight, but
allows so many composite bodies of fire to exist separately,
and does not imperatively collect into one lump all the stars
that be, and demand that there should be one common body
of all upward tending and fiery particles."

IX. "But," said I, "you assert that the sun, my dear Apollonides, is distant infinite myriads of miles from the superior
circumference, while the Morning Star, and Mercury, and the
other planets, all placed below him, keeping far aloof from
the fixed stars, and at great distances from each other, pursue
their course; whereas for the ponderous and earthy particles
you suppose the universe offers no free space, nor interval
between each other in its whole extent. You see it is ridiculous
if we shall assert that the moon is not an earth *because* she
is posted remote from the lower space, but should call her a
star, seeing her thrust away so many myriads of miles from
the superior circumference, and crept as it were into some
hole and corner of creation: at least she is so much below the
other stars that one cannot express the measure of the distance, but arithmetic fails you mathematicians in calculating
the same; whereas, in a manner, she touches Earth. . . .

"For neither does she often overpass the shadow [of Earth],
and elevate herself a little, by reason that the illuminating
body is exceeding great, but she appears to revolve so close
to, and as it were in the embrace of Earth, as to be screened
against the Sun by it, without ever soaring above this shady

terrestrial and darksome region which is the allotment of Earth. Wherefore I think we must confidently declare the moon to be within the limits of Earth, and to be overcast by the point of Earth's shadow.

X. "And consider, leaving out of the case the other fixed stars and planets, what Aristarchus points out in his treatise 'Upon Magnitudes and Distances,' that the distance of the sun is more than eighteen times, but less than twenty times the distance of the moon, by which she is separated from us: and yet the computation that gives the greatest elevation to the moon says she is distant from us fifty-six times the space from the centre of the earth [to the circumference]: this length is of forty thousand stadia, according to those who make a moderate calculation of it. And, calculated from this basis, the sun's distance from the moon amounts to over four thousand and thirty myriads of stadia. So far, then, is she separated from the sun by reason of her weight, and approximated to earth, that if one must define substances by localities, the constitution and beauty of Earth attracts the moon, and she is of influence in matters and over persons upon Earth, by reason of her relationship and proximity. . . .

XV. "In the same way, therefore, is it probable the world is constituted, that is, if it be a *living thing,* containing earth in many places, in many others water and fire, and air, not forcibly compressed, but arranged in order by Reason. For neither is the eye *squeezed out* of the mass into the place it now fills in the body, in consequence of its levity, nor did the heart slip down and fall into the breast by reason of its weight, but because it was better each of the two should be so placed. Therefore, let us not think, of the parts of the world, either that Earth is lying here because she hath tumbled down through her own weight, or the Sun (as Metrodorus the Chian supposed) was shot up into the upper region, through his levity, after the manner of a bubble, or that the other stars got into the places where they now are, because they gravitated thither as though according to the discrimination of a pair of scales. But, inasmuch as He that rules by *reason* is the master, they, like light-giving eyes, are fixed in

the brow of the universe, and stray about: whilst the sun fills
the place of a heart, and, like blood and breath, distributes
and disperses from out of himself both heat and light. Earth
and sea the world uses according to Nature for whatever purposes an animal uses its belly and bladder: whilst the moon
placed between Heaven and Earth, like the liver between
the belly and the heart, or some other soft intestine, diffuses
here the warmth from above, and the exhalations rising hence
she subtilizes by a certain process of digestion and purification,
around herself, and emits them again. . . .

XVI. . . . "That the moon, then, is illuminated, not like glass
or crystal, by the direct or transmitted light of the sun, is a
probable supposition; nor again, by reason of collected illumination or collected reflection, in the same way as torches do,
when the light is augmented; for in that case it will be full
moon to us none the less at the times of new moon, or first
and third quarters, if she neither covers nor blocks out the
sun; but the light rather passes through her by reason of her
fluidity, or else it shines into her by way of intermixture, and
lights up all around her. For it is not possible to lay the blame
in the case of her dark quarters upon her deviations, or re-
treatings, as in the cases when she shows half her orb, or the
same gibbous or crescent-shaped; but, according to Democritus, she stands in a vertical line to the illuminating body, and
receives and takes in the sun: so that it were probable that
she at the same time is illuminated and illuminates that body.
But she is very far from doing this; for at that moment she is
invisible, and she frequently hides, and causes him to disappear, 'she strips him of his beams,' as Empedocles says,

" 'Till up aloft, she veils so much his face
As the width measures of the *blue-eyed* moon:'

as though the [sun's] light fell upon night and darkness, and
not upon another star. And as to what Posidonius says, that
'the light of the sun does not pass through her, on account of
the depth of the moon,' is plainly confuted by the fact; for
the air, though unlimited and having a depth many times
greater than the moon's, is entirely illuminated and shone

upon by his rays. There is left, therefore, the doctrine of Empedocles, that it is by means of a certain reflection of the sun upon the moon that the illumination which proceeds from her here below is brought about. Consequently it [her light] comes to us neither warm, nor brilliant, naturally enough, as there has been a kindling and a mingling of different lights in that case; but just as voices in the case of reflections send back the echo of the sound more dull, and the blows of shots that rebound from an object fall with greatly diminished force,

     " 'So the ray striking on the moon's broad disk,'

makes a feeble and dull rebound upon us, being deprived of its strength by reflection."

XVII. Then Sylla taking up the conversation said: "Certainly, this notion possesses some degree of probability, but the thing that is the strongest of those that make against it, pray, does it admit of any softening down, or has it escaped my companion's observation?" "What is this?" replied Lucius, "do you mean the question about the half-moon?" "Yes, certainly," answered Sylla; "for the assertion has some reason on its side, that, since all reflection takes place at equal angles, when the moon, showing but half her disk, rides in midheaven, the light from her does not travel towards us, but glides off to the part opposite to earth; for the sun, being upon the horizon, touches the moon with his rays; consequently, being refracted at an equal angle, it [the light from the sun] will rebound to the other extremity, and not throw the light so far as to us; or else there will be a great distortion and parallax of the angle, which thing is not possible." "Nay, but indeed," replied Lucius, "this thing has been asserted;" and looking, as he was talking, towards Menelaus the mathematician, "I am ashamed, my dear Menelaus, to take up a mathematical question in your presence, which serves as the very foundation for the whole science of Opticks, but there is no help for it," he continued, "for the fact that all reflection extends itself at equal angles, is neither self-evident nor universally admitted, but is contradicted in the case of convex mirrors, when they make images larger than the objects themselves to one point of vision. It is also contradicted in the case of double mirrors, which being inclined to each other, and an angle formed between them, each of the surfaces presents the appearance of a double one, and gives four images from one face, two of them looking towards the left parts from outside, and two others, indistinct, looking to the right, in the depth of the mirror. Of the production of which images, Plato explains the cause; for he has said that in consequence of the mirror's having got height, on this side and on that, the eyes transfer the reflection, as they change their place from one side to the other. If, therefore, of the images some run back directly to us, whilst some slipping to the other side of the mirror are thrown back again from thence to us, it is not possible that all reflections take place in equal angles, as many as . . . joining battle, they demand to do away with the equality of angles by means of the *emanations* flowing from the moon upon the earth, because they suppose this theory more plausible than the former. Not but that if we must needs gratify your great darling, Geometry, and concede the point,—in the first place it is likely enough that such happens in the case of reflectors made very exact as to their polished surfaces; whereas the moon offers many inequalities and asperities of surface, so that rays from a great body [like the sun] going astray at considerable elevations, that allow of their reflecting and exchanging with one another, are reflected in all sorts of ways, and entangled with each other, and kindle up the lustre in itself, because it is thrown upon us from several reflectors at once. In the next place, even though we allow the reflections upon the moon herself to be at equal angles, it is not impossible that the rays, travelling through so vast a distance, may get reflections and circular slips of their own, so that the light is brought into one, and made to shine. Some, too, write to show that she casts many of her beams upon earth in the line . . . under the inclined, subtended. To construct a diagram in illustration of this theory, and that too, for many spectators, would be quite impracticable.

XVIII. "To sum up, I wonder how they manage about the

half-moon's reaching us, together with the full round, and the crescent. For if the mass of the moon, illuminated by the sun, were made of aether, or of fire, he would not have left her hemisphere shaded, and without lustre to the sense [perceptible], but had he touched here in ever so small a degree, in going around her, it would have been a natural consequence that the sun should fill her substance, and penetrate through the whole of it with his all-pervading light, from the want of any resistance. For where wine touches water at the edge, or a drop of blood falls into any liquid, the whole quantity turns red, and changes to the colour of blood; in like manner, they pretend that the air itself is illuminated, not by emanations of any sort, or rays mingling themselves in it, but by a conversion and transformation due to impact and contagion: how do they imagine that star touches star, and light light, without mixing together or making any confusion or change at all, but to illume those objects only which they touch upon their surface? For the circle which the sun, as he goes round, traces and turns about with reference to the moon, at one time falls upon the line which divides the visible from the invisible portion of her body, at another time rises up vertically so as to cut them, and to be cut by the moon, producing various inclinations and relations of the lighted to the darkened part, the complete circle and the crescent forms in her appearance, all which proves more than anything else that her illumination is not the result of *mixture* but of *contact,* not *ignition* but *irradiation.* And since not only she is lighted up, but transmits hither the image of her light, she supplies yet further reason for our insisting upon our own explanation of her nature; for reflections are produced by no object that is porous or of loose texture. There is no such thing as light rebounding back out of light, or fire out of fire, easily conceivable; but the object that will produce opposition and fracture must necessarily be something ponderous and solid in order there may be impact *against* it, and resilience *from* it. At any rate the sun himself penetrates the air because it neither furnishes obstacles, nor offers resistance; whereas from sticks and stones and clothes exposed to the light the same sun gives back many reflections and irradiations. Thus, in fact, we see the entire earth illuminated by her, for she does not admit the light to a depth like water, nor through the whole substance like air, but whatever kind of orbit of the sun moves round the moon, and for as large a portion of her as is cut off thereby, just such another circle goes round the earth, and just so large a portion is there illuminated, and leaving the other not lighted up; for the hemisphere that is illuminated seems to be little larger in either case. Allow me to speak geometrically according to analogy, that if, there being three things which the light from the sun touches, namely, the earth, the moon, and the air, we see the moon illuminated, not in the same way as the air, but rather in the same way as the earth; it necessarily follows the two have the same nature, being made to be affected in the same way as the earth; it necessarily follows the two have the same nature, being made to be affected in the same way by the same agent." . . .

XIX. . . . The rest, with the accurate calculations of mathematicians, has been worked out and brought to a certainty; namely, that night is the shadow of the earth, and the eclipse of the sun is the shadow of the moon, when the light comes to be in it. For the sun when setting, is blocked up by the earth against the sight; but when eclipsed he is blocked up by the moon, and both phenomena are occultations, but that of setting is due to the earth, that of eclipse to the moon, because she intercepts the view of him with her shadow. What takes place is easily understood from the following considerations. If the effect is the same, the agents are the same; for it is a matter of necessity that the same things should happen in the same case from the same causes. But that the darkness attending eclipses is not complete darkness, and does not condense the atmosphere in the same degree that night does, is a circumstance we ought not to be surprised at; for the *substance* is the same of the object that causes night and that causes the eclipse, but the *magnitude* of each is not equal; for the Egyptians, I think, say the moon is the seventy-second part of the earth in size; Anaxagoras, that she is as big as the Peloponnesus. But Aristarchus proves that the moon's diameter bears a proportion [to that of the earth] which is less than sixty to nineteen, but somewhat greater than one hundred and eight to forty. Consequently earth entirely takes away the sun from sight, by reason of her magnitude; for the obstruction she presents is extensive, and endures the space of a night, whereas the moon, even though she may occasionally hide the sun, the occultation has no time to last, and no extensiveness, but some light shows itself round his circumference that does not allow the darkness to become deep and unmixed. . . . XX. Then Lucius remarked: "These are about the most important of the theories current; but first of all, take in hand, if you please, the explanation derived from the *figure* of the shadow; for it is a cone, as though a great fire or light projected a mass, less indeed than a sphere, but still spherical in form, for which reason in eclipses of the moon the outlines of the darkened parts against the bright ones have their edges circular; for whatever sections a round thing coming in contact with another thing, may either receive or produce, as they go off in all directions, they are made circular by reason of their resemblance [to what produced them]. In the second place, I fancy you know that the moon is first eclipsed on the parts towards the east; whereas the sun is on those towards the west, because the earth's shadow moves towards the west from the east. The sun and the moon, on the contrary, move towards the east. All this, visible facts enable us to discover, and may be understood without very lengthy explanations, and from them the shadow as the cause of the eclipse is established. For when the sun is eclipsed by being *overtaken* by, and the moon by *meeting* that which causes the eclipse, probably, or rather, necessarily, the sun is first overtaken from behind, the moon from the front, for the occultation begins from that side where the object in front first casts the shadow, and the moon first casts it upon the sun from the west, as she is racing against him, but upon *her* he casts it from the east, because she is moving below in a contrary direction, from the east. Thirdly, then, consider the question of the *duration,* and of the *extent* of her eclipses.

When she is eclipsed high in heaven and at her apogee she is obscured for only a short time, but being in her perigee and low when thus affected, she is greatly oppressed, and emerges with difficulty from the shadow. And yet, when she is low, she is making the greatest movements, but when high the smallest of all. But the cause of the difference lies in the shadow, for it is broadest at the base, as all cones are, and contracting gradually, at the top it ends in a sharp and fine point. Consequently, the moon entering into this shadow when she is low down, is caught by it in its largest circumference and passes through its deepest and darkest part, but when up high, just grazing the shadow, as though in shallow water, she quickly makes her escape. . . . If then the moon possesses an infantine and ineffective fire, being a 'feminine star,' as these philosophers pretend, it befits her to be affected in none of the ways in which she is affected at present, but altogether the contrary of them all; she ought to appear where now she is hidden, and be hidden exactly where she now appears: that is to say, be hidden for the rest of the time as being obscured by the circumambient aether, but emerge and become visible every six months, and again every five, when she enters into the shadow of the earth. For the 365 revolutions of the ecliptic full moons contain 404 periods of six months, and the rest of five months each.[1] It would therefore be necessary that the moon should be visible at intervals of so many months, because she became conspicuous in the shadow; but she . . . becomes eclipsed and loses her light, but recovers it again, when she emerges from the shadow, and often shows herself by day, as being anything rather than a fiery or star-like substance."

XXI. Lucius having said this, Pharnaces and Apollonides in a way came into collision with each other [in their eagerness to answer him], but when Apollonides gave up the turn, Pharnaces continued, "This fact *does* most of all prove the moon to be fire or a star, for she is not *entirely* invisible during eclipses, but displays the hot-coal and grim colour which is her own proper hue." . . . "I will turn now to you, Pharnaces,

1. These figures do not make astronomical sense.—Ed.

for that coal-like and glowing colour, which you pretend is the natural complexion of the moon, is really that of a body that possesses density and depth; for in things unsubstantial no remnant or vestige of flame is accustomed to remain; nor is there any food for fire except in a solid body that will receive and nourish the spark kindling it; as Homer also hath sung,

" 'When the fire-flower was spent and quenched the blaze, Spreading the ashes wide.'

For the 'charcoal' is probably not *fire,* but an ignited substance, and affected by fire dwelling upon, and wearing itself out upon a mass which is both solid and possessed of durability; whereas the flames are but the lighting up and jets of an unsubstantial nutriment and material, speedily consumed by reason of its weakness. Consequently, nothing could have been so convincing a proof that the moon is an earthy and dense substance, than if 'smouldering coal' were proper to her as her colour. . . . Wherefore let us believe that we do not offend in supposing her an earth; and as for her *face* visible to us, just as our own earth contains deep recesses [let us believe that] in the same way she too is opened out into vast gulfs, containing either water or darkened air, into which the sun's light doth not descend, or even touch, but falls short of them entirely, and produces a reflection that is dispersed and lost in those places."

XXII. Then Apollonides, scornfully interrupting, exclaimed; "What, then, in the Moon's own name, does it seem to you possible that this appearance is nothing but shadows of streams or of deep ravines, and comes all the way from the moon to us here to our sight? Perhaps you do not consider the consequences, must I tell them? Listen, then, even though you be not ignorant of them already. The diameter of the moon measures twelve fingers' breadth, as it appears to the eye, at her mean distances; whilst of the black and shaded parts each one appears larger than a half digit, so as to be larger than the twenty fourth part of the diameter; and, again, if we should estimate the circumference of the moon at thirty thousand stadia [1] only, and the diameter at ten thousand, according to the rule, then each one of the shaded parts in her, will not be less than five hundred stadia.[2] Consider, pray, in the first place, whether it be possible that such cavities and such great inequalities of surface should exist in the moon as to produce an obscuration of this extent. In the next place, being so large, why are they not perceptible to us?" And I, smiling at him, replied, "Well done, Apollonides, to have invented such a demonstration, on the strength of which you will make out both yourself and me to be bigger than those Aloads of old; not however, at all times of day, but chiefly at sunrise and sunset; you think that because the sun makes our shadows enormous, the fact furnishes this fine argument to the sense, that if the shadow cast be big the thing casting the shadow must be exceeding great. . . ."

XXVI. Almost whilst I was still speaking, Sylla took up the discourse with "Stop, Lamprias, and shut to the wicket of your speech lest you unwittingly run the fable aground, and throw this play of mine into confusion, for it has a different scene and plot. Now, I am the player, but first I will tell you the author of the piece, if there is no objection, who begins after Homer's fashion with,

" 'An isle Ogygian lies far out at sea,' "

distant five days' sail from Britain,[3] going westwards, and three others [4] equally distant from it, and from each other, are

1. 3,750 miles English.—Tr.
2. Fifty-two miles.—Tr.
3. Ireland, probably, which lies at this distance from Rutupiae, the only British port known to Plutarch. The Romans had marched across the island as far as Anglesea in Nero's reign.—Tr.
4. The three other islands may be the Shetlands, since for one month the sun is below the horizon less than an hour each day. Interest in this passage has been aroused by identifying the great continent surrounding the sea with America, an identification made possible by supposing the distance five myriads of stadia instead of five thousand. But the description of the sea as muddy, difficult of passage because of the currents, and the fact that it calls to mind the Maeotis, or sea of Azov, are

more opposite to the summer visits of the sun; in one of which
the barbarians fable that Saturn is imprisoned by Jupiter,
whilst his son lies by his side, as though keeping guard over
those islands and the sea, which they call 'the Sea of Saturn.'
The great continent by which the great sea is surrounded on
all sides, they say, lies less distant from the others, but about
five thousand stadia from Ogygia, for one sailing in a rowing-
galley; for the sea is difficult of passage and muddy through
the great number of currents, and these currents issue out of
the great land, and shoals are formed by them, and the sea
becomes clogged and full of earth, by which it has the appearance of being solid. That sea-coast of the mainland Greeks are
settled on, around a bay not smaller than the Maeotis, the
entrance of which lies almost in a straight line opposite the
entrance to the Caspian Sea. Those Greeks call and consider
themselves *continental* people, but *islanders* all such as inhabit
this land of ours, inasmuch as it is surrounded on all sides by
the sea; and they believe that with the peoples of Saturn were
united, later those who wandered about with Hercules, and
being left behind there, they rekindled into strength and numbers the Greek element, then on the point of extinction, and
sinking into the barbarian language, manners, and laws;
whence Hercules has the first honours there, and Saturn the
second. But when the star of Saturn, which we call the 'In-
former,' but they 'Nocturnal,' comes into the sign of the Bull
every thirty years, they having got ready a long while beforehand all things required for the sacrifice and the games . . . .
they send out people appointed by lot in the same number of
ships, furnished with provisions and stores necessary for persons intending to cross so vast a sea by dint of rowing, as well
as to live a long time in a foreign land. When they have put to

indications that the sea is the Baltic and the continent which surrounds
it is Scandinavia. The Caspian Sea may have been connected with the
Maeotis, though the difference in levels would render unlikely any
navigable waterway. More probably the Caspian was open to the Arctic
Ocean, a hypothesis which would explain the existence of seals in the
Caspian alone of all inland seas. (Cf. also Chapter XXIX near the end.)
The religious exercises mentioned are thought to be Druidic.—Ed.

sea, they meet, naturally, with different fates, but those who escape from the sea, first of all, touch at the foremost isles, which are inhabited by Greeks also, and see the sun setting for less than one hour for thirty days in succession; and this interval is night, attended with slight darkness, and a twilight glimmering out of the west. Having spent ninety days there, treated with honour and hospitality, being both considered and entitled 'holy,' thenceforward they voyage with the help of the winds. No other people inhabit the islands save themselves and those that had been sent out before; it is, indeed, allowed to such as have served thirteen years in waiting upon the god, to return home, but the greatest part prefer to remain there, partly out of habit, partly because they have all things in abundance without toil and trouble, as they pass their time in sacrifices and hymn singing, or in studying legends and philosophy of some sort. For wonderful are both the island and the mildness of the climate; whilst the deity himself has been an obstacle to some when contemplating departure, by manifesting himself to them as to familiars and friends, not by way of dreams or by tokens, but conversing with them in a visible form with many apparitions and speeches of genii. For Saturn himself is imprisoned in a vast cavern, sleeping upon a rock overlaid with gold; for his sleep has been contrived by Jupiter for his chaining—whilst birds fly down from the rock, which are ordained to carry ambrosia to him, whilst the island is overspread with fragrance, diffused from the rock as from a fountain. Those genii wait upon and nurse Saturn, who had been his companions at the time when truly he used to reign over both gods and men; and they, being endowed with prophecy, foretell, on their own account, many things, but important matters, and such as concern the highest things, they go down into the cavern and report as the dreams of Saturn; for whatsoever things Jupiter is devising for the future, Saturn dreams what they are about, and that which is kingly and divine. The stranger having been carried there, as he told us, and waiting upon the god at his leisure, he gained acquaintance with astrology and geometry as far as it is possible to advance, whilst he took up 'natural science' for his department of philosophy.

But, seized at last with a desire and longing to become ac-
quainted with the 'great island,' for so, as was natural, they
denominate the territories inhabited by ourselves; when the
thirty years had expired, and the successors were come from
home, he took leave of his friends and sailed away, having
provided himself carefully with all other stores, and carrying
his travelling expenses in [the shape of] cups of gold. All that
he endured, and how many nations he passed through, con-
sulting their sacred books, and receiving initiation into all
their mysteries, would take a whole day to enumerate in the
way that he related it to us, describing the circumstances very
well and particularly; but as much of them as is connected
with the present inquiry you must now hear, for he spent a
very long time at Carthage, inasmuch as he received great
honours amongst us for having discovered, deposited in the
earth, some sacred parchments, which had been secretly carried off at the time when the former city was destroyed, and
which had been concealed a very long time. Of the visible
powers, he said we ought (and exhorted me also) especially to
worship the moon, as being in reality, and also reputed, the
sovereign of life." . . .

XXVIII. "What, pray, is this, Sylla?" said I. "Do not ask
questions about it," replied he, "for I am going to relate it all.
Man most people rightly think a *composite* being, but wrongly
think a composite of *two* parts only, for they reckon the *mind*
as only a part of the *soul*, being no less in error than they who
think the soul to be only part of the *body;* for the mind is as
much better and more divine than the soul, as the soul is superior to the body. For the conjunction of body and soul produces [1] . . . *Reason*, whereof the one is the origin of pleasure
and pain, the other, of vice and virtue. Of these three combined things, the earth furnished for the birth the *body*, the
moon the *soul*, the sun the *mind*, just as he supplies light to the
moon. The death which we die makes the man *two* instead of
three, the second [death] makes him *one* out of *two*. The first
takes place in the region of Demeter [because the earth] and

1. "Sensation" must be the word lost here; as plainly appears from
what comes next.—Tr.

also the dead are subject to her, whence the Athenians of old used to call the [dead] "Demetrians." The second [death] takes place in the moon, the dominion of Persephone; and of the former the consort is the Earthly Hermes, of the latter, the Heavenly. The former separates the soul from the body, hastily and with violence; but Persephone gently and slowly loosens the mind from the soul, and for this reason she has been named the "Only-begotten," [1] because the best part of the man becomes *single* when separated from the rest by her means. Each of these changes happens, according to nature, as follows: every soul, whether without mind, or joined to mind, on departing from the body, is ordained to wander in the region lying between the moon and earth for a term, not equal in all cases; but the wicked and incontinent pay a penalty for their sins; whereas the virtuous, in order, as it were, to purify themselves and to recover breath, after the body, as being the source of sinful pollution, must pass a certain fixed time in the mildest region of air, which they call the "Meadow of Hades." Then, as though returning to their native land after enforced banishment, they taste of joy, such as the initiated into mysteries feel, mingled with trouble and apprehension, joined with a peculiar hope, for it drives off and tosses away many of them when already making for the moon; and they [the virtuous] also see the ghosts of people there turned upside down, and, as it were, descending into the abyss.[2] Such as are arrived above, and have got firm footing there [on the moon], like victors in the games, crowned with wreaths, encircle their heads with crowns called crowns of "Constancy," made of feathers, because the irrational and passionate part of the soul they have in life presented to Reason, manageable and kept in restraint. In the next place, their sight resembles a sunbeam, and the soul, wafted on high by the air surrounding the moon, gains tone and vigour from the same, just as here below steeled

1. Perverted into an active sense, as "begotten of one."–Tr.

2. The spirits of the good rest above in a fearful hope, for from their place of rest they can see the ghosts of the wicked repelled by the circumference of the moon, tossed about, and falling headlong, as they fancy, into the abyss below.—Tr.

tools gain it by the tempering; for that which was unsubstantial and diffuse becomes solid and transparent, so as to be nourished by the exhalation it meets with there; and Heraclitus hath well said that 'Souls in Hades have the sense of smell.' "

XXIX. "They contemplate, in the first place, the magnitude and beauty of the moon; also her nature, which is not simple and unmixed, but as it were a combination of star and earth; for just as earth mixed with air and moisture becomes soft, and the blood mingling itself with the flesh produces sensibility, in like manner they say the moon being mixed up from her inmost depth, becomes both animated and generative, and at the same time has the symmetrical arrangement of its levity around the centre of the mass for a counteracting force to its own gravity. For it is in this way that our world, being composed out of elements that by their own nature tend some upwards, some downwards, is free from all motion in its place. These facts Xenocrates appears to have discovered through a certain admirable process of reasoning, having taken his starting-point out of Plato. For it is Plato who proved that also each one of the stars is composed of earth and fire, by means of the ascertained analogy of the intervening substances; because nothing comes within the reach of sense that has not some portion of earth and of fire mingled with it. Now Xenocrates says the sun is composed of fire and the First Solid; but the moon of the Second Solid and her own air; and the earth out of water, fire, and the Third of the Solids; and, generally, that neither the solid, taken by itself, nor the fluid, is capable of a soul. Thus much, then, for the physical constitution of the moon. The breadth, and the magnitude of her is now what the geometricians assert, but much larger; for she measures the shadow of the earth only a few times with her own magnitude, not in consequence of her smallness, but because she puts out all her speed, that she may pass through the darkened spot, and carry out with her the souls of the good, that are eager for it and cry aloud to her; because they hear no longer, whilst they are in the shadow, the harmony of the heavens, and at the same time, the souls of those suffering punishment rush up

owards her from below through the shadow, wailing and
shouting (for which reason, during eclipses, most people clat-
er their brass pots and clap their hands, and make a noise to
scare away the ghosts), for the so-called Face frightens them
when they come nigh, looking grim and horrible. Such it is
not really, but like as our earth has deep and great gulfs—one
of them flowing inwards towards us through the Pillars of
Hercules; others flowing outwards as the Caspian, and those
in the Red Sea—in like manner there are deep places and
gulf-like in the moon, whereof the largest is called 'Hecate's
dungeon,' in which the souls either suffer or inflict punishment, for the things which they have either done or endured,
when they have already been made genii: as for the two
smaller depths, because the souls pass through them on the
way towards heaven and towards earth back again, the one is
denominated the 'Elysian Plain,' the other the 'Passage of
Persephone the Terrestrial!' "

XXX. "The genii do not always pass their time upon her
[the moon], but they come down hither and take charge of
Oracles; they are present at and assist in the most advanced of
the initiatory rites [in several Mysteries], as punishers and
keepers of wrong-doers they act, and shine as saviours in battle
and at sea; [1] and whatsoever thing in these capacities they do
amiss, either out of spite, unfair partiality, or envy, they are
punished for it, for they are driven down again to earth and
coupled with human bodies. Of the best of these genii they
told him were those who wait upon Saturn now, and the same
in old times were the Idaei Dactyli in Crete, the Curetes in
Phrygia, the Trophonii in Boeotia Lebadea, and others without number in various parts of the world, of whom the holy
places, honours, and titles still remain; though of some the
powers have ceased since they have experienced a removal of
their virtue to another locality. This change they suffer, some
sooner, some later, when the *mind* has been separated from
the *soul*. The mind separates itself out of a desire of reaching
the Image in the sun, through which shines forth the Desir-

1. Appearing as the twin star, St. Elmo's Fire, upon the ship's
mast.—Tr.

able, and Beautiful, and Divine, and Blissful, to which every
unmixed nature aspires in different ways. For the moon herself, out of desire for the sun, revolves round and comes in
contact with him, because she longs to derive from him the
generative principle. The nature of the soul is left behind the
moon, retaining vestiges as it were and dreams of life; and on
this account you must suppose it rightly said:

" 'Like to a dream, the soul took wing and fled.'

For the soul does not suffer this all at once; nor as soon as
separated from the body, but afterwards when she has become
desolate and solitary, when the mind is departed. And Homer
(said he) appears to have spoken especially through divine inspiration about the whole question:

" 'There midst the rest strong Hercules I marked,
His spectre—for himself dwells with the gods.'

For each individual of us is not anger, nor fear, nor desire
just as he is neither pieces of flesh nor humours; but that
wherewith we think and understand is the soul, impressed by
the mind, and in its turn impressing the body, and impinging
upon it from all parts it models the form; so that, though it
may continue a long time separated from both [the mind and
the body], yet as it retains the likeness and imprint, it is properly denominated the "Image" [or *Spectre*]. Of these images
the moon is the element: for they are resolved into her substance, like as bodies into earth, of the dead. Quickly resolved
are the temperate, such as have led a tranquil, philosophic, and
leisurely life on earth; for being let go from the mind, and no
longer subject to the passions, they wither away. Of those am-
bitious, busy, amorous, and irascible when in the body, the
souls visited, like dreams, with recollections of their past life
and are troubled with them; like that of Endymion of old. For
their restless and passionate character stirs them up, and draw
them away from the moon towards a second birth; she suffer
them not, however [to escape], but recalls them to herself, and
soothes them to remain. For it is far from quiet or orderly
work, when souls, separated from mind, get possession of

body subject to passions. Of such souls came perchance the Tityi and the Typhons, and that Typhon who used to hinder and trouble the oracular power at Delphi: for they are destitute of reason, and actuated by the passionate part, puffed up with pride and self-conceit. But, in time, even these the moon absorbs into herself, and reduces to order. In the next place, the sun having *impregnated* [1] the mind with vital force, produces new souls. And, thirdly, earth furnishes a body: for earth takes back after death that which she gave at birth; whereas the sun *takes* nothing, only *takes back* the mind, which he gave: but the moon both takes and gives, and puts together, and separates; in virtue of two different powers, of which the combining power is named 'Elithyia,' the separative one 'Artemis.' And of the three Fates, Atropos, seated in the sun, supplies the origin of birth; Clotho, moving about the moon, unites together and mingles the various parts; lastly, Lachesis, on earth, who has most to do with Fortune, puts her hand to the work. For the inanimate part is powerless, and liable to be acted upon by others; but the mind is impassive and independent; and the soul is of mixed nature, and intermediate between the two: just as the moon hath been made by the Deity a mixture of things above and of things below, 'a great, full horn,' bearing the same relation to the sun that the earth bears to the moon.

"All this," said Sylla, "I heard the stranger recounting; and the chamberlains and ministers of Saturn had related it, as he said, to him. You, Lamprias, are at liberty to make what use you please of the story."

1. This doctrine explains a curious gem (Matter, "Hist. Crit. du Gnosticisme," Pl. I. F., No. 1), exhibiting the Mithraic Lion copulating with a woman, *quadrupedum ritu,* in a cartouche placed over an outstretched corpse.—Tr.

PHILO JUDAEUS

PHILO was a Jewish scholar who, at the beginning of our era, lived in Alexandria. This great city, having eclipsed Athens in learning and not yet superseded by Rome, accounts for many elements in Philo's philosophy; but his zeal and his motives, his literary style, and not a little of the contents of his system come from devotion to his ancient Israel.

Although for many years the Jews, as a result of the plans of Alexander the Great for a cosmopolitan city with religious toleration for all, had enjoyed civil protection and religious immunity, a persecution connected with emperor-worship overtook them toward the end of Philo's life. As a venerable and distinguished member of their community, he was chosen to head a delegation to obtain alleviation from Caligula. The date (A.D. 39) of the mission, which unfortunately met with no success, is the only accurate date known of Philo's life. Since his fame must have been earned prior to his selection for this important, although distasteful position, it follows that his thought and writings could not have been influenced by Christianity; nor is it probable that he influenced the writers of the New Testament. The similarities are to be explained by the common Hebrew background.

For nearly three centuries there had been a Jewish community in Alexandria, and during these years a semi-conscious syncretism was in progress. Even the Greek translation of the Old Testament, known as the Septuagint, contains slight traces of Greek influence. For example, many of the anthropopathisms were modified; in one or two places the concept of creation was made to approximate the Platonic picture of formation; and in at least one case the influence of Stoicism is discernible in the choice of a technical term. While these peculiarities cannot be explained as the normal result of translating, on the other hand, there is no good reason to suppose that the translators knew and intentionally promoted the later Alexandrian philosophy.

An apocryphal writing, *The Wisdom of Solomon,* advances the progress of syncretism. In the Old Testament, particularly in *Proverbs,* wisdom is personified and closely related to God. With this personification, together with "the angel of the Lord," and the use of the word *Logos,* a person inclined toward Platonism could find comfortable material to develop. *The Wisdom of Solomon,* accordingly, went a step further in understanding creation as a formation of chaotic material. The role of the Logos in framing the world, whether he is a person or whether it is an Idea, is still not clear. The transcendence of God is somewhat emphasized and the method of allegorical interpretation, so characteristic of Philo, begins to make its appearance.

The culmination of the fusion of Hebrew theology and Greek philosophy is precisely the work of Philo. His writings may be divided roughly into three groups. First, there are some early writings that come directly from his study of Greek philosophy and contain nothing Jewish. *De aeternitati mundi* and *De providentia* are such. Second, he wrote commentaries on the Pentateuch. Under the general title of *Allegorical Commentary on Genesis* there are particular pieces, such as, *De cherubim, De sacrificiis Abelis et Caini, Quod Deus sit immutabilis,* and others. In addition to other commentaries, he wrote, in the third place, several historical essays; for example, *De vita Mosis, Contra Flaccum,* and *Legatio ad Gaium.*

In order to harmonize the revelation from God in the Old Testament with clear, rational Greek philosophy, Philo made large use of the allegorical method of interpretation. Egypt is a type of Greece, and as the Israelites at their exodus asked jewels of the Egyptians, so the people of God living in Alexandria are justified in appropriating the precious philosophy of the Greeks.

Philo defended his method of allegorizing on the basis of the anthropomorphisms included in the Old Testament. Scripture itself teaches that anthropomorphism is not to be taken literally. Inclusion of such forms of speech, however, indicates the presence of a hidden meaning, not merely a hidden meaning in the anthropomorphic verses alone, but throughout the text. The literal history is of course true: the Israelites without question escaped from Egypt. The moral lessons are more important than the bare history. But the deepest sense of the revelation, the sense that is truly philosophical, is discovered only by the allegorical method.

Out of the many problems which Philo discusses, it may be wise to select two of the most important, *viz.* his conception of God and his Logos doctrine.

That God exists and rules the world should be evident to anyone who considers the excellence and artistry of its appointments. But Philo was less inclined than Aristotle to trust the standard cosmological and teleological arguments; his favorite approach was more Platonic in retrospect and Augustinian in prospect. The world reveals God in his works, but an examination of the mind of man, of his faculty of spiritual discernment, will eventually reveal God himself. Certain conditions must be fulfilled before one has the intuition of God. Solitude and freedom from bodily distractions are necessary because God himself is a solitary being, and one must try to resemble him in this point at least. After instruction and meditation the vision of God in varying degrees of clarity may be experienced. There is no assurance that any given man will be granted a clear vision, but in any case the search for God is worth while.

However, since our knowledge of God is obtained by introspection, by an analogy between our mind and the universal mind, since we are limited to our own faculties, it follows that we can form no adequate conception of God. The analogy is not strict, because while God, the mind of the universe, formed the universe, it was not our mind that formed our body. Limited as we are, we must use, even the Scripture must use, language that is not philosophically justifiable. Especially for the uneducated, anthropomorphisms are necessary; but God is transcendent.

The dangers of anthropomorphism are in reality slight. Reflection leads one to deny of God any attribute characteristic of a created being, such as wrath or anger. But one should not refuse to ascribe reason to God, for human reason is divine.

A more serious danger than anthropomorphism is man's inability to know his own mind. Just as the eye cannot see itself, the mind, contrary to what Plotinus later argues, cannot know its own essence. How, then, can one know God? "God has shown his nature to none, and who can say either that the Cause is body or that it is incorporeal, or that it is of a certain quality, or that it is destitute of quality, or in general express himself with certainty about his essence, or quality, or habit, or motion?" [1]

This quotation is perhaps one of Philo's most extreme statements, for ordinarily, while he says we cannot know what God is, he is certain that God is *not* corporeal or other ignoble quality.

In any case the transcendence of God is emphasized. He is without qualities, that is, God is superior to all classification. Classification is possible only when two or more objects have a common quality by means of which they can be included in one genus. Therefore, since there must be an object, which is one thing, and a quality, which is second, it follows that all objects capable of classification are compounds and are capable of dissolution. Obviously God is not subject to dissolution or classification. God no doubt has properties: he is omnipotent. But his omnipotence, and his other properties likewise, far from making him similar to other objects, make him superior to all classes. This superiority holds, not only for the objects of this world, but also for the Ideas that Plato would regard as the highest. "God, then, has been ranked according to the one and the unit; or rather even the unit has been ranked accord-

1. *Leg. All.* VI 73.

ing to the one God, for all number, like time, is younger than the cosmos, while God is older than the cosmos and its creator." [1]

When the unity and transcendence of God are maintained without qualification, difficult problems arise with regard to God's relation to the world. In Neo-Platonism the supreme term is so unitary that multiplicity receives a barely plausible explanation. In Plutarch and in many other authors transcendence, particularly in respect to goodness or holiness, not only involves the question of the origin of evil, but also the problem of how a good God can come into a contact with imperfect things, a contact apparently degrading or contaminating. These problems plague Philo also.

As for the origin of evil, Philo takes the easy way out and posits an eternal dualism. Although it is completely inconsistent with the Hebrew background, Philo asserts the eternity of matter. Then, as God forms the world out of matter, it is discovered that even if matter is not positively evil or wicked, it is none the less too imperfect and recalcitrant to receive the perfect goodness and order God wishes to bestow. The other phases of the problem, contact with matter and the existence of multiplicity, are to be satisfied by the theory of the divine powers under the inclusive Logos.

The sun and the moon, for example, are the results of forces impressing matter. Were the forces withdrawn, the bodies would lapse again into formless matter. Dependent on God, and thus inferior to him, the powers are still too great to be explained in human language. They are as infinite as God himself, independent of

1. *Leg. All.* II 1.

time, and unbegotten. In short, they are the Platonic Ideas.

"It is only one of the forms of error maintained by impious and unholy men to say that the immaterial ideas are an empty name without participation in real fact. Those who affirm this, remove from things the most necessary substance, which is the archetypal pattern of all the qualities of substance, in accordance with which everything is ideally formed and measured. Thus, the opinion which destroys ideas confounds all things, and reduces them to that formlessness which was prior to the elements. Now, what could be more absurd than this? For God generated everything out of matter, not touching it himself, for it was not fitting for the Wise and Blessed to touch indefinite and confused matter, but he made use of the immaterial powers, whose real name is ideas, in order that the suitable form might engage each genus. But the opinion in question introduces great disorder and confusion; for by destroying the things through which qualities arise, it destroys at the same time qualities themselves." [1]

The first and most universal of all the powers or ideas is the Logos. As the thought of God the Logos is the place of the cosmos and comprehends the whole intelligible world. Sometimes Philo's wording seems to imply that the Logos is a thinking soul rather than the world of Ideas. Apart from the literary device of personification, this mode of expression can be explained in virtue of a contrast between God and men. An architect, for example, has many plans, his human logos thinks many thoughts, and accordingly it is easy to distinguish be-

1. Sacrificantibus 13.

tween his reason and one of his thoughts. But God has one plan only, and hence reason or soul in God becomes identical with its product. In this way reason or the Logos can be both a power and the world of Ideas.

God originally existed in perfect solitude. His first act of creation, therefore, could not have required an agent or mediator. Thus the Logos or universal reason is, while dependent on and inferior to God, a most faithful image of God. Other things are expressions of thought, but thought is an expression of God alone.

Because Philo used the term *Logos,* because he spoke of the Logos as the image of God, the first begotten Son of God, because of the repeated use of personification, Christians have at times believed they have discovered in Philo an anticipation, if not of the Trinity completely, at least of the second Person of the Trinity. And perchance an inability on the part of Philo sharply to distinguish between Platonic Ideas and Hebrew angels made the divine powers as a solution of the problem of mediation more plausible at that stage of the history of philosophy than now.

At the risk of making Philo a little more clearheaded than he may have been, it seems justifiable to understand the powers and the Logos as Ideas. For although the Logos is the Son of God, on the other hand, Laughter is also a Son of God, God is the husband of Wisdom, Wisdom is the daughter of God, Wisdom is the mother of the Logos, and Wisdom is the *father* of instruction. The number *seven* is also an image of God and a motherless virgin, sprung from the head of Zeus. If the logoi are called angels, Sarah is virtue and Hagar is education. Philo's use of allegory and personification

is amazing. In *De cherubim* Philo explains the statement that God "drove out Adam."

"Why," asks Philo, "does the writer now say 'drove
out' when he had previously said 'sent out'? The words
are carefully chosen; for he who is sent out may return,
but he who has been driven out by God incurs an eternal exile. Thus we see that encyclical education Hagar
twice went forth from the ruling virtue Sarrha. The first
time she returned, for she had run away, and not been
banished, and she was brought back to her master's
house, 'an angel, who is divine Reason, having met her';
but the second time she was driven out never to come
back. The reason was that in the first instance Abram,
'the high father,' had not yet changed into Abraham,
'the elect father of sound,' that is, had not ceased to be
the natural philosopher and become the wise lover of
God, and Sara had not been changed into Sarrha, specific
into generic virtue; and therefore Hagar, encyclical education, though she might be eager to run away from
the austere life of the virtuous, will return to it again;
but when the change takes place, the preliminary
branches of instruction called after Hagar will be driven
out, and her sophist son, called Ishmael, will be driven
out also. What wonder, then, if, when Adam, the mind,
became possessed of folly, an incurable disease, God
drove him out forever from the region of the virtues,
when he banished even the sophist and his mother, the
teaching of the preliminary branches of education, from
wisdom and the wise, whose names he calls Abraham
and Sarrha?"

In view of passages like this, it is extremely difficult
to prove that Philo has abandoned the realm of abstract

Ideas to anticipate a second Person in the Godhead. His language may be extreme, but his thought is fairly sober; and while the Neo-Pythagoreans and Plutarch took their demons seriously, Philo with his divine powers remains a relatively pure Platonist.

PHILO JUDAEUS

THE CREATION OF THE WORLD

II. For some men, admiring the world itself rather than the Creator of the world, have represented it as existing without any maker, and eternal; and as impiously as falsely have represented God as existing in a state of complete inactivity, while it would have been right on the other hand to marvel at the might of God as the creator and father of all, and to admire the world in a degree not exceeding the bounds of moderation. But Moses, who had early reached the very summits of philosophy, and who had learned from the oracles of God the most numerous and important of the principles of nature, was well aware that it is indispensable that in all existing things there must be an active cause, and a passive subject; and that the active cause is the intellect of the universe, thoroughly unadulterated and thoroughly unmixed, superior to virtue and superior to science, superior even to abstract good or abstract beauty; while the passive subject is something inanimate and incapable of motion by any intrinsic power of its own, but having been set in motion, and fashioned, and endowed with life by the intellect, became transformed into that most perfect work, this world. And those who describe it as being uncreated, do, without being aware of it, cut off the most useful and necessary of all the qualities which tend to produce piety, namely providence; for reason proves that the father and creator has a care for that which has been created; for a father is anxious for the life of his children, and a workman aims at the duration of his works, and employs every device imaginable to ward off everything that is pernicious or injurious, and is desirous by every means in his power to provide everything which is useful or profitable for them. But with regard to that which has not been created, there is no feeling of interest as if it were his own in the breast of him who has not created it.

It is then a pernicious doctrine, and one for which no one should contend, to establish a system in this world, such as anarchy is in a city, so that it should have no superintendent, or regulator, or judge, by whom everything must be managed and governed.

But the great Moses, thinking that a thing which has not been uncreated is as alien as possible from that which is visible before our eyes (for everything which is the subject of our senses exists in birth and in changes, and is not always in the same condition), has attributed eternity to that which is invisible and discerned only by our intellect as a kinsman and a brother, while of that which is the object of our external senses he had predicated generation as an appropriate description. Since, then, this world is visible and the object of our external senses, it follows of necessity that it must have been created; on which account it was not without a wise purpose that he recorded its creation, giving a very venerable account of God.

III. And he says that the world was made in six days, not because the Creator stood in need of a length of time (for it is natural that God should do everything at once, not merely by uttering a command, but by even thinking of it); but because the things created required arrangement; and number is akin to arrangement; and, of all numbers, six is, by the laws of nature, the most productive; for of all the numbers, from the unit upwards, it is the first perfect one, being made equal to its parts, and being made complete by them; the number three being half of it, and the number two a third of it, and the unit a sixth of it, and, so to say, it is formed so as to be both male and female, and is made up of the power of both natures; for in existing things the odd number is the male, and the even number is the female; accordingly, of odd numbers the first is the number three, and of even numbers the first is two, and the two numbers multiplied together make six. It was fitting therefore, that the world, being the most perfect of created things, should be made according to the perfect number, namely, six: and, as it was to have in it the causes of both, which arise from combination, that it should be formed according to a mixed number, the first combination of odd and even numbers, since it was to embrace the character both of the male who sows the seed, and of the female who receives it. And he allotted each of the six days to one of the portions of the whole, taking out the first day, which he does not even call the first day, that it may not be numbered with the others, but entitling it one, he names it rightly, perceiving in it, and ascribing to it the nature and appellation of the limit.

IV. We must mention as much as we can of the matters contained in his account, since to enumerate them all is impossible; for he embraces that beautiful world which is perceptible only by the intellect, as the account of the first day will show: for God, as apprehending beforehand, as a God must do, that there could not exist a good imitation without a good model, and that of the things perceptible to the external senses nothing could be faultless which was not fashioned with reference to some archetypal idea conceived by the intellect, when he had determined to create this visible world, previously formed that one which is perceptible only by the intellect, in order that so using an incorporeal model formed as far as possible on the image of God he might then make this corporeal world, a younger likeness of the elder creation, which should embrace as many different genera perceptible to the external senses, as the other world contains of those which are visible only to the intellect.

But that world which consists of ideas, it were impious in any degree to attempt to describe or even to imagine: but how it was created, we shall know if we take for our guide a certain image of the things which exist among us.

When any city is founded through the exceeding ambition of some king or leader who lays claim to absolute authority, and is at the same time a man of brilliant imagination, eager to display his good fortune, then it happens at times that some man coming up who, from his education, is skilful in architecture, and he, seeing the advantageous character and beauty of the situation, first of all sketches out in his own mind nearly all the parts of the city which is about to be completed—the temples, the gymnasia, the prytanea, the markets, the harbor, the docks, the streets, the arrangement of the walls, the situations of the dwelling houses, and of the public and other buildings. Then, having received in his own mind, as on a waxen tablet, the form of each building, he carries in his heart the image of a city, perceptible as yet only by the intellect, the images of which he stirs up in memory which is innate in him, and, still further, engraving them in his mind like a good workman, keeping his eyes fixed on his model, he begins to raise the city of stones and wood, making the corporeal substances to resemble each of the incorporeal ideas. Now we must form a somewhat similar opinion of God, who, having determined to found a mighty state, first of all conceived its form in his mind, according to which form he made a world perceptible only by the intellect, and then completed one visible to the external senses, using the first one as a model.

V. As therefore the city, when previously shadowed out in the mind of the man of architectural skill had no external place, but was stamped solely in the mind of the workman, so in the same manner neither can the world which existed in ideas have had any other local position except the divine reason which made them; for what other place could there be for his powers which should be able to receive and contain, I do not say all, but even any single one of them whatever, in its simple form? And the power and faculty which could be capable of creating the world, has for its origin that good which is founded on truth; for if any one were desirous to investigate the cause on account of which this universe was created, I think that he would come to no erroneous conclusion if he were to say as one of the ancients did say: "That the Father and Creator was good; on which account he did not grudge the substance a share of his own excellent nature, since it had nothing good of itself, but was able to become everything." For the substance was of itself destitute of arrangement, of quality, of animation, of distinctive character, and full of all disorder and confusion; and it received a change and transformation to what is opposite to this condition, and most excellent, being invested with order, quality, animation, resemblance, identity, arrangement, harmony, and everything which belongs to the more excellent idea.

VI. And God, not being urged on by any prompter (for who else could there have been to prompt him?) but guided by his own sole will, decided that it was fitting to benefit with unlimited and abundant favours a nature which, without the divine gift, was unable of itself to partake of any good thing; but he benefits it, not according to the greatness of his own graces, for they are illimitable and eternal, but according to the power of that which is benefited to receive his graces. For the capacity of that which is created to receive benefits does not correspond to the natural power of God to confer them; since his powers are infinitely greater, and the thing created being not sufficiently powerful to receive all their greatness would have sunk under it, if he had not measured his bounty, allotting to each, in due proportion, that which was poured upon it. And if any one were to desire to use more undisguised terms, he would not call the world which is perceptible only to the intellect anything else but the reason of God, already occupied in the creation of the world; for neither is a city, while only perceptible to the intellect, anything else but the reason of the architect, who is already designing to build one perceptible to the external senses, on the model of that which is so only to the intellect—this is the doctrine of Moses, not mine. Accordingly he, when recording the creation of man, in words which follow, asserts expressly, that he was made in the image of God—and if the image be a part of the image, then manifestly so is the entire form, namely, the whole of this world perceptible by the external senses, which is a greater imitation of the divine image than the human form is. It is manifest also, that the archetypal seal, which we call that world which is perceptible only to the intellect, must itself be the archetypal model, the idea of ideas, the Reason of God.

VII. Moses says also: "In the beginning God created the heaven and the earth:" taking the beginning to be, not as some

men think, that which is according to time; for before the
world time had no existence, but was created either simultaneously with it, or after it; for since time is the interval of the
motion of the heavens, there could not have been any such
thing as motion before there was anything which could be
moved; but it follows of necessity that it received existence
subsequently or simultaneously. It therefore follows also of
necessity, that time was created either at the same moment
with the world, or later than it—and to venure to assert that
it is older than the world is absolutely inconsistent with philosophy. But if the beginning spoken of by Moses is not to be
looked upon as spoken according to time, then it may be natural to suppose that it is the beginning according to number
that is indicated; so that, "In the beginning He created," is
equivalent to "first of all He created the heaven;" for it is
natural in reality that that should have been the first object
created, being both the best of all created things, and being
also made of the purest substance, because it was destined to be
the most holy abode of the visible Gods who are perceptible
by the external senses; for if the Creator had made everything
at the same moment, still those things which were created in
beauty would no less have had a regular arrangement, for there
is no such thing as beauty in disorder. But order is a due consequence and connection of things precedent and subsequent,
if not in the completion of a work, at all events in the intention
of the maker; for it is owing to order that they become accurately defined and stationary, and free from confusion.

In the first place therefore, from the model of the world,
perceptible only by intellect, the Creator made an incorporeal
heaven, and an invisible earth, and the form of air and of
empty space: the former of which he called darkness, because
the air is black by nature; and the other he called the abyss, for
empty space is very deep and yawning with immense width.
Then he created the incorporeal substance of water and of air,
and above all he spread light, being the seventh thing made;
and this again was incorporeal, and a model of the sun, perceptible only to intellect, and of all the light-giving stars, which
are destined to stand together in heaven.

VIII. And air and light he considered worthy of the pre-eminence. For the one he called the breath of God, because it is air, which is the most life-giving of things, and of life the causer is God; and the other he called light, because it is surpassingly beautiful: for that which is perceptible only by intellect is as far more brilliant and splendid than that which is seen as I conceive the sun is than darkness, or day than night, or the intellect than any other of the outward senses by which men judge (inasmuch as it is the guide of the entire soul), or the eyes than any other part of the body. And the invisible divine reason, perceptible only by intellect, he calls the image of God. And the image of this image is that light, perceptible only by the intellect, which is the image of the divine reason, which has explained its generation. And it is a star above the heavens, the source of those stars which are perceptible by the external senses, and if any one were to call it universal light he would not be very wrong; since it is from that the sun and the moon and all the other planets and fixed stars derive their due light, in proportion as each has power given to it; that unmingled and pure light being obscured when it begins to change, according to the change from that which is perceptible only by the intellect, to that which is perceptible by the external senses; for none of those things which are perceptible to the external senses is pure.

IX. Moses is right also when he says, that "darkness was over the face of the abyss." For the air is in a manner spread above the empty space, since having mounted up it entirely fills all that open, and desolate, and empty place, which reaches down to us from the regions below the moon. And after the shining forth of that light, perceptible only to the intellect, which existed before the sun, then its adversary darkness yielded, as God put a wall between them and separated them, well knowing their opposite characters, and the enmity existing between their natures. In order, therefore, that they might not war against one another from being continually brought in contact, so that war would prevail instead of peace, God, turning want of order into order, did not only separate light and darkness, but did also place boundaries in the mid-

dle of the space between the two, by which he separated the
extremities of each. For if they had approximated they must
have produced confusion, preparing for the contest, for the
supremacy, with great and unextinguishable rivalry, if boundaries established between them had not separated them and
prevented them from clashing together, and these boundaries
are evening and morning; the one of which heralds in the good
tidings that the sun is about to rise, gently dissipating the darkness: and evening comes on as the sun sets, receiving gently
the collective approach of darkness. And these, I mean morning and evening, must be placed in the class of incorporeal
things, perceptible only by the intellect; for there is absolutely
nothing in them which is perceptible by the external senses,
but they are entirely ideas, and measures, and forms, and
seals, incorporeal as far as regards the generation of other
bodies. But when light came, and darkness retreated and
yielded to it, and boundaries were set in the space between the
two, namely, evening and morning, then of necessity the
measure of time was immediately perfected, which also the
Creator called "day," and He called it not "the first day," but
"one day;" and it is spoken of thus, on account of the single
nature of the world perceptible only by the intellect, which has
a single nature.

X. The incorporeal world then was already completed, having its seat in the Divine Reason; and the world, perceptible
by the external senses, was made on the model of it; and the
first portion of it, being also the most excellent of all made by
the Creator, was the heaven, which he truly called the firmament, as being corporeal; for the body is by nature firm,
inasmuch as it is divisible into three parts; and what other idea
of solidity and of body can there be, except that it is something
which may be measured in every direction? Therefore he, very
naturally contrasting that which was perceptible to the external senses and corporeal with that which was perceptible only
by the intellect and incorporeal, called this the firmament.
Immediately afterwards he, with great propriety and entire
correctness, called it the heaven, either because it was already
the boundary of everything, or because it was the first of all

visible things which was created; and after its second rising
he called the time day, referring the entire space and measure
of a day to the heaven, on account of its dignity and honor
among the things perceptible to the external senses.

*   *   *   *   *

XIV. And on the fourth day, after he had embellished the
earth, he diversified and adorned the heaven: not giving the
precedence to the inferior nature by arranging the heaven subsequently to the earth, or thinking that which was the more
excellent and the more divine worthy only of the second
place, but acting thus for the more manifest demonstration of
the power of his dominion. For he foreknew with respect to
men who were not yet born, what sort of beings they would
be as to their opinions, forming conjectures on what was likely
and probable, of which the greater part would be reasonable,
though falling short of the character of unadulterated truth;
and trusting rather to visible phenomena than to God, and
admiring sophistry rather than wisdom. And again he knew
that surveying the periods of the sun and moon, to which are
owing the summers and winters, and the alternations of spring
and autumn, they would conceive the revolutions of the stars
in heaven to be the causes of all the things which every year
should be produced and generated on the earth, accordingly
that no one might venture either through shameless impu-
dence or inordinate ignorance to attribute to any created thing
the primary causes of things, he said: "Let them run over in
their minds the first creation of the universe, when, before the
sun or the moon existed, the earth brought forth all kinds of
plants and all kinds of fruits: and seeing this in their minds
let them hope that it will again also bring forth such, according to the appointment of the Father, when it shall seem good
to him, without his having need of the aid of any of the sons
of men beneath the heavens, to whom he has given powers,
though not absolute ones." For as a charioteer holding the
reins, or a helmsman with his hand upon the rudder, he guides
everything as he pleases, in accordance with law and justice,

needing no one else as his assistant; for all things are possible to God.

* * * * *

XVII. The aforesaid number therefore being accounted worthy of such pre-eminence in nature, the Creator of necessity adorned the heaven by the number four, namely by that most beautiful and most godlike ornament the light-giving stars. And knowing that of all existing things light is the most excellent, he made it the instrument of the best of all the senses, sight. For what the mind is in the soul, that the eye is in the body. For each of them sees, the one beholding those existing things which are perceptible only to the intellect, and the other those which are perceptible to the external senses.

But the mind is in need of knowledge in order to distinguish incorporeal things, and the eyes have need of light in order to be able to perceive bodies, and light is also the cause of many other good things to men, and particularly of the greatest, namely philosophy. For the sight being sent upwards by light and beholding the nature of the stars and their harmonious movement, and the well-ordered revolutions of the fixed stars, and of the planets, some always revolving in the same manner and coming to the same places, and others having double periods in an anomalous and somewhat contrary manner, beholding also, the harmonious dances of all these bodies arranged according to the laws of perfect music, causes an ineffable joy and delight to the soul. And the soul, feasting on a continuous series of spectacles, for one succeeds another, has an insatiable love for beholding such. Then, as is usually the case, it examines with increased curiosity what is the substance of these things which are visible; and whether they have an existence without having been created, or whether they received their origin by creation, and what is the character of their movement, and what the causes are by which everything is regulated. And it is from inquiries into these things that philosophy has arisen, than which no more perfect good has entered into human life.

XVIII. But the Creator having a regard to that idea of light perceptible only by the intellect, which has been spoken of in the mention made of the incorporeal world, created those stars which are perceptible by the external senses, those divine and superlatively beautiful images, which on many accounts he placed in the purest temple of corporeal substance, namely in heaven. One of the reasons for his so doing was that they might give light; another was that they might be signs; another had reference to their dividing the times of the seasons of the year, and above all dividing days and nights, months and years, which are the measures of time; and which have given rise to the nature of number. And how great is the use and how great the advantage derivable from each of the aforesaid things, is plain from their effect. But with a view to a more accurate comprehension of them, it may perhaps not be out of place to trace out the truth in a regular discussion.

Now the whole of time being divided into two portions day and night, the sovereignty of the day the Father has assigned to the Sun, as a mighty monarch: and that of the night he has given to the moon and to the multitude of the other stars. And the greatness of the power and sovereignty of the sun has its most conspicuous proof in what has been already said: for he, being one and single has been allotted for his own share and by himself one half portion of all time, namely day; and all the other lights in conjunction with the moon have the other portion, which is called night. And when the sun rises all the appearances of such numbers of stars are not only obscured but absolutely disappear from the effusion of his beams; and when he sets then they all, assembled together, begin to display their own peculiar brilliancy and their separate qualities.

XIX. And they have been created, as Moses tells us, not only that they might send light upon the earth, but also that they might display signs of future events. For either by their risings, or their settings, or their eclipses, or again by their appearances and occultations, or by the other variations observable in their motions, men oftentimes conjecture what is about to happen, the productiveness or unproductiveness of the crops, the birth or loss of their cattle, fine weather or cloudy weather, calms and violent storms of wind, floods in the rivers or droughts, a tranquil state of the sea and heavy waves, unusual changes in the seasons of the year when either the summer is cold like winter, or the winter warm, or when the spring assumes the temperature of autumn or the autumn that of spring. And before now some men have conjecturally predicted disturbances and commotions of the earth, from the revolutions of the heavenly bodies, and innumerable other events which have turned out most exactly true: so that it is a most veracious saying that "the stars were created to act as signs, and moreover to mark the seasons." And by the word seasons the divisions of the year are here intended. And why may not this be reasonably affirmed? For what other idea of opportunity can there be except that it is the time for success? And the seasons bring everything to perfection and set everything right; giving perfection to the sowing and planting of fruits and to the birth and growth of animals.

* * * * *

XX. Then when earth and heaven had been adorned with their befitting ornaments, one with a triad, and the other, as has been already said, with a quaternion, God proceeded to create the races of mortal creatures, making the beginning with the aquatic animals on the fifth day, thinking that there was no one thing so akin to another as the number five was to animals; for animate things differ from inanimate in nothing more than in sensation, and sensation is divided according to a five-fold division, into sight, hearing, taste, smell and touch.

* * * * *

XXIII. So then after all the other things, as has been said before, Moses says that man was made in the image and likeness of God. And he says well; for nothing that is born on the earth is more resembling God than man. And let no one think that he is able to judge of this likeness from the characters of the body: for neither is God a being with the form of a man, nor is the human body like the form of God; but the resemblance is spoken of with reference to the most important part of the soul, namely, the mind: for the mind which exists in each individual has been created after the likeness of that one mind which is in the universe as its primitive model, being in some sort the God of that body which carries it about and bears its image within it. In the same rank that the great Governor occupies in the universal world, that same as it seems does the mind of man occupy in man; for it is invisible, though it sees everything itself; and it has an essence which is undiscernible, though it can discern the essences of all other things, and making for itself by art and science all sorts of roads leading in divers directions, and all plain; it traverses land and sea, investigating everything which it contained in either element. And again, being raised up on wings, and so surveying and contemplating the air, and all the commotions to which it is subject, it is borne upwards to the higher firmament, and to the revolutions of the heavenly bodies. And also being itself involved in the revolutions of the planets and fixed stars according to the perfect laws of music, and being led on by love, which is the guide of wisdom, it proceeds onwards till, having surmounted all essence intelligible by the external senses, it comes to aspire to such as is perceptible only by the intellect: and perceiving in that, the original models and ideas of those things intelligible by the external senses which it saw here full of surpassing beauty, it becomes seized with a sort of sober intoxication like the zealots engaged in the Corybantian festivals, and yields to enthusiasm, becoming filled with another desire, and a more excellent longing, by which it is conducted onwards to the very summit of such things as are perceptible only to the intellect, till it appears to be reaching the great King himself. And while it is eagerly longing to behold him pure and unmingled, rays of divine light are poured forth upon it like a torrent, so as to bewilder the eyes of its intelligence by their splendour.

But as it is not every image that resembles its archetypal model, since many are unlike, Moses has shown this by adding to the words "after his image," the expression, "in his likeness," to prove that it means an accurate impression, having a clear and evident resemblance in form.

XXIV. And he would not err who should raise the question why Moses attributed the creation of man alone not to one creator, as he did that of other animals, but to several. For he introduces the Father of the universe using this language: "Let *us* make man after our image, and in our likeness." Had he then, shall I say, need of any one whatever to help him, he to whom all things are subject? Or, when he was making the heaven and the earth and the sea, was he in need of no one to co-operate with him; and yet was he unable himself by his own power to make man an animal so short-lived and so exposed to the assaults of fate without the assistance of others? It is plain that the real cause of his so acting is known to God alone, but one which to a reasonable conjecture appears probable and credible, I think I should not conceal; and it is this.

Of existing things, there are some which partake neither of virtue nor of vice; as for instance, plants and irrational animals; the one, because they are destitute of soul, and are regulated by a nature void of sense; and the other, because they are not endowed with mind or reason. But mind and reason may be looked upon as the abode of virtue and vice; as it is in them that they seem to dwell. Some things again partake of virtue alone, being without any participation in any kind of vice; as for instance, the stars, for they are said to be animals, and animals endowed with intelligence; or I might rather say, the mind of each of them is wholly and entirely virtuous, and insusceptible of every kind of evil. Some things again are of a mixed nature, like man, who is capable of opposite qualities, of wisdom and folly, of temperance and dissoluteness, of courage and cowardice, of justice and injustice, in short of good and evil, of what is honourable and what is disgraceful, of virtue and vice. Now it was a very appropriate task for God the Father of all to create by himself alone, those things which were wholly good, on account of their kindred with himself. And it was not inconsistent with his dignity to create those which were indifferent since they too

are devoid of evil, which is hateful to him. To create the
beings of a mixed nature, was partly consistent and partly inconsistent with his dignity; consistent by reason of the more
excellent idea which is mingled in them; inconsistent because
of the opposite and worse one.

It is on this account that Moses says, at the creation of man
alone that God said, "Let *us* make man," which expression
shows an assumption of other beings to himself as assistants,
in order that God, the governor of all things, might have all
the blameless intentions and actions of man, when he does
right, attributed to him; and that his other assistants might
bear the imputation of his contrary actions. For it was fitting
that the Father should in the eyes of his children be free from
all imputation of evil; and vice and energy in accordance with
vice are evil. And very beautifully after he had called the
whole race "man," did he distinguish between the sexes, saying, that "they were created male and female;" although all
the individuals of the race had not yet assumed their distinctive form; since the extreme species are contained in the genus,
and are beheld, as in a mirror, by those who are able to discern acutely.

XXV. And some one may inquire the cause why it was
that man was the last work in the creation of the world. For
the Creator and Father created him after everything else as
the sacred scriptures inform us. Accordingly, they who have
gone most deeply into the laws, and who to the best of their
power have investigated everything that is contained in them
with all diligence, say that God, when he had given to man
to partake of kindred with himself, grudged him neither
reason, which is the most excellent of all gifts, nor anything
else that is good; but before his creation, provided for him
everything in the world, as for the animal most resembling
himself, and dearest to him, being desirous that when he was
born, he should be in want of nothing requisite for living,
and for living well; the first of which objects is provided for
by the abundance of supplies which are furnished to him for
his enjoyment, and the other by his power of contemplation
of the heavenly bodies, by which the mind is smitten so as

to conceive a love and desire for knowledge on those subjects; owing to which desire, philosophy has sprung up, by which, man, though mortal, is made immortal. As then, those who make a feast do not invite their guests to the entertainment before they have provided everything for festivity, and as those who celebrate gymnastic or dramatic contests, before they assemble the spectators, provide themselves with an abundance of competitors and spectacles, and sweet sounds, with which to fill the theatres and the stadia; so in the same manner did the Ruler of all, as a man proposing games, or giving a banquet and being about to invite others to feast and to behold the spectacle, first provide everything for every kind of entertainment, in order that when man came into the world he might at once find a feast ready for him, and a most holy theatre; the one abounding with everything which the earth, or the rivers, or the sea, or air, brings forth for use and enjoyment, and the other being full of every description of light, which has either its essence or its qualities admirable, and its motions and revolutions worthy of notice, being arranged in perfect order, both as to the proportions of its numbers, and the harmony of its periods. And a man would not be far wrong who should say that in all these things there might be discovered that archetypal and real model music, the images of which the subsequent generations of mankind engraved in their own souls, and in this way handed down the art which is the most necessary and the most advantageous to human life.

* * * * *

XXVIII. And besides all this, another is also mentioned among the necessary causes. It was necessary that man should be the last of all created beings; in order that being so, and appearing suddenly, he might strike terror into the other animals. For it was fitting that they, as soon as they first saw him should admire and worship him, as their natural ruler and master; on which account, they all, as soon as they saw him, became tame before him; even those, who by nature

were most savage, becoming at once most manageable at the
first sight of him; displaying their unbridled ferocity to one
another, and being tame to man alone. For which reason
the Father who made him to be a being dominant over them
by nature, not merely in fact but also by express verbal appointment, established him as the king of all the animals, beneath the moon, whether terrestrial or aquatic, or such as
traverse the air. For every mortal thing which lives in the
three elements, land, water or air, did he put in subjection
to him, excepting only the beings that are in heaven, as creatures who have a more divine portion. . . .

*   *   *   *   *

XLVI. After this, Moses says that "God made man, having
taken clay from the earth, and he breathed ínto his face the
breath of life." And by this expression he shows most clearly
that there is a vast difference between man as generated now,
and the first man who was made according to the image of
God. For man as formed now is perceptible to the external
senses, partaking of qualities, consisting of body and soul,
man or woman, by nature mortal. But man, made according
to the image of God, was an idea, or a genus, or a seal, perceptible only by the intellect, incorporeal, neither male nor
female, imperishable by nature. But he asserts that the formation of the individual man, perceptible by the external senses,
is a composition of earthy substance and divine spirit. For
that the body was created by the Creator taking a lump of
clay, and fashioning the human form out of it; but that the
soul proceeds from no created thing at all, but from the Father
and Ruler of all things. For when he uses the expression, "he
breathed into," etc., he means nothing else than the divine
spirit proceeding from that happy and blessed nature, sent to
take up its habitation here on earth, for the advantage of our
race, in order that, even if man is mortal according to that
portion of him which is visible, he may at all events be immortal according to that portion which is invisible; and for
this reason, one may properly say that man is on the bound-

aries of a better and an immortal nature, partaking of each
as far as it is necessary for him; and that he was born at
the same time, both mortal and the immortal. Mortal as to
his body, but immortal as to his intellect.

*   *   *   *   *

LII. And with great beauty Moses has attributed the giving
of names to the different animals to the first created man, for
it is a work of wisdom and indicative of royal authority, and
man was full of intuitive wisdom and self-taught, having been
created by the grace of God, and, moreover, was a king. And
it is proper for a ruler to give names to each of his subjects.
And, as was very natural, the power of domination was excessive in that first-created man, whom God formed with
great care and thought worthy of the second rank in the creation, making him his own viceroy and the ruler of all other
creatures. Since even those who have been born so many
generations afterwards, when the race is becoming weakened
by reason of the long intervals of time that have elapsed since
the beginning of the world, do still exert the same power over
the irrational beasts, preserving as it were a spark of the
dominion and power which has been handed down to them
by succession from their first ancestor.

Accordingly, Moses says, that "God brought all the animals to man, wishing to see what names he would give to
each." Not because he was in doubt, for nothing is unknown
to God, but because he knew that he had formed in mortal
man a rational nature capable of moving of its own accord,
in order that he might be free from all participation in vice.
But he was now trying him as a master might try his pupil,
stirring up the disposition which he had implanted in him;
and moreover exciting him to a contemplation of his own
works, that he might extemporise them names which should
not be inappropriate nor unbecoming, but which should well
and clearly display the peculiar qualities of the different subjects. For as the rational nature was as yet uncorrupted in the
soul, and as no weakness, or disease, or affliction had as yet

come upon it, man having most pure and perfect perceptions
of bodies and of things, devised names for them with great
felicity and correctness of judgment, forming very admirable
opinions as to the qualities which they displayed, so that their
natures were at once perceived and correctly described by
him. And he was so excellent in all good things that he speedily arrived at the very perfection of human happiness.

LIII. But since nothing in creation lasts for ever, but all
mortal things are liable to inevitable changes and alterations,
it was unavoidable that the first man should also undergo
some disaster. And the beginning of his life being liable to
reproach, was his wife. For, as long as he was single, he re-
sembled, as to his creation, both the world and God; and
he represented in his soul the characteristics of the nature of
each, I do not mean all of them, but such as a mortal constitution was capable of admitting. But when woman also was
created, man perceiving a closely connected figure and a
kindred formation to his own, rejoiced at the sight, and approached her and embraced her. And she, in like manner,
beholding a creature greatly resembling herself, rejoiced also,
and addressed him in reply with due modesty. And love being engendered, and, as it were, uniting two separate portions
of one animal into one body, adapted them to each other, im-
planting in each of them a desire of connection with the other
with a view to the generation of a being similar to themselves.
And this desire caused likewise pleasure to their bodies, which
is the beginning of iniquities and transgressions, and it is owing to this that men have exchanged their previously immortal and happy existence for one which is mortal and full
of misfortune.

LIV. But while man was still living a solitary life, and before woman was created, the history relates that a paradise
was planted by God in no respect resembling the parks which
are seen among men now. For parks of our day are only lifeless woods, full of all kinds of trees, some evergreen with a
view to the undisturbed delectation of the sight; others bud-
ding and germinating in the spring season, and producing
fruit, some eatable by men, and sufficient, not only for the

necessary support of nature as food, but also for the superfluous enjoyment of luxurious life; and some not eatable by men, but of necessity bestowed upon the beasts. But in the paradise, made by God, all the plants were endowed in the souls and reason, producing for their fruit the different virtues, and, moreover, imperishable wisdom and prudence, by which honorable and dishonorable things are distinguished from one another, and also a life free from disease, and exempt from corruption, and all other qualities corresponding to these already mentioned. And these statements appear to me to be dictated by a philosophy which is symbolical rather than strictly accurate. For no trees of life or of knowledge have ever at any previous time appeared upon the earth, nor is it likely that any will appear hereafter. But I rather conceive that Moses was speaking in an allegorical spirit, intending by his paradise to intimate the dominant character of the soul, which is full of innumerable opinions as this figurative paradise was of trees. And by the tree of life he was shadowing out the greatest of the virtues—namely, piety towards the gods, by means of which the soul is made immortal; and by the tree which had the knowledge of good and evil, he was intimating that wisdom and moderation, by means of which things, contrary in their nature to one another, are distinguished.

LV. Therefore, having laid down these to be boundaries as it were in the soul, God then, like a judge, began to consider to which side men would be most inclined by nature. And when he saw that the disposition of man had a tendency to wickedness, and was but little inclined to holiness or piety, by which qualities an immortal life is secured, he drove them forth as was very natural, and banished him from paradise; giving no hope of any subsequent restoration to his soul which had sinned in such a desperate and irremediable manner. Since even the opportunity of deceit was blameable in no slight degree, which I must not pass over in this place.

It is said that the old poisonous and earthborn reptile, the serpent, uttered the voice of a man. And he on one occasion coming to the wife of the first created man, reproached her with her slowness and her excessive prudence, because she delayed and hesitated to gather the fruit which was completely beautiful to look at, and exceedingly sweet to enjoy, and was, moreover, most useful as being a means by which men might be able to distinguish between good and evil. And she, without any inquiry, prompted by an unstable and rash mind, acquiesced in his advice, and ate of the fruit, and gave a portion of it to her husband. And this conduct suddenly changed both of them from innocence and simplicity of character to all kinds of wickedness; at which the Father of all was indignant. For their actions deserved his anger, inasmuch as they, passing by the tree of eternal life, the tree which might have endowed them with perfection of virtue, and by means of which they might have enjoyed a long and happy life, preferred a brief and mortal (I will not call it life, but) time full of unhappiness; and, accordingly, he appointed them such punishment as was befitting.

LVI. And these things are not mere fabulous inventions, in which the race of poets and sophists delights, but are rather types shadowing forth some allegorical truth, according to some mystical explanation. And any one who follows a reasonable train of conjecture, will say with great propriety, that the aforesaid serpent is the symbol of pleasure, because in the first place he is destitute of feet, and crawls on his belly with his face downwards. In the second place, because he uses lumps of clay for food. Thirdly, because he bears poison in his teeth, by which it is his nature to kill those who are bitten by him. And the man devoted to pleasure is free from none of the aforementioned evils; for it is with difficulty that he can raise his head, being weighed down and dragged down, since intemperance trips him up and keeps him down. And he feeds, not on heavenly food, which wisdom offers to contemplative men by means of discourses and opinions; but on that which is put forth by the earth in the varying seasons of the year, from which arise drunkenness and voracity, and licentiousness, breaking through and inflaming the appetites of the belly, and enslaving them in subjection to gluttony, by which they strengthen the impetuous passions, the seat of which is beneath the belly; and make them break forth. And they lick up the result of the labours of cooks and tavern-keepers; and at times some of them in ecstasy with the flavor of the delicious food, moves about his head and reaches forward, being desirous to participate in the sight. And when he sees an expensively furnished table, he throws himself bodily upon the delicacies which are abundantly prepared, and devotes himself to them, wishing to be filled with them all together, and so to depart, having no other end in view than that he should allow nothing of such a sumptuous preparation to be wasted. Owing to which conduct, he too, carries about poison in his teeth, no less than the serpent does; for his teeth are the ministers and servants of his insatiability, cutting up and smoothing everything which has a reference to eating, and committing them, in the first place to the tongue, which decides upon, and distinguishes between the various flavors, and subsequently, to the larynx. But immoderate indulgence in eating is naturally a poisonous and deadly habit, inasmuch as what is so devoured is not capable of digestion, in consequence of the quantity of additional food which is heaped in on the top of it, and arrives before what was previously eaten is converted into juice.

And the serpent is said to have uttered a human voice, because pleasure employs innumerable champions and defenders who take care to advocate its interests, and who dare to assert that the power over everything, both small and great, does of right belong to it without any exception whatever.

* * * * *

LVIII. But what has been already said is sufficient to show what the reasons were on account of which the serpent appears to have uttered a human voice. And it is on this account that Moses appears to me in the particular laws also which he issued in the respect to animals, deciding what were proper to be eaten, and what were not, to have given especial praise to the animal called the serpent fighter. This is a reptile with jointed legs above the feet, by which it is able to leap and to raise itself on high, in the same manner as the tribe of locusts. For the serpent fighter appears to me to be no other than temperance expressed under a symbolical figure, waging an interminable and unrelenting warfare against intemperance and pleasure. For temperance especially embraces economy and frugality, and pares down the necessities to a small number, preferring a life of austerity and dignity. But intemperance is devoted to extravagance and superfluity, which are the causes of luxury and effeminacy to both soul and body, and to which it is owing that in the opinion of wise men life is but a faulty thing, and more miserable than death.

LIX. But its juggleries and deceits pleasure does not venture to bring directly to the man, but first offers them to the woman, and by her means to the man; acting in a very natural and sagacious manner. For in human beings the mind occupies the rank of the man, and the sensations that of the woman. And pleasure joins itself to and associates itself with the sensations first of all, and then by their means cajoles also the mind, which is the dominant part. For, after each of the senses has been subjected to the charms of pleasure, and has learned to delight in what is offered to it, the sight being fascinated by varieties of colors and shapes, the hearing by harmonious sounds, the taste by the sweetness of flowers, and the smell by the delicious fragrance of the odors which are brought before it, these all having received these offerings, like handmaids, bring them to the mind as their master, leading with them persuasion as an advocate, to warn it against rejecting any of them whatever. And the mind being immediately caught by the bait, becomes a subject instead of a ruler, and a slave instead of a master, and an exile instead of a citizen, and a mortal instead of an immortal. . . .

LX. . . . Therefore, the race of mankind, if it had met with strict and befitting justice, must have been utterly destroyed, because of its ingratitude to God its benefactor and its Saviour. But God, being merciful by nature, took pity upon them, and moderated their punishment. And he permitted the race to continue to exist, but he no longer gave them food as he had done before from ready prepared stores, lest if they were under the dominion of his evils, satiety and idleness, they should become unruly and insolent.

LXI. Such is the life of those who originally were men of innocence and simplicity, and also of those who have come to prefer vice to virtue, from whom one ought to keep aloof. And in his beforementioned account of the creation of the world, Moses teaches us also many other things, and especially five most beautiful lessons which are superior to all others. In the first place, for the sake of convicting the atheists, he teaches us that the Deity has a real being and existence. Now, of the atheists, some have only doubted of the existence of God, stating it to be an uncertain thing; but others who are more audacious, have taken courage, and asserted positively that there is no such thing; but this is affirmed only by men who have darkened the truth with fabulous inventions.

In the second place he teaches us that God is one; having reference here to the assertors of the polytheistic doctrine; men who do not blush to transfer that worst of evil constitutions, ochlocracy, from earth to heaven.

Thirdly, he teaches, as has been already related, that the world has created; by this lesson refuting those who think that it is uncreated and eternal, and who thus attribute no glory to God.

In the fourth place we learn that the world also which was thus created is one, since also the Creator is one, and he, making his creation to resemble himself in its singleness, employed all existing essence in the creation of the universe. For it would not have been complete if it had not been made and composed of all parts which were likewise whole and complete. For there are some persons who believe that there are many worlds, and some who even fancy that they are boundless in extent, being themselves inexperienced and ignorant of the truth of those things of which it is desirable to have a correct knowledge.

The fifth lesson that Moses teaches us is, that God exerts his providence for the benefit of the world. For it follows of necessity that the Creator must always care for that which he has created, just as parents do also care for their children. And he who has learned this not more by hearing it than by his own understanding, and has impressed on his own soul these marvellous facts which are the subject of so much contention —namely, that God has a being and existence, and that he who so exists is really one, and that he has created the world, and that he has created it one as has been stated, having made it like to himself in singleness; and that he exercises a continual care for that which he has created—will live a happy and blessed life, stamped with the doctrines of piety and holiness.

HERMES TRISMEGISTUS

THE legendary literature written by Hermes was in ancient times optimistically estimated as running into thousands of volumes. Today one is interested in fourteen tractates to which the name Poimander or Poemandres is sometimes given. More properly the title Poimander belongs only to the first of the fourteen. Published with these there are also two other pieces, one a small collection of fragments, the other, *The Definitions of Asclepius to Ammon the King.*

The entire collection bears the name of Thrice Greatest Hermes because of the identification of the Greek god Hermes with the Egyptian god whose name is variously spelled Tat, Thot, or Theuth. The mythology is not consistent, however, for Hermes is given as the father of Tat, and Tat is a descendant of Uranus and Cronos. And further, the identity of Asclepius is obscured because he is said to be the grandson of the inventor of medicine.

In general the tractates claim to be, and until modern times were frequently thought to be, a revelation of Christian truth to the ancient Egyptians. Although, of course, this claim and this opinion are mistaken, it cannot be denied that some ideas from Egyptian theology, and some Persian influence as well, may have been incorporated in several of the chapters. The significant sources of its philosophy, however, are to be sought in

184

popular Platonism, Neo-Pythagoreanism, and Stoicism. The religious note, which is dominant throughout, is colored by the mysteries, both Greek and Eastern, and to a noticeable degree by Judaism and Christianity.

The corpus as a whole is not the work of a single author, and attempts to formulate a consistent system of theology or cosmology from its teachings must result in confusion. The critical problems are difficult. None of the tractates was written before the Christian era and they were not collected into a single group much before A.D. 300. The dates of the separate parts cannot be fixed with any accuracy, for Kroll considers Poimander the latest, while Zielinski asserts that it is the earliest. Zeller, in order to account for similarities with Neo-Platonism makes the interesting assumption that Hermes as well as Plotinus studied under Ammonius Saccus. But Zeller seems to have overemphasized the similarities. Without sufficient evidence to warrant greater exactitude, the safest thing to do is to consider the tractates as having been produced sometime during the second and third centuries.

It is even possible that a Semitic original underlay the Greek text, or parts of it. For example, the last phrase of Poimander, paragraph five, makes no sense as it stands in Greek. The phrase "which had leaped into it," is an emendation for the words "unto hearing." But one may suppose that a Greek translator confused the Semitic (Syriac or Coptic) roots meaning *hearing* and *heaven;* in which case the author would have said, "the pervading Spiritual word in heaven." Another illustration is found in the peculiar statement of paragraph eighteen that love is the cause of death. If the author of the Greek text is translating a Syriac original, he may have mistaken *darkness* for *love*. Other examples could be listed.

Another critical problem, and a very interesting one, is the relation between this literature and the New Testament. Reitzenstein, in his effort to prove that the theology of the Pauline epistles is derived from Hermes, asserts that Poimander was written in the first century of our era. This date is now generally rejected, and the alleged influence of any Hermetic theology on Christianity is inherently improbable. Two points among others destroy Reitzenstein's theory. First, the salvation which Poimander offers is deification procured by a cosmological revelation; but for Paul salvation is not deification and the message by which salvation is mediated, instead of being cosmological, is an account of recent historical facts—the death and resurrection of Jesus Christ. Second, in the two religions the roles of soul and spirit, on which Reitzenstein places so much emphasis, are in direct conflict.

Corroborating the later date usually assigned Poimander, the internal evidence favors an influence of Christianity on Hermes. The text of Poimander betrays verbal similarities with the Septuagint, and, while the case is not so clear, there seem to be phrases taken from the New Testament also. Furthermore, the prayer which closes Poimander is found in a collection of Christian prayers—a fact which indicates that someone mistook this tractate for a Christian production. Such a mistake requires the confusion of mind, characteristic of the second century, in which recent converts from paganism could not well distinguish which of their old ideas could be harmonized with the new religion. Consequently one must judge that the Hermetic literature is a less popular form of Gnosticism, showing Christian influence in its phraseology, but even more pagan in its philosophy than the better known Gnostic systems.

Poimander opens with a mystic vision induced, not by corybantic frenzy, but, as in Plotinus, by a study of metaphysics or cosmology. In this vision, the human subject expects to receive scientific information; and while the bodily senses are to be held in abeyance the blank consciousness of quietism is nowhere held to be the method or the goal.

In the beginning was God, the Intellect. A part of God becomes chaotic nature. Then a holy Logos from God descends upon nature with the result that the four elements separate and assume their proper places. The Father God, represented by light in the vision, consists of countless powers arranged in a cosmos. Undoubtedly this means that Plato's world of Ideas has been definitely identified with the mind of God. The elements of nature came into being because the mind of God, in conjunction with the Logos, imitated itself and constructed a world from its own elements. If the Stoics had encountered difficulty in defending materialism, Poimander has learned the lesson only too well, for here the stuff out of which the world is made is nothing else than the mind of God.

The Intellect God next produced, with the aid of the Logos, a demiurge, also an intellect. This third God is the maker of the planetary spheres, and these in the guise of Fate govern the sensible cosmos. The Logos and the demiurge then bring forth the various living beings which inhabit the earth; but the original God alone who is Life and Light, begat man equal with himself. Man, then, in the image of God, contemplating the work of the demiurge his brother, obtained from the Father authority to do some creating of his own. Therefore he broke through the sky, which held the element fire in its proper place, and exhibited himself to nature below. Nature, entranced with the beauty of this image of God, loved him; he, too, seeing his form reflected in the water and his shadow on the earth, embraced it and her and so came to inhabit an irrational form. For this reason, man today is partially mortal because of his body and partially, in fact essentially, immortal because of his origin. If, therefore, a man understands this account of the origin of the world and of himself, if he learns that he has come from Light and Life, and consists of them, he shall proceed back to Life. In the attempt to return, men who are holy and good receive aid from the Intellect God. He aids them in understanding, in turning from sensation and the body, and in cutting off thoughts which tempt. The description of the ascent to God is that type of celestial geography, also found in Plutarch, which pictures psychological purification. Finally the pilgrim comes to be in God; "this is the good end for them that have acquired gnosis— to be deified."

The thirteenth tractate is closely related to Poimander. While there are differences between them, the latter expands the general view of salvation presented in the former. There is a vision in which one passes beyond the body into a sort of dreamlike existence. Man in this state is no longer corporeal, but colorless, formless, shin-

ing, immutable—in other words, a pure spirit. In this
tractate it is not so clear that this state is induced by
rational study in the ordinary sense of the words; it is
more mystical and moral—"Withdraw into thyself and
it will come; *will,* and it will come to pass; make idle
thy body's senses and it will be the birth of the Divinity;
cleanse thyself of Matter's irrational Avengers." The
Avengers are vices, such as avarice and anger. Thus the
tone of the discourse is more moral than cosmological.
In Poimander the gnosis by which salvation is accomplished is a knowledge both of the universe and of the
self, for in fact this knowledge is one; but here knowledge of self on a relatively superficial level receives practically all the emphasis. The new birth produced by self-
knowledge does not affect the natural body, for the aim
of salvation here, as it was in Poimander also, is deification. "Knowest thou not that thou art in thy nature
God?"

The tractate ends with a hymn that is not devoid of
devotional charm. Contrary to the teaching of Poimander, the new birth is to be kept a secret and not divulged
to the mass of men.

With this summary of Poimander and its companion
piece, the question of their relations to the New Testament may again be raised. Both chronology and content
prevent them from having influenced Paul. It may be
possible to connect Poimander with the Prologue of
John's Gospel and with his first Epistle. The connection, however, is not one of dependence, in either direction, but of opposition. For Poimander the Logos was
not in the beginning, as John asserts; for John, "all
things were made by him and without him was not any

thing made that was made," and this Poimander denies. While the more popular forms of Gnosticism at least made some mention of Jesus Christ—an almost indispensable requirement for a work to be Christian—Poimander not only ignores him, but the nature of the system and the conception of salvation by a cosmological gnosis, tacitly excludes the Christian idea of an historical Incarnation according to which "the Logos became flesh and dwelt among us."

Because these points are not merely differences but pointed contradictions, it may not be too improbable to assume that John included the Prologue in his Gospel for the purpose of opposing prevalent notions similar to those in Poimander; for even though the tractate cannot be placed in the first century, it may in more systematic form reflect the opinions of an early fringe of semi-Christian thought.

The title of tractate six, *In God Alone is the Good and Nowhere Else,* might lead one at first to expect a negative theology and an emphasis on God's transcendence. However, the teaching turns out to be an insistent pantheism. When the author says that God is the reality or substance of motion and genesis, he may not completely identify God with the processes of the world, for later he distinguishes between God and "this living being which is greater than all" particular things; but at most he implies that God is the abiding form of the world. In a certain sense the theology may be called negative—in the sense that all the qualities, activities, and attributes common in the phenomenal world involve evil and limitation, and hence all that can be said of God is that he is Good. In this predication nothing concrete is signified—it means merely that God has no needs, desires, pain, or jealousy.

If the pure Good of God remains negative and without content, the good in the cosmos is not less so. The processes of generation in some way participate in the Good, but it is more proper to speak of degrees of Evil. "Only the name of the Good is found among men, the thing itself nowhere." In fact the Cosmos is a pleroma of evil.

The ninth tractate, apparently written later, and probably an excerpt from an Asclepius-corpus not now known, directly attacks this view. Here it is blasphemy to call the Cosmos a pleroma of evil. To be sure no part of the Cosmos is empty of a demon, and demons plant evil thoughts in the minds of men. Yet the Cosmos is an instrument of God's will and is the son of God as also the things in the cosmos are sons of the cosmos. More profoundly, God not merely contains all existent objects, he is himself all things, producing them, presumably by emanation, but at least producing them out of himself.

Whether these tractates represent a merely literary religion, as some have suggested, or whether they came from some small sect, as is more probable, they form one stage, an early and very incomplete stage, in the fusion of Hebrew-Christian views with Hellenistic philosophy. Gnosticism included more of Christianity, and Plotinus admitted none of it.

THRICE GREATEST HERMES [1]

I. POIMANDER

1. Once upon a time, when I had been meditating upon the Existents and my reason was exalted exceedingly and my bodily senses held in check as are sleeping men weighed down by a gorge of nutriment, or by fatigue of body, methought Someone more than vast, in measure boundless, was calling my name, saying to me:

"What wouldst thou hear and see and, upon apprehending, learn and comprehend?"

Say I, "Who indeed art thou?"

2. "I," said he, "am Poimander, the Intellect of the Dominion; I know what thou wouldst and I am with thee everywhere."

3. Say I, "I wish to learn the Existents and to apprehend their nature and to comprehend God. This," said I, "I wish to hear."

He replies to me: "Hold in thy intellect whatsoever things thou wouldst learn and I shall teach thee."

Upon saying this he was changed in appearance, and immediately all things were opened to me in a twinkling.

4. And I beheld a Vision, indefinite, but all things became Light, mild and cheering, and I was delighted upon seeing it. And after a little the lower portion had become in part Darkness, awesome and gloomy, sinuously extended, so that I supposed the darkness to be changing into a kind of Liquid Substance, indescribably agitated, emitting smoke as though from a fire and producing a sound suppressed like wailing. Then an inarticulate cry came forth from it, the voice, one would think, of Fire. 5. And from the Light . . . a Holy Word descended upon the Nature, and unmixed Fire leaped out of the Liquid Substance up and aloft; buoyant was it and keen and active too. The Air, too, being buoyant, followed after the Fire, ascending from Earth-and-Water up to the Fire so that it seemed suspended therefrom. But Earth

---

1. Translated by W. R. Newbold.

and Water remained by themselves commingled so that the
Earth could not be seen apart from the Water; but they were
kept in motion through the pervading Spiritual Word which
had leaped into it.[1]
6. Saith Poimander to me:
"Hast thou apprehended this Vision, what it means?"
"May I indeed comprehend," said I.
"That light," said he, "am I, Intellect, thy God, who existed before the Liquid Substance which appeared from Darkness; but the Luminous Word which appeared out of Intellect
is the Son of God."
"What then?" say I.
"Comprehend thou this: that which sees and hears in thee
is the Word of the Lord, but Intellect is the Father God, for
they do not part one from the other, for Life is union of
these."
7. "I thank thee," said I.
"Well, then, apprehend the Light and recognize what follows."
After saying this he gazed for a long time upon me, so
that I trembled at the look of him. But when he raised his
head, I behold in my Intellect the Light as consisting of
countless Powers and become a boundless Cosmos, and the
Fire being on all sides restrained by a very mighty Power and
come to a stop, subdued. These things I understood merely
by seeing them through the word of Poimander.
8. But as I was in great astonishment, he saith again to me:
"Thou has seen in the Intellect the Archetypal Form which
began before the limitless beginning."
These things said Poimander to me. Said I, "the Elements,
then, of nature—whence came they into being?"
To this he replied, "From the Decree of God, which ac-
quiring the Word and beholding the beautiful Cosmos, copied
it by making herself into a Cosmos [2] through her own naked
elements and offspring. 9. But the Intellect, God, being bi-

1. Or, *the pervading Spiritual Word in heaven.*
2. i.e., the planetary spheres. This cosmology is purely Stoic; its pro-
totype is outlined as from Zeno by Diogenes Laertius VII 134 ff.

sexual, existing as Life and Light, brought to birth by the
Word another Intellect as Maker, who, being God of the Fire
and Wind, made certain seven Governors, in circles enclosing
the sensible cosmos. And their government is called Fate.
10. There leaped straightway out of the Elements down below
the Word of God into Nature's pure formation and was united
to the Maker-Intellect, for it was consubstantial with it. And
the irrational Elements of Nature, those down below, were
left behind so as to be bare Matter. 11. But the Maker-
Intellect, together with the Word, which restrains the Circles
round about and spins them in a whirl, set his formations
turning and let them turn from an indefinite beginning to a
limitless end, for it begins where it leaves off. But their revolution, in accordance with the will of the Intellect, brought
forth from the Elements down below irrational living beings,
for it did not extend reason to them. The Air brought forth
winged things, the Water those that swim, and the Earth
and the Water were separated one from the other in accordance with the will of the Intellect, and the Earth brought
forth from herself the living beings she had, quadrupeds and
reptiles, beasts wild and tame. 12. But the Father of All, the
Intellect, being Life and Light, brought forth Man, co-equal
to himself, with whom he fell in love, as being his own child,
for he was exceeding beautiful, the image of his Father. For
in reality even God fell in Love with his own form, and to
him he gave all his own formations. 13. And having observed the Maker's Creation in the Father, he also wished
himself to make, and it was granted him by the Father. When
he had come to be in the Sphere of Making, seeing that he
was going to possess full authority, he observed his Brother's
formations. And they fell in love with him and each gave
him a share of his own Rank. And after he had well learned
their essence and had received a share of their Nature, he
resolved to break through the circumference of the circles
and to subdue the might of that which [1] held down the Fire.
14. So he that possesses full authority over the Cosmos of living creatures looked down through the Celestial System after

1. i.e., the Valentinian Horos.

breaking through that might, and exhibited to Nature down
below the beautiful form of God. And when she saw him endowed with beauty which can never satiate, and possessing
in himself the entire active power of the Governors and the
form of God, she smiled with love, inasmuch as she saw the
exquisitely beautiful form of Man reflected in the water and
his shadow upon the earth. And he, upon seeing the form
like to himself in her in the water, loved it and resolved to
dwell there. With the resolve came its actualization and he
inhabited the irrational form.   15. And Nature, upon receiving the Beloved, wrapped all herself around him and they
were commingled, for they were lovers. And this is why,
beyond all living beings upon the earth, Man is two-fold:
mortal indeed because of the body, but by virtue of the Man
which is his essence, immortal. For although he is immortal
and possesses authority over all things, he suffers the vicissi-
tudes of a mortal, being subjected to Fate. For although he
is above the Celestial System, within the System he has become a slave. Although he is bisexual, because sprung from
a bisexual Father, and unsleeping because sprung from an
unsleeping Father, yet he succumbs to sleep."
16. And after this, "O Intellect of mine, even I myself am
amorous of thy teaching."
    Poimander said, "this is the mystery kept hid until this day.
Nature blended with Man brought forth a wonder most wonderful. For as he had the Nature of the Celestial System of
the Seven, who, as I said to thee, were made of Fire and
Wind, Nature delayed not but immediately brought forth
seven men, in correspondence with the natures of the Seven
Governors, bisexual and belonging on high."
    And after this I said, "O Poimander, . . . for now a great
longing has seized me and I crave to hear; do not haste
away."
    And Poimander said,
"Keep silence, for I have not yet completed for thee the first
discourse."
    "Lo! I am silent," said I.
    "In such wise then as I have said the generation of these

Seven came to pass. 17. Earth was feminine, the Water
fertilizing, the ripeness came from Fire, from the Ether she
took Breath,[1] and Nature brought forth Bodies corresponding
to the appearance of man. And Man from Life and Light
changed into Soul and Intellect, from Life into Soul and from
Light into Intellect. And all the parts of the Sensible Cosmos
remained thus until the period of the end. 18. Now hear the
rest of the discourse which thou dost long to hear. The period
being completed, the bond of them all was loosened [2] by the
Will of God. For all the living beings, being bisexual, at the
same time with Man were loosed apart; some became male
and some female in like manner. And God straightway spoke
by his Holy Word, 'Increase ye in increase and multiply in
multitude, ye creatures and formations all, and let him that
possesses intellect recognize himself as being immortal and
Love [3] as the cause of Death, and all the Existents.' 19. When
he had said this, his Providence, through Fate and the Celestial System, brought about the couplings and established the
generations. And all things were multiplied according to their
kind. And he that hath recognized himself is come into that
abounding Good, but he that hath delighted, through Love's
seduction, in the body, he stays in the Darkness wandering,
sensibly suffering the pains of Death."
20. "Why is the sin so great," said I, "of them that fail to
know, that they should be deprived of immortality?"
    "Thou seemest, my son, not to have given heed to the
things thou hast heard. Did I not tell thee to think?"
    "I am thinking and remember, and I give thanks also."
    "If thou hast thought, tell me, why are those worthy of
Death who are in Death?"
    "Because the Substratum-body originated in the gloomy
Darkness, from which came the Liquid Substance of which
the body is composed in the Sensible Cosmos from which the
draught of Death is drawn."

    1. Or, *Spirit.*
    2. Corresponding to the fall of Adam; the "spoiling" of Valentinus.
    3. Or, and the cause of death-love; i.e., the love of man for his image,
which imprisoned him in matter.

"Thou hast thought aright, my son. 21. But in what respect doth 'he that hath apprehended himself proceed to him' as the Word of God hath it?"

Say I, "Of Light and Life doth the Father of the Whole consist from whom Man is come into being."

"Thou speakest aright; the God and Father is Light and Life and of him Man came into being. If then thou learnest that thou thyself art from Life and Light and that thou dost in fact consist of them thou shalt proceed back into life."

These things Poimander said. "But tell me further, how shall I proceed into Life, O Intellect of mine," said I. "For God saith, 'Let the man possessed of Intellect recognize himself.' Then do not all men possess Intellect?"

"Speak reverently, my son," said he. 22. "I, the Intellect come to the holy and good and pure and merciful and devout, and my coming results in help and straightway they understand all things and solicit the Father's favor affectionately and give him thanks, invoking on him blessings, and chanting hymns, intent on him with ardent love. And ere they give the body up to its proper death, they turn them with disgust from sensations, knowing their effects; nay, rather shall I myself the Intellect not suffer the effects of the body which assail the soul to be completed, for, being door-keeper, I shall close the entrances against evil and base effects by cutting off the thoughts. But to those who are devoid of Intellect and to the evil and the wicked, the envious and the covetous and murderers and the impious I am far off, yielding my place to the Avenging Spirit who, by increasing the sharpness of the fire, sensibly infects him and arms him the more for transgressions that he may meet greater punishment, nor does he ever cease to have appetites inordinate, insatiably fighting in the dark; and he torments him and causes the fire to wax still more against him."

24. "Well hast thou taught me all things, as I wished, O Intellect. Furthermore, tell me about the Ascent which is now beginning." [1]

1. Poimander's instruction has already furnished the disciple with some knowledge of himself, and so the ascent is already begun.

In reply Poimander said, "In the dissolution of the Sub-
stratum-body, first thou surrenderest it to Change and the
form which thou hadst becometh invisible, and thy temperament thou surrenderest to the Spirit in a state of inactivity,
and the senses of the body withdraw into their proper founts,
becoming parts [1] and again combining for their activities,
and impulse and Lust proceed into the irrational Nature.
Thus it is that Man doth speed his way upward through the
Celestial System. To the first Zone [2] he gives the Activity of
Waxing and Waning, to the second, the Contriving of Evils,
it being inactive, and to the third the Deception of the Desires, inactive, and to the fourth his Domineering Arro-
gance(?), inactive, and to the fifth Unholy Boldness and
the Rashness of Audacity, inactive, and to the sixth Evil Seek-
ings for Wealth, and to the seventh zone Lurking Falsity,
inactive. And then, stripped naked of the effects of the system, he cometh to the Eighth Nature, clothed in his proper
Power, and with the Existing Ones hymns the Father. And
they that are there rejoice with him at his coming, and
when he has become like to those that sojourn there, he hear-
eth certain Powers which are above the Eighth Substance
hymning God in a voice of their own. And then in order they
ascend to the Father, and themselves surrender themselves to
Powers, and upon becoming Powers they come to be in God.
This is the Good End for them that have acquired Gnosis—to
be deified.   25. Why then dost thou tarry? Seeing that thou
hast received all, wilt thou not become a Guide [3] to the
worthy, so that the race of Humanity through thee may be
saved by God?"

Upon saying this Poimander was commingled with the
Powers. But I, after I had given thanks and had blessed the

1. Or, *organs*.
2. The first zone is that of the Moon. Craft is given to Mercury, the
second zone; Lust to Venus; and so on. Note the implied hostility to the
popular religion; this is not Stoic. Cumont, *After-Life in Roman Paganism*, p. 107, attributes a similar scheme to Numenius.
3. In XIII 13, Hermes is told not to betray the secret of the new birth
to the many.

Father of the Whole, dedicated myself, strengthened by him and instructed in the Nature of the All and in the vision most sublime, and have begun to proclaim to men the beauty of piety and of gnosis: "O ye peoples, men born of earth, who have given yourselves over to drunkenness and sleep and ignorance of God, become sober, shake off your stupor, the spell of irrational sleep." And when they had heard, they came with one accord. And I say, "Why, O men born of earth, have ye given yourselves over unto death while yet ye have the power of sharing immortality? Repent ye, ye that make Error your fellow traveller and Ignorance your partner. Get ye out from the darksome light, share in immortality, forsaking corruption." And some of them replied with silly chatter and turned away, because they had given themselves over to the Way of Death, but others entreated to be taught, casting themselves before my feet. But I have raised them up and have become Guide of the Race, teaching the Words, how and in what way they shall be saved. And I have sowed in them the Words of Wisdom and they have been nourished by the Water Divine. But when even had come and all the radiance of the sun was beginning to set, I bade them give thanks to God. And when they had fulfilled their thanksgiving each man turned away to his own resting-place.

But I recorded for myself the benefaction of Poimander and with my every wish fulfilled rejoiced exceedingly. For the sleep of my body proved to be my soul's waking, and the closing of my eyes a true vision, and my silence pregnant with the Good, and the issue of my Word begettings of the good. This fell to my lot, being received from the Intellect, that is from Poimander, the Word of the Dominion, whence I have become inspired and have come to the Circle of the Truth. Wherefore of my whole soul and strength I give blessing to the Father, God:—

26. Holy are thou O God,[1] Father of the Whole,

1. Berliner Klassikertexte, Heft VI, Altchristliche Texte, bearbeitet von C. Schmidt u. W. Schubart, Berlin 1910, pp. 110-114, contain six Christian prayers, of which the fourth is taken direct from Poimander, a fact not observed by the editors.

Holy are thou O God, whose counsel is accomplished by
thine own Powers,

Holy art thou O God, who willest to be known and art
known to thine own,

Holy art thou, who by the Word didst cause the Existents to subsist, of whom all Nature hath become an
image.

Holy art thou whom Nature hath not shaped,

Holy art thou who art mightier than all Power,

Holy art thou who art greater than all pre-eminence,

Holy art thou who art superior to all Praises:

Receive rational offerings, pure, from soul and heart up-
lifted to thee, O thou Unutterable, Ineffable, by Silence in-
voked.

As I pray that I fail not of the Gnosis appropriate to our
Being, nod me thine assent and strengthen me and fill me
with this grace, in order that I may enlighten those in
ignorance of their Race, my brethren but thy sons.

Wherefore I believe and bear witness—I am going into
Life and Light. Blessed art thou O Father! Thy Man would
be holy as thou art, even as thou hast given him the full
power to be holy.

II. THRICE GREATEST HERMES TO ASCLEPIUS:
A UNIVERSAL DISCOURSE [1]

1. Either God or the divine, by which I now mean not the
Generated but the Ungenerated. If Divine it is substantial,
if God it is in consequence non-substantial. Moreover, God
is rationally apprehensible in the sense now to be explained.
God first of all things is apprehensible to us, but not to himself. For the Apprehensible is submitted to the Apprehending by Sense-perception. God, then, is not apprehensible to
himself, for he is not, as Apprehending, something other
than the Apprehended, and so cannot be apprehended by
himself. But to us he is a something other than ourselves and
so is apprehended by us.   2. Now if Place is apprehensible,

1. Apparently the opening paragraphs of this tractate have been lost.

it is not as God but as Place, and if it is also apprehended as God, it is not as Place, but as an activity of comprehending [other things within itself]. Now every Moved is moved, not in a Moved, but in something at rest, and the Mover therefore is at rest, for it cannot move with the Moved.

How then, O Thrice Greatest, do the things here below move with those moving on high? For you have said that the erratic spheres are moved by the unerring sphere.

This, Asclepius, is not a moving with but a moving against, for they are not moved in the same but in opposite directions one to another, and the contrariety keeps the contrary tendency of the motion [of the unerring sphere] at rest, for its contrariness to rest *is* motion. 3. Hence the erratic spheres, being moved contrariwise to the unerring sphere, because of their mutually opposed directions, are moved, by virtue of that very opposition, by the sphere at rest. And it cannot be otherwise. Do you think that the Great and Little Bear, which you see neither setting nor rising but always revolving about the same point, are in motion or at rest?

In motion, O Thrice Greatest.

What sort of motion, O Asclepius?

That which revolves about the same point.

But revolution about the same point is a motion controlled by rest. For the limitation, "around the same point" prevents its moving beyond it. And if that which is prevented from moving beyond it stands still in the motion about it, so also the motion in the opposite direction stands still, being kept steady by the opposition. 4. I will give you an illustration which meets your eyes. Consider terrestrial animals while swimming, a man for example. If the water is moving, the resistance of his feet and hands results in the man's keeping still so as not to be carried away by the water.

You have given a very clear illustration, O Thrice Greatest.

All motion, then, moves in rest and because of rest. The motion of the Cosmos therefore and of every material living creature does not owe its being to things outside the Cosmos, but comes from the Intelligibles within, soul or spiritus or some other incorporeal thing, to that which is without. For Body does not move an animate body, nor does it move Body at all, even though the Mover be animate.

5. What do you mean by this, O Thrice Greatest? Are not the things which move sticks and stones and all other inanimates, bodies?

Not at all, O Asclepius. For that which is within the body that moves the inanimate, that which moves both, both the body of the bearer and the body of the borne, is not a body. Hence it is a something animate *per se,* since it causes motion. Hence you see the soul overladen when alone she carries two bodies. And that things moved are moved in something and by something, is manifest.

6. But things moved must move in the Empty, O Thrice Greatest.

Hush, O Asclepius. None of the Existents is empty as regards Existence; only the Non-Existent is empty of and alien to Existence, but the Existent could not have been Existent were it not full of Existence. For that which exists can never become empty.

Are there not some things which are empty, O Thrice Greatest? They are such as an empty jug, an empty jar, an empty vat, and the like.

Alas, what a stupendous mistake, O Asclepius. The things which are most full and stuffed you think to be empty!

What do you mean, O Thrice Greatest?

Is not the Air a body?

It is.

Does not this body pervade all the Existents and in pervading them fill them?

Yes.

But is not Body blended out of the four elements?

Yes.

Then all the things which you call empty are full of air. But if of air, they are full of the four elements also. The opposite of your doctrine then becomes self-evident, that the things which you call full are all empty of the air, which is crowded out by other bodies that cannot receive the air into their place. The bodies therefore which you call empty ought to be called hollow, not empty, for in fact they are full of air and spiritus.

Your argument is unanswerable, O Thrice Greatest. The air is body and this body pervades all the existents and in pervading them fills them. What then shall we call the place in which the All moves?

7. Incorporeal, O Asclepius.

What then is the Incorporeal?

Intellect and Logos, Whole from Whole, Self-embracing, free of all Body, unerring, impassive, intangible, self-existent, capable of containing all others and preservative of the Existents, whereof the Good, the Truth, the Archetypal Light, the Archetype of the Soul, are rays.

What then is God?

He that is not any one of these but is the Cause of their being, both of them all and of each single part in each of all these Existents, nor has he in the least failed the Nonexistents anymore than the Existents. All things owe their being to Existents, not to Non-existents. For Non-existents are not of such a nature as to be able to become Existents, but are of such a nature as not to be able to become anything real, and again the Existents are not of such a nature as at any time not to be.

8. What then do you mean by "not at any time to be"?

Now God is not Intellect but is the Cause of its existing, nor is he spiritus or light, but is the Cause of the light's existing. Wherefore God ought to be worshipped under these two titles, which are appropriate to him alone and to no one else. For none of the other beings called gods, no man, no spirit, can *be* good in any degree whatever; God alone can, and he is this only and is nothing else. All things else are without capacity for the Nature of the Good. For they are Body and Soul, which possess no place capable of accommodating the Good. The Magnitude of the Good indeed is as great as is the subsistence of all the other Existents, both Bodies and things Incorporeal, sensible and Intelligible;

this is God. Call not then anything else Good, for it would be an impious act, nor ever call God anything except The Good, for, again, it would be an impious act. 9. The expression, "The Good" is used by all, but *what it is* is by all not comprehended. Therefore God is also by all not comprehended; in their ignorance they call both gods and some men "good," although they could never either be or become good. For Becoming good is utterly alien to God, just as being good is inseparable from him, seeing that he himself is the Good. Now all the other immortal gods are honored with the title "god," but God is the Good, not by way of honor, but by virtue of his nature. For the Good is the sole and only nature of God; the two constitute one Order, from which come all the other Orders. For it is "He that is good" that gives all and takes nothing. God then is the Good and the Good is God. 10. His other title is "Father," again because of the attribute of making all things. For making is a father's part, hence for right-minded men child-making is life's greatest and most God-fearing occupation, and the greatest calamity and offence against God is that one should depart from amongst men childless. Such a man pays penalty after death to the spirits, and this is the penalty— the soul of the childless man is condemned to a body possessing the nature neither of man nor of woman, which is accursed under the sun. Therefore, O Asclepius, rejoice with no man who is childless; rather pity his misfortune, knowing what punishment awaits him.

Regard these statements, O Asclepius, in number and in kind as above given, as a kind of introduction to the Nature of the Universe.

VI. THRICE-GREATEST HERMES' DISCOURSE: IN GOD ALONE IS THE GOOD AND NOWHERE ELSE

1. The Good, O Asclepius, is in nothing save in God alone, nay rather God himself is the Good always. If so, he must be the Reality of all motion and genesis. And nothing is

bare of that Reality, which has around about it a fixed activity, nothing lacking and boundless, a most copious Supplier continuously in every way. For seeing that it supplies all Good, when I say continuously in every way, it implies that it is always good. This is found in nothing else, but in God alone. For there is nothing which he needs that he should desire to get it and get it in some evil way and become evil, nor can any of the Existents fall away from him by which falling away he would suffer pain. For pain is a part of evil. Nor is anything superior to him with which he would be at war, nor has he any consort by whom to be wronged and therefore also no one with whom he would be in love, nor anyone disobedient with whom he would be enraged, nor wiser of whom he would be jealous. 2. Since his Reality has none of these attributes, what remains except the Good alone? For just as none of the evils is in such a Reality as I have described so also will the Good be found in none of the others. For all the others are in all, both in the small and in the great and in each individual and in this Living Being which is greater than all of them and most mighty. For generated things are full of passions because Genesis itself is subject to passion, but where passion is, God is not, anywhere, and where the Good is, there is not even a single passion, anywhere. For where day is, night is not, anywhere, and where night is, day is not, anywhere. Wherefore it is impossible that the Good should be in Genesis; it is in the Ungenerated alone. But just as a participation in all things has been bestowed upon the matter, so also in the Good. In this way the Cosmos is good in that it also makes and does all so as to be good as regards its making and doing, but in all things else it is not good. For it is subject to passion and motion and is a maker of things subject to passion. 3. Now in Man, Good is graded by comparison with Evil, for the less degrees of Evil are accounted "good" but the "good" of this world is the least part of Evil. It is then impossible that the good of this world should be pure of Evil. For the Good in this world is becoming evil and while becoming evil it no longer remains

good, and not so remaining it becomes evil. The Good then
is in God alone, or rather, God himself is the Good. Only
the name, O Asclepius, of the Good is found among men,
the thing itself nowhere, for it is impossible. For it cannot
be contained in material body, pressed on all sides by wickedness and toils and sufferings and desires and rages and deceits and foolish beliefs and, what is worst of all O Asclepius,
that each of these which I have mentioned is firmly believed in this world to be the greatest good. But the un-
surpassable evil, the supplier of all evils, Error, is the absence in this world of the Good.   4. And I am grateful to
God who has put into my mind even an inkling of the
gnosis of the Good to the effect that it cannot possibly be
in this Cosmos. For the Cosmos is a plenitude of Evil, but
God of the Good and the Good of God. For the pre-
eminences [1] of the beautiful are in the neighborhood of the
Substance both more pure and more simple—possibly indeed they *are* his substance. For I must venture to say, O
Asclepius, that the substance of God, if indeed he has a
substance, is the Beautiful, but the Beautiful and Good
cannot be grasped by any of the things in the Cosmos. For
all things that fall under the eye are images and, so to say,
shadow-pictures, but the others are not things falling under
the eye, and especially is this true of the substance of the
Good and Beautiful. And just as the eye is not able to see
God, so also can it not see the Beautiful and Good. For
these members of God are complete, peculiar to him alone,
proper, inseparable, most lovable, which either God himself
loves or they love God.   5. If you are able to apprehend
God you will apprehend the Beautiful and Good, that which
is exceeding luminous, that which is thus illuminated by
God. For that Beauty is incomparable and that Good in-
imitable, just as God himself is. As you think God therefore, so also think the Beautiful and Good, for of them the
other living beings cannot partake because they are inseparable from God. If you seek after God you are seeking
after the Good, for one is the road which leads to him,

1. Possibly, the immediate emanations of God.

namely, godliness with gnosis. Wherefore those who knew
not and journey not along the way of godliness, dare to
call man beautiful and good, who has not even in dream
seen whether there is any Good but is preoccupied with
every evil and believes evil to be good and so employs it
insatiably and fears to be deprived of it and strains every
nerve not only to keep it but also to increase it. Such are
the goods and the beauties of men, O Asclepius, which we
can neither escape nor hate, for the hardest of all is this,
that we have need of them and cannot live without them.

IX. THRICE-GREATEST HERMES' DISCOURSE ABOUT THOUGHT AND SENSATION, SHOWING ALSO THAT IN GOD ALONE IS THE BEAUTIFUL AND THE GOOD, AND NOWHERE ELSE.[1]

1. Yesterday, O Asclepius, I delivered the Perfect Doctrine;
now I judge it necessary to expound in detail that which
follows thereupon, namely the doctrine of sense-perception.
For sense and thought are regarded as distinguished in that
the former is material, the latter substantial, but I regard
both as united and not sundered—in men, I mean. For in
the other animals it is sense that is united to their natures
but in men, thought. Now intellect differs from thought as
God from the Divine. For the Divine owes its being to God
and thought to intellect, being the sister of speech and each
the instrument of the other. For speech is not uttered without thinking, nor is thinking made manifest without speech.
2. So sense and thought stream into man simultaneously
each with the other as though intertwined, for it is not possible to employ thought without sense-perception or to perceive by sense without thinking, but it is possible to ap-

1. This tractate reflects Stoic and Platonic theses: God as demiurge,
an animate cosmos, salvation by Gnosis. There is no allusion to the
Ideas; no connection with Poimander; the author obviously knows
and attacks tractate six.

prehend intelligent thought without sense-perception, as do those to whom visions are presented in dreams. But I am of the opinion that in seeing dreams both these activities are concerned. For in waking life sense is divided between the body and the soul, and when both these parts of sense agree one with the other, then thought comes to view, being conceived by intellect. 3. For intellect conceives all the thoughts, good thoughts when it receives the seeds from God, and the contrary kind when from some one of the demons, for no part of the Cosmos is empty of a demon which, insinuating himself into him who is planted by God, sows the seed of his own activity and the intellect bears that which was sown—adulteries, murders, beatings of one's father, temple-robberies, impious acts, garottings, plungings over precipices, and all the other deeds of demons.

4. For the seeds of God are few but great and beautiful and good—virtue and temperance and piety. Now piety is the gnosis of God [1] and he that has come to know him becomes full of all the goods and keeps his thoughts divine and not like the many. Therefore those that are in gnosis do not please the many nor the many them; they are regarded as lunatics and incur ridicule, are hated and despised and possibly even murdered. For we hold that here is the proper dwelling of wickedness, being indeed its place, for its place is the earth, not the cosmos,[2] as some persons at times blasphemously assert. The godfearing man will endure all things in the consciousness of his gnosis, for all things to such a man, even though evil to others, are good, and when snares are laid for him he refers everything to his gnosis and he alone makes the evils good.

5. I return to the discourse about sense. It is human for man to participate in thought, but not every man, as I said above, enjoys thought. One man is material, another substantial, for he that is associated with wickedness and is material gets, as I have said, the seed of his thinking from the demons, but those who are associated with the Good get

1. Lactantius II 15 quotes this phrase.
2. This is a polemic against VI 3–4.

it substantially, being saved by God. For God is the maker of all things, and in making all things makes them indeed like himself and supervises them while they are becoming good by the performance of their function. For the course of the cosmos, as it grinds out the generations, gives them their characteristics, soiling some with wickedness, cleansing others with the Good. The cosmos indeed, O Asclepius, has a sense-perception and thought of its own, not like the human and variegated, so to speak, but in a different way superior and more simple. 6. For the sense-perception and thought of the cosmos is one because it makes all things and unmakes them into itself, being an instrument of God's will, and really made an instrument in order that, receiving the seeds from God and keeping them in itself, it might patently make all things and by dissolving all things renew them, and when they have been dissolved with this end in view, as Life's good husbandman, by its planting while revolving it provides them with renewal. There is nothing, therefore, upon which it does not confer life and by revolving it causes all things to live and is at once the place and the maker of life.

7. The bodies which come from matter are diverse, for some come from earth, some from water, some from air, and some from fire; but all are composite, some more so, some more simple—more composite are the heavier, less so the lighter. The speed of its revolution produces the variety of the diverse kinds of generations. For a breath which is exceedingly dense bestows upon bodies their qualities with a single filling—life. 8. Now God is the Father of the cosmos and the cosmos is the father of the things in the cosmos, and the cosmos is the Son of God and the things in the cosmos are the sons of the cosmos. And with good reason is it called Cosmos, for it adorns the totality of things with the variety of generation and with the uninterruptedness of life and with the unflaggingness of activity and with the velocity of Necessity and with the compounding of the elements and with the orderliness of all things that come into being. It then should both necessarily and properly be

called Cosmos. Now in the case of all living beings sense-perception and thought enter from without, breathing in from that which surrounds them; but the cosmos, after receiving them once for all simultaneously with its coming into being, receiving them from God, retains them.   9. But God is not, as some maintain, unknowable to sense and intellect—they blaspheme indeed by reason of superstition. For all things which exist, O Asclepius, are in God and through God they come into being and thence do they depend, some operating through the bodies, others causing motion through psychic substance, others giving life through spirit, others receiving things worn out. And with good reason, for the sense and thought of God are just this—his ever giving motion to all things. And there never will be a time when any of the existents will fail. Now when I say "of the existents" I mean "of God." For God contains the existents—I mean rather, not that he contains them but—I am declaring the truth—he is himself all things, not taking them to himself from without but giving them out from himself. And nothing is outside him nor is he outside anything.

10. If you ponder upon these things, O Asclepius, they will seem to you true; if you ignore them they will seem incredible. For to comprehend is to believe; to disbelieve is not to comprehend. Now my discourse just barely attains the truth, but intellect is great and, after being escorted by speech for a certain distance is able to attain the truth and after surveying the totality of things and discovering that they are concordant with the statements of speech, it believes and finds rest in this beautiful belief. To those then that have comprehended the statements above made about God, they will be credible; to those that have not, they will be incredible.

Let the above, no more, no less, suffice for sense-perception and thought.

XIII. THRICE-GREATEST HERMES' SECRET SERMON TO HIS SON TAT ON THE MOUNTAIN ABOUT REBIRTH AND THE PROCLAMATION OF SILENCE.[1]

1. In the General Sermons, O Father, thou didst speak in riddles and not distinctly when discoursing upon the Divine, nor didst thou reveal thy meaning in saying that no man could be saved before Rebirth. Further, when I became thy suppliant in descending from the Mount after thy conversation with me, and longed to learn the doctrine of the Rebirth, for this alone among all things I know not, thou saidst, when [2] thou wast on the eve of becoming a stranger to the world, thou wouldst give it me. Wherefore I have

1. This tractate is clearly by another hand than Poimander, for, whereas Poimander is promulgated as a revelation which Hermes the recipient is to proclaim to all men, the same doctrine of rebirth is here represented as the secret privilege of the few initiated. Hence the title, taken from the language of the mysteries. The author also aims to supplement the revelation of Poimander. Poimander represents man as a divine mind incarcerated in a material body; it is surrounded by evil passions which have been conferred upon it, during its descent from heaven, by the planets through whose spheres it passed, and which it must return to them after death, while ascending. There is an allusion to an Avenging Spirit who punishes the wicked, and to the Powers of the Ogdoad, but no further details. Here instead of seven, there are twelve evil passions; they are not the same as the seven, they are not implanted in or wrapped about the spirit while descending, but are evil spirits which enter into the body during life. They are in fact the Avenging Spirit. They must be expelled by the influx of the Ten Powers, which are here named. Clearly this is an expansion and modification of Poimander. Moreover the author refers to Poimander, and claims to have received the additional revelation there promised. He is, then, a later claimant to honors already given Poimander.

2. i.e., just before Hermes' ascension to heaven. With this tractate compare Philo, *The Migration of Abraham*, XXXI, 168–175, where mind ascends to God accompanied by the powers at first, led by the Logos, but finally keeping pace with his guide.

made me ready and have made the thought within m
strange to the world's deceitfulness; only, do thou fill up m
deficiencies with the teachings which thou saidst woul
convey Rebirth to me, setting them forth in speech or se
cretly. I know not, O Thrice-Greatest, of what kind o
womb or of what kind of seed thou [1] wast reborn.

2. The Womb, O Child, is Wisdom, conscious in silence
and the seed is the true Good.

Who was the Sower, Father? For I am altogether at ;
loss.

The Will of God, O Child.

And of what kind is he that is begotten, Father? Was h
indeed without share of the substance which is in me an
other than the Intelligible?

He that is begotten is God, Child of God; the All in All
composed of all Powers.

Thou tellest me a riddle, Father, and dost not speak a
father unto son.

This Race, O Child, is never taught, but whensoever i
wills its memory is restored by God.

3. Thou tellest me, O Father, things impossible and forced
hence would I have answers direct to these things. Am I ;
son of a nature strange to my paternal Race? Begrudge m
not Father: I am a true-born son; explain to me the manne.
of the Rebirth.

What shall I say, O child? I have naught to tell save this
While beholding within myself a certain Vision, not imagi
nary, called into being by the mercy of God, I find I hav
passed through myself into an immortal body and now an
not what I was before but have been born in Intellect. Thi
matter is never taught, nor can it be seen by this body o
thine which is moulded of the elements. And my origina
composite form has been dismembered. 4. I no longer pos
sess color nor do I have touch and dimension. I am strang
to them now. Thou "seest me," O Child, "with eyes" whei
thou dost observe with strain of body and of sight; not witl
these eyes am I now contemplated, O Child.

1. An emendation. The text reads: *man was begotten.*—Ed.

Into no little madness and frenzy of brain hast thou plunged me, O Father, for now I no longer see myself.

O Child, thou too hast passed through thyself, like those in sleep dreaming, without sleep.

5. Tell me this also, who is the Author of the Rebirth?

The Child of God, One Man, by the Will of God.

Now in addition, O Father, hast thou reduced me to speechlessness. For, bereft of my former mind, I behold thy Size, O Father, with the same distinctive figure.

In this thou art deluded too, for the mortal form daily changes, for with Time it turns to waxing and waning, seeing that it is a Lie.

6. What then is true, O Thrice-Greatest?

That which is never made turbid, O Child, that which cannot be bounded, which is colorless, formless, inflexible, naked, shining, perceptible to itself, immutable, incorporeal.[1]

I rave indeed, O Father. Just when I thought to be made wise by thee I find the senses of this mind of mine blocked up.

Thus is it, O Child. The one [sight] is upward bearing like fire, another is downward-bearing like earth [touch], and [another, taste, is] liquid like water, and [another, hearing, is] affected by breath as is air; how shalt thou sensibly apprehend Itself, that which is not hard, not liquid, that which cannot be constrained, that which never slips away, that which is only by power and activity apprehensible, 7. but [2] needing one who is able to apprehend the Birth in God.

Then am I unable, O Father?

Nay, God forbid, O Child. Withdraw into thyself and it will come; *will,* and it will come to pass; make idle thy body's senses and it will be the Birth of the Divinity; cleanse thyself of Matter's irrational Avengers.

Have I indeed tormenters within myself, O Father?

Not a few, O Child, nay fearful ones and many.

1. Intended to exclude the conception of God as space, this passage is important as a clear formulation of *spirit.*

2. Or, It requires only mind to apprehend the Birth in God.

I do not know them, Father.

One torment, O Child, is this Ignorance; second is Grief; third, Intemperance; fourth, Desire; fifth, Injustice; sixth, Avarice; seventh, Deception; eighth, Envy; ninth, Guile; tenth, Anger; eleventh, Rashness; twelfth, Malice. These are in number twelve, but under them there are many more, O Child, and through the prison-cell, the body, they compel the inner Man to suffer sensibly. 8. Now these depart, though not all at once, from him that has found mercy with God, and this constitutes the method and the theory of the Rebirth. And now, my Child, keep still and solemn silence. Thus shall the mercy of God towards us not cease. Moreover rejoice, O Child, seeing that thou art being cleansed by the Powers of God for the articulation of the Word.[1] There has come to us the Gnosis of God; when it has come, Ignorance is driven out. There has come to us Gnosis of Joy; when it has come, O Child, Sorrow will flee away to them that give it room.

9. I invoke a Power in addition to Joy—Self-Control. O Power most sweet! Let us receive it, O Child, most gladly. How with its coming hath it chased Intemperance away! And now a fourth I invoke, Firmness, that power which is directed against the Desires. This Step, O Child, is the Seat of Righteousness, for behold how without a judgment it hath driven out Injustice. We have been justified, O Child, seeing that Injustice is gone. A sixth Power I call to us, that which is directed against Avarice, namely Sharing. And now that Avarice has left, I invoke Truth. Flee, Deception, Truth is arriving. See how the Good is fulfilled, O Child, now that Truth has arrived. For Envy hath gone from us and unto Truth is joined the Good as well, with Life and Light. And no longer doth any Torment of the Darkness attack, but vanquished they have flown away with whirring wings. 10. Thou hast learned, O Child, the manner of the Rebirth. When the Ten is come, O Child, which driveth out the Twelve, the Intellectual Birth is complete and we are deified by that Birth. Whosoever then doth by mercy obtain the

1. i.e., as shown by his ability to articulate the secret hymn (?).

Birth according to God, upon abandoning the body's sensation recognizeth himself as consisting of these and rejoiceth.

Made steadfast by God, O Father, I mentally behold, not by the sight of the eyes, but by the activity of Intellect through the Powers. I am in heaven, in earth, in water, in air, I am in animals, in plants, in the womb, before the womb, after the womb, everywhere. 11. But further, tell me this, how is it that the Torments of Darkness which are twelve in number, are repelled by ten Powers? What is the way of it, O Thrice-Greatest?

This tabernacle through which, O Child, we have just passed, is constructed by the life-bearing [1] Circle, and when it has been constructed [the Torments also are constituted] of [passions] twelve in number, of one Nature, of manifold appearance,[2] 12. for the misleading of men. But there are disjunctions among them, O Child, although conjoined in conduct, for in conduct Rashness is inseparable from Anger, yet are they nevertheless separable. It is not surprizing, then, that in accord with Right Reason they take their departure once for all when driven away by ten Powers, that is to say by the Ten. For the Ten, O Child, is soul-engendering. Now Life and Light are united where the number One, that of the Spirit, naturally is.[3] With reason then the One contains the Ten and the Ten the One.

13. Father, I see the All, and myself in the Intellect.

This is the Rebirth, O Child, to receive impressions no longer as regards the body which is extended in three dimensions through this doctrine of the Rebirth, upon which I have touched briefly, that we may not be betrayers of it all

---

1. Perhaps a pun, for the zodiac is meant.

2. In the text the sentence ends here. The emendations do not seem necessary. Twelve elements constitute the zodiac. The following phrase begins the next sentence. Newbold wrote: "I have done the best I can with this corrupt passage, but am not sure of the results."—Ed.

3. In Plutarch's vision of Timarchus, *De gen. Soc.*, there are four powers, Life, Motion, Generation, and Dissolution. The *unit* unites the first and second in the Invisible, νοῦς the second and third in the Sun, and φύσις the third and fourth in the Moon.

to the many to whom indeed God himself wills we should
not.[1]

14. Tell me, O Father, this body which is made up of the
Powers, has it ever dissolution?

Hush! and utter not impossibilities, else wilt thou sin and
the eye of thine Intellect will be quenched. The natural body
perceived by sense is far removed from this essential Birth.
The one is dissoluble, the other indissoluble; the one mortal,
the other immortal. Knowest thou not that thou art in thy
Nature God and Child of the One, even as I myself?

15. I have been wishing, O Father, to learn the Hymn of
Blessing which thou saidst I would hear from the Powers
when I reached the Ogdoad.

Just as Poimander foretold, Child, upon ascending to the
Ogdoad. Well dost thou haste to "strike thy tent," for thou
hast been made pure. Poimander, the Intellect of the Dominion, passed on to me no more than hath been written
down, knowing that of myself I should be able to apprehend all things and to hear whatsoever I would and to see
all things, and it was he that committed to me the doing
of noble deeds. Wherefore as in all, the Powers which are
in me sing.

16. Father, I would hear and wish to apprehend them.

Keep still, O Child, and listen to the Blessing which now
is fitting, the Hymn of the Rebirth, which I would not have
decided to disclose so readily were it not to thee, at the end
of the All; wherefore this is never taught but is kept hidden
in silence. Thus then, O Child, standing in a place open to
the sky, facing the southern wind, about the sinking of the
setting sun, make thine obeisance, and in like manner when
he is rising, facing the east. Be still now, O Child.

THE SECRET HYMN

17. Let every Nature of the Cosmos give attention to the
hearing of my Hymn. Open thou, O Earth, let every storm-
bar be opened for me. O ye Trees, wave not. I am about

1. Note how incompatible with Poimander.

ɔ sing the Lord of the Creation and the All and the One. Ɔpen, O Heavens, and ye Winds, stand still. Let the immortal Circle of God give attention to my word. For I am ɓout to sing him that created all things, that fixed the earth ɩnd hung up heaven and commanded sweet water to be ɪupplied by the ocean to the inhabited and the uninhabited ɛarth for the nourishment and possession of all men, that ːommanded fire to present itself for every deed of gods ɪnd men. Let us all together give the Blessing to him who ɪs exalted upon the heavens, Creator of every Nature. He ɪt is that is the Eye of the Intellect; may he accept the Blessɪng of my Powers. 18. Ye Powers that are in me, hymn ɣe the One and the All. Sing in unison with my Will, all ɣe Powers that are in me. O Holy Gnosis, illumined from ːhee, through thee hymning the Intelligible Light, I rejoice ɪn the Joy of Intellect. O all Powers, sing ye with me; sing ːhou, O Self-Control; O Justice, sing thou the Just through ɪme; O Community that is in me, sing thou the All through ɪme; O Truth, sing thou the Truth; Goodness, sing the Good. O Life and Light from us to you our Blessing goes. I give thanks to thee, O Father, Actuality of my Powers; I give thanks to thee, O God, Power of my Activities. Thy thought through me hymns thee. Through me receive the All in thought, a thought offering. 19. These are the cries of the Powers that are in me, thee the All they hymn, thy Will they perform. Thy Will from thee proceeds, to thee the All returns. Receive from all a thought offering. The All that is in us do thou, O Life, preserve; O Light, illumine; O Spirit, inspire; for thy thought is pastured by the Intellect. O thou Maker instinct with the Breath of Spirit, thou art God. These are the cries thy Man makes through fire, through air, through water, through wind, through thy creatures. From thy Aeon [1] have I found the Blessing, and of the object of my seeking I am by thy Wish relieved. 20. I have seen this Blessing uttered by thy will, O Father; I have placed it in my Cosmos too.

1. He is now in the Ogdoad and receives the Blessing from the Aeon just outside the Ogdoad.

O Child, say, "in the Intelligible Cosmos."

In the Intelligible Cosmos am I able, O Father, by thy Hymn to place it, and by thy Blessing hath mine Intellect been illumined. Moreover I also would send forth from mine own mind a Blessing to God.

O Child, not aimlessly.

21. What I behold in the Intellect, O Father, that I say. To thee, First Parent of my generation, God, I Tat send thought offerings. O God and Father, thou art the Lord, thou art the Intellect; receive thought offerings which thou wouldst have of me, for when thou willest, all things are accomplished.

Do thou, O Child, send an acceptable offering to the Father of all things, God, but add also, O Child, "through thought."

I thank thee, O Father, for having prayed that I should utter these praises.

I rejoice, O Child, that thou hast brought the good fruits forth of Truth, immortal offspring. And now that thou hast learned of me this lesson of Virtue, proclaim silence, revealing, Child, to no one the tradition of the Rebirth, that we may not be accounted informers. And now we both have given heed sufficiently, both I the speaker and thou the hearer. Thou hast apprehended thyself intellectually and our common Father.

PLOTINUS

NEO-PLATONISM is the culmination of all Greek philosophy. The problems that had arisen during the previous seven or eight centuries, the antagonisms of conflicting solutions, the commendable desire of the eclectics—however poor their practice—to choose the best from all thinkers, are, within the world of Greek thought, in large measure satisfied.

From Ammonius Saccas in Alexandria, Plotinus (205–270) received his philosophic instruction, inspiration, and perhaps the chief principles of his system. However, the extent of this indebtedness cannot be ascertained with accuracy, since Ammonius refrained from publication. When Plotinus was about forty years of age he made Rome his permanent residence and addressed himself to the establishment of a school. In addition to his seminars, where he developed his views by explicating the ancient texts, he wrote fifty-four tractates, which Porphyry after his death collected, edited, and rearranged into six groups of nine, for which reason they are called *Enneads*.

Porphyry, of course, was a disciple of Plotinus. Because of his introduction to Aristotle's *Categories*, translated into Latin by Boethius, Porphyry both kept alive logical discussion through the Dark Ages and in conjunction with other factors caused the Middle Ages to view the world in Neo-Platonic perspective. Although

Plotinus attacked Gnosticism, he does not seem to have been familiar with the main current of Christianity. Porphyry and later Neo-Platonists could not escape it. Porphyry himself argued that several books of the Bible were spurious; and Julian the Apostate, besides being an emperor, was a Neo-Platonic philosopher, and an opponent of the growing religion in both capacities. While Plotinus and Porphyry repudiated the superstitions of idolatry and were rationalistic in their approach to religious questions, Julian, although he considered the Homeric legends fabulous or allegorical, interested himself, along with the Neo-Platonic school in Pergamum, in theurgy and mystery religions. The formal history of Neo-Platonism and of Greek civilization ends with the mathematical school of Hypatia (-415) in Alexandria, and with the great Proclus (410–485) who with dignity closed Plato's Academy in Athens, and with some obscure Latin remnants in the west.

To be a culmination of a philosophical development, a proposed system must satisfy at least two conditions. First, there must be a dominating, integrating principle, for otherwise an attempt to sum up the history of opposing schools is mere eclecticism. There is no doubt that Plotinus had such a principle. But this is not all. Hegel, in the Preface to his *Phenomenology of Mind,* criticizes Schelling's "ecstatic enthusiasm which starts straight off with absolute knowledge, as if shot out of a pistol, and makes short work of other points of view simply by explaining that it is to take no notice of them." Hegel complains that this type of philosophy is but "the shapeless repetition of one and the same idea, which is applied in an external fashion to different material, the wearisome

reiteration of it keeping up the semblance of diversity."
The avoidance of monotonous formalism, therefore, requires not merely a dominating, integrating principle,
but also a content of concrete detail to be integrated.
Plotinus has this too.

As an illustration of careful attention to minutiae, mention might be made of the penetrating analysis of Aristotle's system of categories and their rejection in favor
of the five categories of Plato's *Sophist*. Or, to turn to
another field of investigation, mention might be made of
the medium presupposed by the transmission of light.
Aristotle had argued for such a medium, the transparent,
which, though not strictly visible in itself, was so by reason of extrinsic color; unaware, however, that light has
a finite velocity, he used the principle of actualization to
explain the change from the potential state of the medium,
darkness, to its actuality, light. The theory of Plotinus
does not admit a medium for sight. To be sure the universe is a continuum and there is no empty space: in this
sense there is a medium between the eye and an object,
but the medium is not essential to the explanation of vision. When a stone falls, it falls through the air, but no
one would argue that air is a medium essential to the
stone's fall. If a medium is required in the sense that the
object first affects the air with which it is in contact, and
this portion of air affects the contiguous portion, and so
on until the portion of air in contact with the eye affects
the eye, then three impossible consequences follow: we
would not see the object but only a portion of air; the
sensation would have occurred by contact, and, therefore,
the object if placed on the eyeball would be all the more
visible, a conclusion factually untrue; and third, if suc-

cessive portions of the medium were affected, then at night a distant fire or star, seen clearly, would illumine the air and dispel the darkness. The first of these three considerations betrays a fundamental motivation. Plotinus was, in the ancient sense of the word, a realist. The intellect and even the senses grasp their objects; no image stands between to prevent real knowledge of the objects themselves. To defend the possibility of knowledge against skepticism Plotinus therefore rejected not only the crude Epicurean form of image-transmission, but also the more refined theory of Aristotle, and even the theory of Plato whom in general he followed. The explanation he accepted is that of the sympathy of similar parts of the same universe. As Plato had taught in the *Timaeus*, with a few modifications adopted from Stoicism, the universe is a living being with a soul. Certain groups of parts in an animal, although relatively far apart in distance, are by reason of their similarity sympathetically affected. The parts in the intervening distance do not ordinarily suffer the same affection. Therefore they are not properly a medium of transmission. The two similar parts act the one on the other at a distance, and in some such way sensation is to be explained.

The theory of imagination, which may serve as a third illustration of Plotinus' attention to detailed investigation, comes still closer to the general principles which integrate and systematize all his thinking.

While in general Plotinus wishes to re-establish Platonism, and in the analysis of categories rejects Aristotle's ten for Plato's five, yet on the subject of imagination, concerning which Plato's remarks are distressingly brief, Plotinus does not hesitate to make good use of Aristotle's extended discussion. But it is a good use that Plotinus makes. Unlike Aristotle with his clean-cut distinctions, with his hard and fast line between one faculty and its inferior and superior, Plotinus because of his basic metaphysics tends to merge each faculty with its neighbors, or, perhaps more accurately, views all mental activity from the highest to the lowest as a continuous process.

Plotinus had also to take account of the Stoics. With their materialism they had defined both memory-images and sense-presentations either as impressions with elevations and depressions in the waxy substance of the soul or at least as qualitative, chemical changes. Guarding against Stoic materialism and the traces of behaviorism in Aristotle, Plotinus argued that sensation is an activity of an immaterial soul and not an affection, passion, or imprint in matter. The analogy of imprints on wax leads to many impossibilities both with respect to sensation and all the more with respect to imagination, memory, and thinking.

Although an untiring opponent of materialism, although an advocate of a form of spiritualism foreign to the twentieth century, he is by no means blind to the physical conditions of mental activity. A certain bodily organization inclines one to anger; and sick people are more irritable than the healthy. The soul causes fear, shame, and blushing, but it is the body and not the soul that experiences these effects. Emotion and imagination are frequently linked. The imagination of imminent death causes fear; so closely is imagination connected with bodily conditions that it is not in our power, and hence those who act under the influence of imagination and emotion are not free moral agents.

Consequently, and parenthetically, from Plotinus' ethical and mystical standpoint, imagination involves pollution and necessitates purification.

Each organ of the body is animated by the soul and receives power according to its fitness for its work. The origin of the activity of this power is in the brain. The work of the organs and of the motor and sensory nerves belongs strictly to the body; but without the soul and without its participation in the higher principle of reason the power would be lacking.

It cannot be denied, therefore, that Plotinus pays serious attention to the physical conditions of mental activity; but the question of imagination, once this more general view of the soul is accepted, becomes the question whether memory and imagination are functions of sensation. There are reasons for answering this question in the negative. In the first place, if one remembers concepts as well as sense objects, and if memory is the function of the faculty of sensation, it would seem that concepts would have to be sensed. In the second place, those who have the keenest sensation and those who are most brilliant in reasoning do not necessarily have the best memories.

But if memory is a separate function, must it not sense what it is to remember? Not exactly. The sense-presentation becomes, as in Aristotle's theory, a representation-image, so that memory belongs to the faculty of imagination, which is a distinct faculty.

If, however, images are the objects of memory, is it possible to remember conceptions and reasonings? This problem had confronted Aristotle and had not received a complete explanation. If every act of thinking produces an image, then memory of thought is as easily explained as memory of sense objects; but if not, another explanation must be sought. Concepts are strictly indivisible; an image of them is hard to imagine. Furthermore, since the mind is active, it always thinks even though we are not conscious of its activity. Therefore, so long as the concept remains indivisible and internal, it escapes our notice. To remember it, it must first be externalized, made discursive, and reflected as it were in a mirror. This is accomplished by expressing the thought in words, and it is the verbal formula accompanying the concept that is received into the imagination.

The notion of a verbal formula's unfolding a concept and substituting for an image deserves to be signalized. For Aristotle memory depended on the preservation of a sensible affection, and the continuance of the affection results, not from the activity of the soul, but from the physical condition of the organ. Sense objects are properly objects of memory, but concepts are objects of memory per accidens. The insistence by Aristotle that "recollection is a searching for an 'image' in a corporeal substrate," and that the effort to remember, if at first unsuccessful, frequently persists involuntarily by its own momentum, apparently did not satisfy Plotinus as an explanation of the memory of concepts. Certainly when one remembers the proof of a theorem, one does not see the chalk marks on a blackboard. Modern psychologists, in order to retain the general proposition that no thought is possible without imagery, have not only added auditory, gustatory, *etc.,* to visual images—quite properly—but have also extended the term imagination to kinaesthesia when other forms of imagery failed to sustain the proposition. Rather than use the phrase kinaesthetic images, in which the term image has lost all its original flavor, Plotinus prefers to explain the memory of concepts by the retention in the imagination of a verbal formula. That this is not merely a change in terminology that Aristotle might lightly have granted, may be argued from the fact that for Aristotle all images are natural and are the same for all men, while language is conventional and differs from nation to nation.

Underlying all these matters of detail is the basic position of Neo-Platonism. Reality is not reducible to inanimate atoms and void, but all the gross corporeal phenomena are reducible to a fundamental spiritual life. The most important levels of this life are three: the soul, not a passive recipient of impressions, but essentially active; above the soul, the mind, whose unceasing activity we perceive only when the bodily organs are properly disposed; and finally, above mind is the One, the ultimate source of all.

Obviously Plotinus opposes materialism. To say that determinate proportions of material substances produce life is to ignore the fact that the prerequisite of determination is an intelligent agent to decide the proportions and to supervise the mixing. It is still more difficult for materialism to account for sensation. The perception of an object requires the presence of the whole object in the entire soul, not a part of the object on one end of the soul and another part on the other end; therefore the soul must be unitary and unextended. The unity, and hence the immateriality, of the soul is also required for the synthesis of disparate sensations. With these and

many other arguments Plotinus attacks the atomism of
Democritus, the materialism of the Stoics, and the refined behaviorism of Aristotle.

While all these arguments apply to the souls of individual men, it is not in individual men that the soul
in its purity is seen. In ordinary men the soul is sullied
by irrational desire; in a wise man passion has been de-
feated, a measure of purification has been attained, and
the soul's divine nature, which links it with the higher
world, shines forth more clearly. And the more virtuous
a soul it is that we study, the more obvious is it that the
soul is a divine and immortal reality. The more obvious
is it also that the individual souls are parts of, or derive from, a higher, purer soul, the world-soul, which,
unlike the souls of men, never experiences any evil.

Since the individual souls are products of the world-
soul and always remain in contact with it, they are medi-
ately united with each other. This raises the question
how one human soul can have an experience or sensation without every other soul's being aware of it. The
solution is not difficult. Although the same soul pervades
the universe, its combination with one body is not identical with its combination with another body. As in the
case of Ideas, humanity moves when one person moves
and remains at rest in another person, so also the same
soul may have a sensation in one body and be unconscious of it in another body. Or, to use another illustration, when one burns the left hand, the right hand experiences no pain. And further, while the world-soul
affects its parts—the individual souls, some individual
experiences no more affect the world-soul than sub-
limenal stimulation affects the individual person.

If the soul, however, even the world-soul, were the only principle, it would be impossible to account for even ordinary human intelligence. Soul of itself, brought to perfection, is the production of life, but life does not automatically produce intellect. Whenever there exists a soul displaying intelligence, it is clear that a higher principle has been at work. The potential never becomes actual by chance; there must always precede an effective principle to induce actualization. Therefore, above soul one must posit the Divine Mind or, what is the same thing, the world of Ideas. To appreciate the identification of the mind and the objects of thought is difficult for the untutored in any age; to those who are tutored in modern idealism it may be confusing. One should particularly guard against using one's own mind as an illustration of the Divine Mind and a sense object as an illustration of an object of thought. In Neo-Platonism the objects of mind are not sense objects but concepts, and since the essence of mind is thought, since the Divine Mind is always actual, there cannot be, as in the case of a human mind and a sense object, any separation of the mind from the objects which completely characterize it. Or conversely, suppose that the mind and its objects were not the same, and that the essence of the mind were separable from its thought. On such a supposition the mind would be only potentially intellectual, while in itself it would be unintellectual. Therefore the Divine Mind and its objects, the Ideas, are inseparable. In modern idealism the mind alone is ultimate and its ideas are its creations. But Plotinus writes, "Not by its thinking movement does movement arise. Hence it is an error to call the Ideas intellections

in the sense that, upon an intellectual act in this principle one such Idea or another is made to exist." [1] It is
true that the thoughts of the mind are Ideas, but it is
untrue that the Ideas exist because the mind thinks
them.

These Ideas, however, this Divine Mind, is still not
the highest principle of all. For in this realm, duality
remains. Since the Ideas are distinct from each other,
there is multiplicity. In knowledge there is always a
subject and a predicate, a knower and an object known,
and hence duality. But duality is secondary to unity.
Therefore it still remains to climb the steep ascent of
heaven to the source, the One. The climbing of the
ascent and the resting on the summit, let it be noted,
are not the same thing. The rational processes of philosophic dialectic demonstrate the necessary existence of
the One. He who has felt the urge to unity can never
rest in plurality, and is forced to posit a source superior
to all diversity. But if we are to know that source and
not just infer it, we must experience the One in mystic
vision. Four times during the six years of Porphyry's
study under him, Plotinus enjoyed this communion. Of
the many persons who have experienced trances, visions, or states of exaltation, some deliberately induce
the state by self-hypnotization or even by violent physical
frenzies. Such methods were alien to Plotinus; indeed
he did not seek the vision at all, he studied and the
vision was graciously vouchsafed to him. Then the
ordinary conditions of consciousness are suspended and,
having become oblivious of self and the world, the soul
sees the One alone. The soul no longer knows whether

1. V ix 7.

it has a body, and cannot tell whether it is a man, or a living being, or anything real at all. In this happiness the soul knows beyond delusion that it is happy; delusion there cannot be, because Truth has revealed itself and nothing is truer than the True. The vision is a direct contact with the One, a divine illumination. All knowledge is rather like our sight of sense objects on a cloudy day; in the vision we see the Source of the light which made knowledge possible, and we see it directly in all its brilliance. No other light illumines the Source, but, as in the case of the sun, so here we see it by its own light, directly and immediately. This experience is not abnormal, it is but the exercise of a faculty which all have though few use. He who has seen, says Plotinus, knows what I mean.

During the vision there is neither time nor power for reasoning and reflection, but afterwards one may talk and make judgments about the experience. The experience itself cannot be written down, it can only be experienced; the place of the experience, and the position of the One in philosophy, can none the less be designated. And that place is at the apex of the whole system.

PLOTINUS

IV iii. DIFFICULTIES CONCERNING THE SOUL

23. Each part of the body illumined and animated by the soul participates in the soul in its own peculiar manner. And according to the fitness of the organ for its work the soul gives it a power suited to that work. 5] Thus/ the power in the eyes is that of sight; the power

of hearing is in the ears; of tasting in the tongue; of
smelling in the nose; and the power of touching is
present everywhere, for with reference to this type of
perception the whole body is present to the soul as an
organ.

10]   Since the organs of touch/ are in the primary nerves,
which also have the power of moving the living being
and from which this power distributes itself; and since
the nerves have their origin in the brain; that is where
[medical men] place the origin of sensation, desire, and
in general all functions of life; on the assumption that
15] where the/ organs take their rise, there is to be situated
that which uses them. But it would be better to say that
the origin of the activity of the power is there, for it
is at the point at which the organ begins to be in motion,
that the power of the operator, that power which is
suited to the tool, must, so to speak, exert its force; or
20] rather, not the power, for the power/ is everywhere; but
the origin of the activity is there where one finds the
origin of the instrument.

Accordingly, the powers of sensation and appetition,
since the soul is a sensitive and imaginative nature, have
reason above them, just as the soul by its lower part
neighbors on that which it is above. Thus the ancients
25] placed the soul/ in the uppermost part of every living
being, in the head, as being not in the brain but in that
principle of sensation by which reason is seated in the
brain. Something must be assigned to body, especially
to that which most of all receives the activity of body;
but also something that has no community with body
30] whatsoever must participate in that/ which is a form
of soul, of soul capable of accepting the perceptions
which come from the reason.

[Such must be the relative positions of these factors]
because the faculty of sensation is a sort of judge, the
faculty of imagination is quasi-intellectual, and appetition and desire follow upon imagination and reason.
Accordingly, discursive reason is not in the brain as in

a place, but because what is there participates in it. And
35] the meaning of/ localization with respect to the faculty
of sensation has been explained.

29. Are we then to refer memory to the faculty of sensation so that the faculty of memory and faculty of
sensation will be the same? But if the shade [1] remembers also, as was said, the faculty of sensation will be
5] double, or if the faculty of sensation is not the/ faculty
of memory, but is another faculty, then that which
remembers will be double. Again, if the faculty of
sensation also deals with things learned, it will be the
faculty of concepts too.[2] Certainly these two must be
different. Shall we then assume a common faculty of
perception and give to it the memory of both [sense
10] objects and concepts]? Now if it is one and/ the same
thing which perceives sensibles and intelligibles, this
suggestion might amount to something, but [since this
reverts to the notion that concepts could be sensed] if
it must be divided into two, there will none the less be
two faculties. And if we give both to each of the two
souls [3] there would then be four. And in general, why
is it necessary to assign memory to that by which we
15] sense, so that both should belong to the same/ power;
and why must one assign the memory of things reasoned
about to that by which we reason? Those who reason
the best are not the same as those who best remember.
Those who benefit equally by sensation do not remember equally well; some have keen senses, but others
remember although their sensation is not so sharp.
20]   Now, in the next/ place, if each of these faculties is

1. The shade or ghost of Hercules in Hades, while his spirit at the
same time is with the gods.

2. Concepts could then be perceived by sensation.

3. The two souls are either the ghost in Hades and Hercules with the
gods, or the soul in the body and the soul detached and purified. The
latter pair is more in keeping with the general context. The *two* which
precedes and the *four* which follows must be faculties, and not memories,
as Bréhier supposes.

distinct, and if the one is to remember the things which
sensation has previously grasped, does it not follow that
memory must sense what it is to remember? [Not
exactly.] Rather, nothing will prevent the sense-image's
being a representation-image to that which will remember it; so that memory and retention belong to the fac-
25] ulty of imagination which is a distinct faculty. For/
sensation culminates in imagination; and when sensation no longer exists the visual image is present to the
faculty of imagination. If, then, the imagination of an
absent object is already in this faculty, it is remembering, even if it endures but a short time. If it remains
a short time, the memory is brief; when the image remains longer, people with the greater strength of this
30] faculty remember better,/ because the image is not easily
changed, with the consequent disappearance of memory. Memory, then, belongs to the faculty of imagination, and such are the objects we remember.[1]

We should explain the differences among memories
either by the differences among the powers themselves,
35] or by exercise or the lack of it, or by bodily admixtures/
inhering or not, which do or do not cause qualitative
changes and disorders. But these matters are discussed
elsewhere.

30. But what about [the memory] of reasonings? Does
the faculty of imagination deal with these also? If indeed an imagination follows upon every act of thinking,
then, perhaps, when such an imagination, like an image
5] of an object of thought, endures, there might thus be/
memory of the thing known. But if not, another explanation must be sought. Perhaps that which is received
into the faculty of imagination is the verbal formula

---

1. Bréhier translates: "The memory of sense objects belongs, therefore, to imagination." It is true that so far only sense objects have been
mentioned; the emphasis, however, is not on sensation, but rather on
images. Therefore, the word *such* refers, not to sense objects, but to
images, and the question of the memory of concepts is left open for
discussion in the following chapter.

which accompanies the concept. For the concept is indivisible, and not yet externalized it remains internal
and escapes our notice. But speech, by unfolding it and
leading it from the state of a thought to the faculty
of imagination, exhibits the thought as in a mirror, and
10] thus/ we have the perception of it, its conservation, and
memory. And therefore, since the soul is always thinking, we have perception whenever it arrives at this stage.
For thinking is one thing, but perception of the thinking is another; and while we always think, we do not
always perceive. This is because the recipient not only
receives thoughts from above, but also sensations from
below.

31. But if memory belongs to the faculty of imagination, and both souls are said to remember, there will be
two faculties of imagination. When the two are separate
such is the case, but when they are the same thing in
us how can there be two and in which of them does
5] imagination occur? For if it occurs in both/ there will
always be two imaginations, for it is not true that one
of them deals with intellectual objects and the other
with sensible. For such an arrangement would in every
case result in there being two persons having nothing in
common with each other. If, then, in both, what is the
difference? And how is it we do not perceive the difference? [There are two possibilities.] When the one is
10] in agreement with the other, so that the/ faculties of
imagination are not separate, though the better dominates, there is but one image, with a sort of shadow
accompanying in the other [faculty], like a dim light
merging into a greater. But when they conflict and
discord arises, the lesser becomes perceptible by itself;
15] but we fail to notice that it is in another/ because also
in general we fail to notice the duality of the souls. For
the two form a unity in which the one drives the other.
The one sees all things, and when it leaves [the union
with the other soul in the body] it retains some images
from the lower stage but dismisses others, just as we

remember little of the conversation of our inferior
20] friends after we have changed to others of higher rank,/
whom we keep in mind very well.

IV vii. ON THE IMMORTALITY OF THE SOUL

1. Is every man of us immortal or do we perish completely? Or do some parts of man pass away in dis-
persion and destruction while other parts, which are
truly the man himself, endure forever? This question
may be answered if one conducts his investigation ac-
5] cording to nature. Man is hardly a simple/ being, for
there is in him a soul and he also has a body, regard-
less of whether the body is our instrument or whether
it is connected in some other way. With this distinction
we must consider the nature and reality of each of the
two parts. Now the body is itself a composite and
10] reason/ shows that it cannot endure. Sensation perceives it in process of dissolution, of casting away, and
of suffering all sorts of loss. Each of its constituent
elements returns to its original state, and one part destroys another, changes it into something else and destroys it, especially when the soul which effects harmony
15] is not present in the/ masses. Even if each constituent
which is subject to becoming is singled out, it is not a
unity, for it admits dissolution into form and matter, of
which by necessity even the simple bodies are composed.
And further, since everything corporeal has magnitude,
it must submit to destruction in that it can be cut and
20] broken into small parts./ Consequently if this is a part
of us, we are not completely immortal; but if it is an
instrument, nature would have given it to us as such for
a certain time. But the chief part, that is the man himself, is either related to body as form to matter or as a
user to his instrument. In either way it is the soul
which is the man himself.[1]

1. Chapters 2–8 criticize in detail all opposing theories, including that
of Aristotle, which views the soul as form or entelechy.

9. [Besides body which comes into being, passes away, but never truly is] There is another nature, having its being of itself, completely and truly being, which neither comes into existence nor is destroyed. Otherwise all sense objects would vanish, and with this nature destroyed nothing later would come into being, for it is the cause of the preservation both of sense objects in
5] particular/ and of the world as a whole, ordered and preserved by soul. For as a principle of motion which furnishes motion to other things, it is self-moved, and as giver of life to besouled bodies it has life of itself, an indestructible life because it has it of itself. For not all
10] things/ use a derivative life. Otherwise there would be an infinite regress. But there must be some nature primarily alive, which needs must be indestructible and immortal, because it is the source of life for the other living things. Here also must be fixed all that is divine
15] and blessed, living of itself and self-existent, primal/ being and primal life, with no share in change of substance, neither coming into being nor perishing. For whence could it come or into what could it be dissolved? And if we must take in strict truth the attribute of reality, it cannot be sometimes existing and sometimes non-existent; just as white, the color itself, cannot be sometimes/ white and sometimes not-white. Now
20] if white were being, with its being white, it would be ever-existent. But it is only white. But that to which being is present of itself and primally, that will always be. This being, accordingly, primal and always existent, is nothing dead like a stone or piece of wood, but it
25] necessarily lives, and/ it enjoys a pure life to the extent that it remains alone. However, when it is commingled with the worse, it experiences difficulties with reference to the best; still its proper nature is not destroyed and it resumes its original state in returning to its own nature.

10. That the soul is generically the same as the divine and eternal nature is clear from the fact that it has

been shown to be incorporeal. It has neither shape nor color, nor can it be touched. But the same can also be shown from the following considerations. Since we
5] agree/ that everything divine and truly existent enjoys a life that is good and wise, we must examine next, from our own soul, what is its nature. Let us then take a soul, not as in a body beset by irrational desires and
10] disturbances and receptive of other passions, but as/ purified from these things and so far as possible without commerce with the body. This sort of soul makes it clear that evils are added to the soul from without, and that in the purified soul the virtues inhere, wisdom and other virtues, as its proper attributes. If then the soul is such a being, when it comes to itself how can it
15] not have/ the nature of that which we said was divine and eternal? For since wisdom and true virtue are divine, they could not arise in anything base or mortal, but such a being is necessarily divine, inasmuch as the divine is with it because they belong to the same genus
20] and are consubstantial. Therefore, whoever of us/ is such would differ little, with respect to his soul, from superior beings, and is inferior only in so far as he is in a body. Therefore, also, if every man were such, or if a great number so exercised their souls, no one would be so incredulous as not to believe that the soul is alto-
25] gether immortal./ But as a matter of fact we frequently see that in most men the soul is impure so that we cannot consider it a thing divine and immortal. It is necessary, however, to investigate the nature of each thing by examining it in its purity, since any addition
30] is always a hindrance to knowing the thing in/ question. Investigate, then, by setting aside the additions, or rather, let the one who sets aside see himself, and he will believe that he is immortal when he beholds himself in the intelligible and pure state. For he will see a mind which sees not something sensible or mortal, but conceiving the eternal by means of the eternal in himself
35] sees everything in the intelligible realm and/ becomes

himself an˙ intelligible and brilliant cosmos being illumined by the truth which comes from the good which
sheds the light of truth on all intelligible beings, so
that frequently one thinks the following verse is well
40] put, "Hail, I am for you an immortal God," [1]/ because
he has risen to the divine and has gazed on his likeness to it. But if purification advances one in the knowledge of the best things, then the various kinds of
knowledge which are truly knowledge, [and their ob-
jects] are obviously internal. For it is not by running
around outside that the soul perceives temperance and
45] justice,/ but it sees them of itself, by reflecting on itself
and on what it was previously—it sees them like images
impressed on itself, which are covered with the rust of
time and which the soul polishes. For example, imagine
a conscious lump of gold; it has removed all its impuri-
ties; prior to this it was ignorant of itself, it did not
50] see that it was gold,/ but now, seeing itself isolated
from everything it may have once used, it is amazed,
and it is convinced that it needs no added beauty; it
itself is supreme if only it is permitted to be independent.

11. With respect to such a being, how could any sane
man doubt that it was immortal? A being, in fact,
which possesses in its own right a life which cannot
be destroyed. How, indeed, for its life is not an accidental addition, nor is the relation of the life to it the
5] same as the relation of heat/ to fire. I do not mean that
heat is an accidental addition to fire, but that, even
while not an addition to fire, to the underlying matter
of fire it is an accident. For by this matter fire can be
extinguished. But the soul does not possess life in this
manner; that is, there is not a matter or substratum

1. Mackenna translates this, *Farewell,* etc., as if "I" were leaving
this world and its associations. The verse comes from Empedocles, D.L.
VIII 62, where the sense is that Empedocles walks among and ministers
to his patients like a god. The greeting therefore is not *Farewell,* but
Hail, or *Rejoice.* Plotinus probably meant that even now we are gods.

on the one hand and on the other a life added to it to
10] produce a soul. For either/ life is reality and such a
reality is alive of itself, which is exactly what we are
looking for, and this is admittedly immortal, or else
as a composite it may be resolved again and again until
we come to something immortal which moves itself and
15] cannot possibly suffer death. Or if one say that life is/
a quality added to matter, one is forced to admit that
the source from which the quality came to the matter
is itself immortal because it cannot receive the opposite
of what it brings. Certainly, then, there is a single nature in actuality alive.

12. Again, if one say that every soul is corruptible, the
universe ought to have disintegrated long ago. But if
one soul perishes and another does not, for example, if
the world soul is immortal but ours is not, the cause
of this must be stated. For both of them are principles
5] of motion, both of them are alive/ in their own right,
and in thinking the things that are in heaven and above
heaven, in investigating everything that exists in reality,
even advancing on to the first principle, they both grasp
the same objects in the same way. The conception of
each object, which the soul of itself draws from the
10] objects it contemplates within itself, arises by/ reminiscence, and prior to incarnation gives to the soul its being. Since then the soul uses eternal knowledge, it too
is eternal. Everything that can be destroyed exists because of composition and naturally can be disintegrated
according as it was composed. But the soul is a single
and simple nature, existing in actuality by the fact that
15] it lives. In the soul, therefore,/ there can be no corruption. But it could perish—so they say—by division
and fragmentation. On the contrary, however, the soul
is not a mass nor a quantity, as has been shown. But
—they counter—it will be destroyed by change of quality. No, because qualitative change, if it result in destruction, removes the form while it permits the matter
to remain; and this type of modification can occur only

20] in a composite. If, then, the soul cannot be destroyed/ in any of these ways, it is necessarily indestructible.

V iii. THE HYPOSTASES WHICH KNOW

[Summary of 1 and 2: For one part of a being to know another part is not true self-knowledge; therefore, either a simple being can know itself or the notion of self-knowledge must be dropped. Sensation can grasp only external objects; can the human mind, or can the divine mind alone, know itself? [1]]

3. For sensation sees a man and transmits the image to the discursive reason. And what does this reason say? It will say nothing yet, but knows only and stands still; unless indeed it asks itself, "Who is this?"—if it
5] has met the man previously—and says/ by making use of memory that he is Socrates. But if it should explain the image, it separates the material imagination gave it. If it should explain whether he is a good man, it would speak out of the things it learned by sensation, but what it said about them would depend on itself because it has a standard of good within itself. How
10] does it contain the good within itself?/ Why, it is good by nature, and was strengthened for the sensation of good objects by the intellect's illuminating it. For this, the pure part of the soul, receives the traces of intellect which are imposed upon it.—Why then is this not intellect itself and the remainder from sensation downward will be soul?—Well, a soul must be able to
15] reason, and all these things/ are functions of the reasoning faculty. But why not finish the matter by giving self-knowledge to this part of the soul? Well, because

1. In Greek philosophy knowledge had regularly been explained by a comparison with sight; but if this is basic there can be knowledge only of external objects. Yet, since Socrates, the center of all good philosophizing was self-knowledge. Note that this is not a question of being conscious that one sees a tree; the question is, how can one "see" his self?

we gave it the investigation of external things, but we
consider that it belongs to intellect to investigate itself
and the things in itself.—But if someone should say,
20] "What prevents discursive reason from examining/ its
own contents by another faculty?"—Such a person is
not seeking the discursive or reasoning faculty but he
grasps pure intellect.—What then prevents pure intellect from being in the soul?—Nothing, we shall say.
But still, is it necessary to call it part of soul? No, we
shall not call it a part of soul; we shall say it is our
25] intellect, but it is different from/ discursion and placed
above it; none the less it is ours even if we may not
count it among the parts of the soul. It is ours and
not ours; therefore, we use it and do not use it; but we
always make use of discursion. When we use it, it is
ours; when we are not using it, it is not ours. What is
30] meant by using it?/ Can it mean that we become intellect, and talk like it or in accordance with it? No,
for we are not intellect; but [we judge] in accordance
with it by the primary part of discursive reason which
receives [its influence]. For we sense by sensation and
it is we who sense. Do we, then, reason in a similar
35] manner? Well, it is we who reason, and we/ ourselves
think the thoughts that are in the discursive reason; for
that [1] is what we are. But the activities of intellect
come from above just as those of sensation come from
below. This *we* is the chief part of the soul, a mean
between two faculties, a better and a worse; sensation
is the worse and the better is the intellect. It is agreed
40] that sensation/ is ours because we are always sensing;
but the case of intellect is doubtful both because we are
not always using it and because it is separated; and it
is separated because it does not incline toward us but

1. Bréhier: we are the thoughts. Zeller, p. 577, n.1: we are the
faculty of discursive reason. To the question, Do we reason in a similar
manner, Bréhier answers "Yes." Mackenna answers "No." The more
indefinite "Well" of this translation seems to follow the text more
closely, and the lines which follow clarify the hesitant answer.

we, rather, incline toward it by looking above. Sensation is our servant, but intellect our king.

4. But we also are king when we act in accord with intellect. This accord is two-fold: either we are filled with intellect by its characters' being written in us like laws, or we are able to see and sense it as present. And

5] we know/ ourselves in that we learn the other things [in intellect] in such a vision; or we learn, by the very power itself, the power which knows such an object; or we become it. Consequently he who knows himself is double: he is a knower of the nature of the discursive reasoning of the soul, and above this sphere, he becomes

10] intellect and/ knows himself by intellect. In this latter state, he no longer knows himself as a man, but he has become completely another person and has carried himself above, taking along only the best part of the soul, which, also, can alone soar to intellection, in order that someone there might deposit what he has seen.[1] But

15] doesn't the discursive faculty/ know that it is discursive and that it is conscious of external things, and that it judges what it judges by the standards in it, which it got from the intellect, and that there is something better than it which does not seek [2] [truth] but has [truth] absolutely? [Of course it knows all this,] but, then, what thing would it not know if it knows what that

20] thing is and what its functions are? [3] If, therefore,/ it says that it had its origin in intellect, and is second only to intellect, and is an image of intellect, having in itself all knowledge engraved as it were, as the engraver There engraved it, will it stop at this point when it knows

1. Mackenna translates this purpose clause, "And gives the man, once established There, the power to appropriate what he has seen." This interpretation is very doubtful, because once established There, we have no more need of what we have seen Here.

2. Mackenna gives the quite possible translation: "which it [discursive reason] has no need to seek, but fully possesses." Lines 20–30 might be understood so as to support MacKenna's interpretation.

3. And since it knows its own functions, it must have self-knowledge.

itself to this extent? Do we, by using another faculty,
see the intellect which knows itself; or is it by partici-
25] pating/ in intellect, since it is ours and we are its, that
we know intellect and ourselves? This is necessarily so,
since we are to know whatever in intellect knows itself. A man becomes a sort of intellect himself, when
setting aside the other phases of himself he looks upon
such an object by means of that object, and knows
30] himself by himself. In fact [we see ourselves] as/ intellect sees itself.

5. Then does one part of the self see another part of
itself?—But that means that one part would do the
seeing and the other part would be seen; and that
would not be self-knowing.—What, then, if every self-
knower be composed of homogeneous parts, so that that
5] which sees differs in nothing from what is/ seen? For
in this way if one part sees another part which is the
same as itself, it would see itself; for there would be
no difference between the part seeing and the part seen.
—Well, first, the division of itself is absurd, for how
can it be divided? Certainly not at random. And who
or what does the dividing? The part which decides to
10] do the contemplating, or the part contemplated?/ Secondly, how can the part which contemplates know itself in the part contemplated when it has decided to
contemplate? For there is no contemplation going on
in the part contemplated. Or if it knows itself, it will
know itself as contemplated, not as contemplating. Consequently, it will neither know all of itself nor know
itself as a whole. What it sees will be the contemplated,
15] but the contemplator it does not/ see; and thus it will
be another and not itself which it sees. [To the object
of knowledge] it must also add from itself the part
contemplating in order to have perfect self-knowledge.
But [1] if [the contemplator knows] the contemplator

1. Lines 17–28 give an excellent statement of the realistic theory of
knowledge. Truth is the possession of the objects themselves, not the
possession of their impressions, which act as a veil between knower and

also, [as distinguished from, or rather, in addition to
the contemplated] [he must also know] at the same
time the objects seen. Granting that the things contemplated exist in the contemplation, if [they exist
merely as] impressions of the objects, [the contempla-
tor] does not have the objects themselves. But if he has

20] them, it is not/ by seeing them as a result of having
divided himself, but they existed [in the contemplation]
before he divided himself and he contemplates and has
them. Therefore, the contemplation must be the same as
the object contemplated, and the intellect the same as
the intelligible. For if they were not the same, truth
would be impossible, for he who has objects different
from the real objects will have an impression [merely],[1]

25] and this is not/ true. For truth cannot belong to something other [than itself], but what it says, that it also
is. So then, intellect, the intelligible, and being are one,
and this is primary being. And also primary intellect
possesses the real beings, or rather it is identical with
them.—But if intellection and the intelligible are one,

30] how does that imply that whatever/ uses intellect
knows itself? For intellection will, as it were, surround
the intelligible, or be the same as the intelligible, but
still it is not clear that intellect knows itself.—But what
if the intellection and the intelligible are the same? For
the intelligible is a sort of activity; it is not a mere
potentiality, nor is it devoid of life, nor even is its life

35] and intellection added as to a different/ reality, such
as a stone or some inanimate object. No, the intelligible
is the primary reality. If, then, [the intelligible] is an
activity, the primary and most noble activity would be
intellection, a substantial intellection, for it is most true.
This sort of intellection, since it is primal and exists

---

object. Sextus Empiricus, as a true skeptic, had assumed a division between knower and known. Plotinus, like any true realist, attacks the
unexpressed basis of skepticism.

1. Or, he who has an impression will have an object different from
real objects.

primally, is the primary intellect. For this intellect is
40] not potential, nor is it itself one thing/ while intellection is something else, for thus again it would be essentially potential. If, then, it is an activity, and its
reality is an activity, it must be one and the same thing
with its activity. Now being and the intelligible are
one with this activity; and so all will be one: intellect,
intellection, and the intelligible. If, therefore, its intellection is the intelligible, it is itself the intelligible, and
so it will know itself. For it will know by the knowing,
45] which/ it itself is, and it will know the intelligible,
which it itself is. In both ways, then, it will know itself, both because the intellection is itself, and because
it itself is the intelligible known in the intellection,
which is itself.

6. The argument has demonstrated that there is something which strictly knows itself. In the soul it knows
after a fashion, but in the intellect it knows quite strictly.
For the soul knows itself because it depends on another, but intellect knows because it is itself just as it
5] is and/ by virtue of its own nature as it introspects.
For by seeing the existent objects [1] it sees itself, and
by seeing it is in activity, and the activity is itself, for
intellect and intellection are one. The whole intellect
knows as a whole; it is not a case of part knowing part.
Has, then, the argument demonstrated this position by
actual persuasion? We have necessity in the argument,
10] but not persuasion./ For necessity is in intellect, but
persuasion in soul. We seek, so it seems, rather to be
persuaded than to contemplate the truth in pure intellect. For as long as we were above in the nature of
intellect, we were satisfied with our thinking; and by
reducing all things to one, we beheld. For it was the
intellect which was thinking and talking about itself;
15] but the/ soul was quiet, giving place to the activity of
the intellect. But when we are come here again to the
level of soul, we seek some persuasion as if we wished

1. i.e., the Platonic Ideas.

to contemplate the archetype in an image. Perhaps, then, it is necessary to teach our soul how the intellect
20] can contemplate itself, or at least to teach it to the/ part of the soul which is in a sense intelligent, which we identify as the faculty of discursive reason, and by naming it so signify that it is a sort of intellect,[1] or that it has its power by and from the intellect. This, therefore, it is fitting to know: how discursive reason knows what it sees and understands what it says. If it were
25] what it says, it would by that fact know itself./ Since the things it sees and says are above or come to it from There, whence also it itself proceeds, it follows that, because it is a logos and grasps objects of the same quality [2] and harmonizes them with the traces [of intellect] in itself, it knows itself in this fashion. Let it therefore place the image beside the true intellect which
30] is identical with truths thought,/ the true and primary beings, because such an intellect cannot be outside itself; so that if it is in itself and with itself and is just what it is—an intellect, [for an intellect could never be unintellectual] it must necessarily know itself, be-
35] cause it is in itself and its function and essence/ are nothing else than pure and simple intellectual existence.[3] This is not a practical intellect, for since practice has regard for externals and does not remain in itself, it will have some sort of knowledge of externals, but if it is wholly practical such an intellect could not have self knowledge. But where there is no practice—for there is no desire of an absent object in pure intellect —there introspection of self not only appears plausible,

1. By etymology.
2. i.e., Because it is a reason, it grasps reasons.
3. The line of argument in lines 18–35 Bréhier summarizes as follows: La connaissance discursive consiste, on l'a vu, à rapporter les traces des intelligibles en nous aux intelligibles eux-mêmes: attenuez, puis supprimer la distance qui sépare ces traces de leur modeles; au lieu de la connaissance affaiblie de l'intelligence par la pensée discursive, vous aurez la connaissance de l'intelligence par elle-même.

but indeed self-knowledge is necessary. For what else
would its life be, released from practical cares and
existing in intellect.

7.—But, we might say, it is contemplation of God.—
But if anyone admits that intellect knows God, he will
be compelled to agree that it knows itself also. For it
will know all that it holds from God, the things God
5] has given, and what God can do./ In the knowing of
these things it will also know itself. For it itself is one
of the things given, or rather, it is all of the things
given. If, therefore, it knows God and his power, it
will, in its self-knowledge, know that it has come from
There, furnished with its particular abilities. But [1] if it
10] cannot see/ God clearly, since the act of seeing and the
object seen are identical, then all the more there remains for it self-seeing and self-knowing, if the act of
seeing is the very object that is seen. For what else
could we give to it? Repose, of course. But for intellect
repose is not a departure from intellect; the repose of
15] the mind is/ an activity which brings freedom from
other things. Even in the case of other things, at least
those whose existence is not potential but actual, when
they have rest from what is foreign to them there remains their own activity, and even more so than before. Now, existence [for intellect] is an activity; and
since there is nothing toward which this activity is directed, it must be directed toward itself. By thinking
20] itself, therefore,/ it restrains its activity to itself and
with itself. And even if anything is produced from in-

1. To this point Plotinus' argument against the religiously orientated
arguments which emphasize the vision of God more than self-knowledge
is clear: if one knows God, he must know himself. Bréhier understands
the remainder of the argument, to line 25, in the same way. But this
would concede too much to the opposing view. Let us, therefore, divide
the argument into two parts, (a) if we see God, we know ourselves—
the ad hominem argument,—and (b) if we do not see God, since what
we see is our seeing all the more we must know ourselves, if truth is to
be possible.

tellect, it is because of its activity in and toward itself.
For it must first act in itself before it can direct its
activity toward something else, or have something proceed from it like itself. For example, only the fire which
25] is first fire in itself and has the activity of fire/ can
produce its own likeness in something else.

And so, to repeat, the intellect is an activity directed
upon itself; but the soul, so much of it as turns toward
intellect, is, as it were, internal, while that part outside
of intellect is directed toward externals. On one side
it resembles that from which it came; on the other side,
30] although unlike its source, none the less it is similar/
even here, whether it engages in practical activity or
production. For even in practical activity it nevertheless
contemplates, and in production it produces forms like
perfect intellections, so that all things are traces of intellection and intellect. They all proceed in conformity
with the archetype and those that are nearer imitate it
35] better while the last preserve an obscure/ image.

8. What are the characteristics of the intelligible which
the intellect sees, and what are its own characteristics?
We must not look for an intelligible as if it were the
color or shape of bodies. For intelligibles exist before
these do. Now the seminal reasons which produce colors
5] and shapes/ are not to be identified with the colors
and shapes, because they are by nature invisible. And if
these are invisible, the intelligibles are still more so;
and there is an identity of nature between the intelligibles and the beings which possess them, just as the
seminal reasons and the souls which have them are alike
in nature.—But the soul does not see what it has.—No,
because it is not the producer but an image of its source
10] as are the reasons also. The source is the/ clear, the
true, the primarily existent, a source, of itself and by
itself. But the soul, unless it arises from another being
and resides in it, cannot continue in existence. For an
image must be the image of something and reside in
something, unless it remains attached to the model.

Therefore, it does not see because it does not have suf-
15] ficient light; or if it sees, then, since its perfection lies/
in another it sees another and not itself.

However, none of this is There; the seeing and the
thing seen are together and the thing seen is such as
the seeing and the seeing is as the thing seen. Who,
then, will say what it is like? The one who sees; and
20] it is intellect which sees. Since even here sight is a light,/
or rather, is unified with a light, it sees light; for it sees
colors. But There vision occurs not through a foreign
medium, but through itself, because it does not see an
external object. One light sees another light, but not
through another medium. Thus a light sees a light;
therefore it sees itself.

25] This light, shining in the soul, illumines it; it/ makes
the soul intelligent, and makes it similar to itself—the
light above. And so, there has arisen in the soul a trace
of this light. If, now, you think of a light similar to this
trace, but greater and brighter and more beautiful, you
will come near to the nature of intellect and the intelligible. Indeed, it is this illumination which has given to
30] the soul its/ brighter life, not its generative life. For,
on the contrary, it causes the soul to turn inward and
prevents it from dissipating; it causes the soul to love
the splendor in intellect. Nor its life of sensation, for
this looks outward to an object which it senses. But
35] he who receives that light of truth sees,/ as it were, not
so much visible objects as their contrary. It remains,
therefore, that the soul has acquired an intelligent life,
a trace of the life of intellect. For There is truth.

Life in the intellect is also an activity, the original
light, giving primary illumination for itself, and shin-
40] ing upon itself, at once that which shines and/ that
which is shone upon, the truly intelligible, that which
thinks and that which is thought, seen by itself and
needing nothing else in order to see, but sufficient to
itself for seeing. For it itself is what it sees. We know
it by virtue of itself, for our knowledge of it comes into

45] being through it. Otherwise how would we be able/ to talk about it? Its nature is such that it grasps itself clearly, and we grasp it through itself. By such arguments our soul rises toward the intellect and asserts itself to be the image of the intellect, because the soul's life is an image and resemblance of the intellect, and

50] when it thinks it becomes divine/ and intellectual. If anyone asks it what is the character of that perfect and complete intellect, which primarily knows itself, it will come into the intellect or give place to the activity in the intellect whose contents it guards in its memory. It

55] will show that it has the same contents. Since it is/ an image, it can through itself see the intellect in some fashion, that is, by resembling intellect to the degree of exactitude with which a part of the soul is able to resemble intellect.

9. For him who is to know what intellect is, it is necessary, so it seems, to contemplate soul and the most divine part of soul. This perhaps will be accomplished if you first separate the body from the man, your true

5] self; then set aside the soul/ which informed the body, and of course sensation, desires, anger, and other such foolish things because they decidedly incline us toward that which is mortal. The remainder of the soul is what we called an image of intellect, preserving some of its light, just as from the sun, below the sphere of its

10] magnitude, comes that around it,/ illuminated by it. Now no one asserts that the light of the sun exists within itself about the sun, since it sets forth from the sun [as well as] remaining around it; but there is always one light proceeding out of the one before it, until it reaches us on earth. It must be remembered, however, that all [the light] about the sun exists in some other

15] [substratum] in order not to admit a space/ void of body below the sun. But the soul, a sort of light from intellect and residing about intellect, depends on it and does not exist in another [substratum] but [is centered] around that intellect, nor does it have place. For neither

has that intellect.[1] The light of the sun is in the air, but
20] the soul is pure, so that of itself it is seen by itself and/
by any other such being.

In its own right it investigates intellect by reasoning,
but intellect studies itself without reasoning. For it is
always present to itself, but we are present to it only
when we turn towards it. For our life is divided, and
there are many lives, but intellect has no need of any
other life or of other things; the lives which it fur-
25] nishes/ it furnishes to others, not to itself. For it does
not need inferior things; nor does it furnish to itself
the lesser thing when it has everything; nor the traces
when it has the primary beings—or rather, not *has*
them but *is* itself these things.

But if anyone is unable to have the primary life of
pure intellection, let him take the faculty of opinion
30] and/ rise from there. But if not even this, let him take
sensation, which attends to the forms as they are more
extended in space—sensation both of itself with its powers and as already existing in the forms.[2] But if anyone
wishes, he may descend even to the reproductive soul
and to the things it produces. From there he may then
35] ascend, from the last/ forms [on the lowest end of the
scale] to the last forms in the other direction, which
are rather the first forms.

V ix. ON THE INTELLECT, THE IDEAS, AND
BEING

1. [Some men, bound to the region of sense, assert
that pleasure is the good; others rise to the conception
of virtue, but limit themselves to a practical life; but
others, of a race divine, ascend above the clouds and
darkness to the region of truth.]

1. For a discussion of lines 7–18, cf. *The New Scholasticism*, Vol. XII,
No. 1, January 1938, pp. 66–68.
2. Bréhier understands this to mean both potential and actual sensation.

2. What kind of a place is it? And how can one get there? He who is by nature a lover and who truly possesses the disposition of a philosopher from the start, he will arrive there, in travail for the beautiful, however,

5] because he is a lover, not captivated by the beauty/ of the body, but fleeing thence to the beauties of the soul, which are virtue, knowledge, fine deeds, and lawful activity; and again he will mount to the cause of the beauties in the soul, and if again there is anything prior to this, he will continue to the end, the first, which is

10] beautiful in itself. When he arrives at/ this point his birth pangs will cease, but not before. But how is the ascension undertaken? And whence comes the ability; and what instruction will teach this love? Is it not as follows? This beauty which attaches to bodies is accidental to them, for these bodily forms exist in them

15] as in matter. For when the subject changes/ it turns from being beautiful to being ugly. The argument shows then that it was beautiful by participation. What then makes a body beautiful? In one sense the presence of beauty, in another sense the soul which fashions them and introduces this form into them. What then? Is the soul of itself beautiful? No, it is not. For one soul

20] is wise and beautiful and another is foolish/ and ugly. So then beauty in the soul comes by wisdom. And what is it that gives wisdom to the soul? Is it not of necessity the intellect? Not an intellect which is sometimes intellect and sometimes without intellect, but the true intellect. And this is beautiful of itself. Must we here make our stand as if we have arrived at the first term, or is it necessary to go beyond even intellect? Now

25] intellect/ precedes the first principle in relation to us, and standing as it were in the vestibule of the good,[1] it of itself announces all things, for it is the image of that good, although it is multiple and the good remains a unity.

1. There are many verbal reminiscences of Plato in Plotinus. Here cf. Philebus 64 c.

3. We must investigate this nature of intellect which the argument shows to be real being and true reality, having previously made certain by another method that such a nature exists. Probably it would be ridiculous
5] to ask whether/ there is an intellect among things that exist, although some might perhaps question even this. But it is more profitable to ask, if it is such as we have described, and if it is separable, and if intellect and the things which exist are the same, and if here we have the nature of the forms—these are the questions which confront us now. Now we see that all the things
10] we say exist are composites, and/ none of them is simple, whether made by art or constituted by nature. For artificial objects have bronze, wood, or stone, but are not complete in these until a given art makes of them a statue or bed by introducing its own immanent
15] form. And also the natural/ compounds, of which some are very complex and are called mixtures, one analyses into the elements of the mixture and the form imposed on them. For example, man reduces to soul and body, and body to the four elements. And each of these is a
20] composite of matter and form, for the matter/ of the elements, of itself, is without form. Hence one must search whence the form comes upon the matter. One must ask whether even the soul is a simple being or whether it has something analogous to matter and something else like form, whether the intellect in it is similar to the form imposed on the bronze and in another sense similar to him who imposes the form on
25] the bronze. Applying the same/ considerations to the universe one must there also rise to, and posit a truly productive intellect and demiurge; and one must say that the substratum which receives forms becomes fire, water, air, or earth, but that these forms come from
30] another. This other is soul. It is soul/ which gives to the four elements the form of a cosmos; but the intellect provides the soul with the logoi, just as the arts provide the souls of the artisans with the principles of

procedure. Intellect, in the sense of form of the soul, has respect to shape, but in another sense intellect furnishes
35] the form as a sculptor furnishes the form of the/ statue in which there inheres all that he gives it. What intellect therefore gives to the soul is virtually real being, but what the body receives is already image and imitation.

4. Why then must one proceed beyond the soul rather than considering it the primary being? Well, first, intellect is different from and better than soul, and the better is naturally prior. For the ordinary conception, that soul when perfected begets intellect, is untrue. For how can a potential being rise to actuality unless there
5] is/ a cause to bring it into actuality? If it were by chance, it might not come to actuality. Therefore it is necessary to assert that the primary beings are actual, independent, and perfect. Imperfect beings are subsequent to these, and become perfect by reason of their
10] generating causes, which are similar to fathers/ who perfect their children which at the beginning were born imperfect. In relation to the primary agent, they are matter which then becomes informed to its complete development. If now soul is passive, there ought to be something impassible, (otherwise everything would perish in time), therefore something must precede soul.
15] And if soul is in the cosmos, and if there/ must be something outside the cosmos, there must also be something prior to soul. For if what is in the cosmos is always corporeal and material, nothing would remain stable; with the consequence that man and all the logoi would neither be eternal nor remain the same. Thus anyone, by these arguments and many others, may see that intellect must be prior to soul.

5. We must take intellect, if we are to apply the term properly, not as a potentiality or as that which passes from an unintelligent state to an intelligent state (for then it would again be necessary to seek another intellect prior to this one) but we must consider it an in-

tellect in actuality and always real. Since, then, think-
5] ing is not a mere addition to it,/ if it thinks something,
it thinks it of itself; and if it has anything, it has it of
itself. Now if it thinks by itself and of itself, it is itself
what it thinks. For if its reality were other than the
reality of what it thinks, its own reality would be un-
thought and therefore would be potential instead of
10] actual. We must not then separate one/ from the other,
although we are accustomed to separate them on the
basis of our own subjective thinking. What is it, then,
that acts and thinks in such a way that we admit it to
be precisely the things it thinks? Obviously it is the
truly real intellect that thinks and conceives the realities. It is then the realities. For it will think them as
15] existing somewhere else or in itself and as being/ itself.
But somewhere else is impossible. For where would that
be? Hence it thinks them in itself and as being itself.
For they are not in sense objects as some believe. For
in no case is the sensible primary; for the form in sense
objects is an image placed on matter, and every form
in something comes to it from a source and is the image
20] of that source. And if/ it is also the maker of this universe, it will not think the forms in a universe which
does not as yet exist, in order to make that very universe. Before the cosmos, therefore, those forms must
exist, not as impressions from something else, but as
primary archetypes and as the reality of intellect. Now
if anyone says that the Ideas are sufficient, it is clear
that they are eternal; but if eternal and impassible, they
25] must exist in an intellect/ which is also such, and which
is prior to habitude, to nature, and to soul; for these
are potential. Intellect then is those beings which truly
exist [the Ideas] and thinks them not as they are elsewhere; for they are not before it nor after it; but it is
like a primary law-giver, or rather it is the law of their
existence. Thus it was correctly stated, "To think and
30] to be are/ the same thing;" and "The knowledge of
immaterial objects is the same as the object itself;" also,

"I investigated myself" as one of the real beings; and
"reminiscence." For none of the real beings is outside
or in space, but they remain ever in themselves subject
neither to change nor destruction. And this is why they
35] are truly real. Things which come into being and/ pass
away enjoy a spurious being, and it is not these but
that other which is true being. Sensible objects are what
they are called by participation; their underlying nature
has received its form from elsewhere, just as bronze receives its form from the art of sculpture and wood receives its from carpentry by means of an entrance into
40] them of an image of the art,/ while the art itself with
its own peculiar properties remains external to the matter and contains the true statue and bed. Thus it is
also in the case of bodies. And this universe shares in
images which are plainly not the real beings; the images
change but the real beings do not; they are established
45] in themselves and do not/ occupy space, for they are
not magnitudes, but have an intellectual and self-sufficient mode of existence. For the nature of bodies desires
conservation from another; but intellect, supporting by
its marvellous nature the things inherently contingent,
does not itself seek a foundation anywhere.

6. Let intellect, therefore, be the real beings. It contains
all things in itself, not as in space but as self-possessed
and as being their unity. All things there are together,
yet none the less they are separated. Since soul too,
which holds together many sciences in itself, has noth-
5] ing/ confused, and each science produces its proper
effect whenever it should, without involving the others,
but rather with each thought acting in its purity apart
from the other thoughts in the soul; similarly, therefore, and even more so, the intellect is all things together and also not together, because each thing is a
10] particular potentiality. But intellect as a whole contains/
all things in the sense that a genus contains species and a
whole contains parts. The powers of seeds illustrate what

is meant. For in the whole seed everything is contained undivided and the logoi are there as in a single center. Yet there is one logos for the eye and another for the hand, and these are recognized as different when seen 15] in the sense objects which they/ produce. Each of the powers in the seeds is a logos and makes with the parts contained in it a single whole. It has a corporeal matter, to wit, the fluid, but it itself is a form, a whole; and the logos is the same as the generative form of a soul 20] which is an image of another better soul./ Nature is what some call the soul in the seed; it springs from what is prior to it yonder, as light is derived from fire, and it nourishes and informs the matter, not by pushing nor by using levers, which people talk so much about, but by conferring reasons on it.

7. Some of the sciences which are in the rational soul deal with sensible objects (if they should be called sciences, when the name of opinion fits them better) and as posterior to things they are images of things. Other sciences deal with intelligible objects, and these are truly 5] sciences,/ for they come to the rational soul from the intellect and grasp nothing sensible. In so far as they are sciences, they are the very things which they think and they have within themselves both the object thought and the thinking, because the intellect, which is the primal beings themselves, is ever within itself and does not rise to actuality by straining toward what it does 10] not/ have or by extending its range or by making progress in an unfinished discussion, for these are affections of the soul; but intellect is established in itself, and is all things at once nor is it by thinking that it causes each thing to exist. For it is not when it thought God that God came into being, nor when it thought motion that motion began. For this reason also, to call 15] the forms thoughts, in the sense/ that the thing comes into being or exists upon the intellect's thinking it, is incorrect. For the thing thought must be prior to this

thinking. Otherwise how could the mind think it? For it is not by chance or at random that the intellect applies itself to an object.

8. If then the object of intellection is internal, that internal form is identical with the Idea. What then is this? It is an intellect, an intelligent reality. Each Idea is not other than the Intellect, but each is an intellect. And all the forms comprise intellect as a whole; each
5] form is each intellect,/ just as science as a whole is comprised of all the theorems, though each part of the whole is not spatially separated, but each has its function in the whole. This intellect, then, exists in itself, and holds itself at rest as eternal satiety. If one considers in-
10] tellect as prior to reality one must say/ that intellect by acting and thinking begets and perfects the realities. Since, however, it is necessary to conceive reality as prior to intellect, one must assume that the realities are in the subject which thinks and that the activity of intellection is in the realities as much as the activity of
15] fire is in fire, so that the internal Ideas have for/ themselves the intellect as their own activity. Reality also is an activity. Accordingly, for both there is one activity, or rather the two are one thing. Reality and intellect are thus one nature; and therefore also the realities, the activity of reality, and this sort of intellect are one; also the intellections so understood, the Idea the form of
20] reality, and the activity. Only in our conception/ are they separated and one made prior to another. For the separating intellect is one thing, but the indivisible intellect which does not separate reality and all things is another.[1]

9. What are those things in the unitary intellect which we separate by thinking? For it is necessary to present them as stable, just as we contemplate the contents of a unitary science. This world which is a living being
5] and which contains all living beings/ derives its ex-

[1]. Or: for the separating intellect is one thing; but the indivisible intellect which does not separate is reality and all things.

istence and character from another. This other is to be
traced back to intellect and therefore the archetype of
the world is to be found in intellect; and intellect is
that intelligible world which Plato in the *Timaeus* called
the living being. For when there is a logos of some
10] living being, and when there is a matter to/ receive
the seminal logos, then of necessity a living being comes
into existence; in the same way when there is an intelligent, all-powerful nature, and when nothing hinders,
or, when nothing intervenes between this nature and
that which can receive it, then of necessity the former
produces order and the latter is ordered. And the thing
on which order has thus been imposed has the form
15] which has been separated/ —in one case the form of
man, in another of the sun. But that which produces
order is all things in one.

10. Whatever is in sense objects as form came from
There; the remainder is not from There. Therefore
nothing contrary to nature is There; just as nothing contrary to art is in art neither is lameness in the seed. A
5] deformity of the feet/ sometimes occurs in birth when
the logos does not control, and sometime it is an accidental maiming of the form. Harmonious qualities and
quantities, both numbers and extensions, generations
and conditions, actions and passions if all these are
according to nature, motions and rests, are There both
in general and in particular. But instead of time, there
is eternity; and place There becomes logical inclusion.
Since all things There are together, whatever you may
grasp is an intelligent reality and each one shares in
life, both same and other, motion and rest, the moved
and the arrested, reality and quality—all these share in
15] reality. For each reality/ is an actuality, not a potentiality. Consequently the quality of each reality is not separated from it.[1]

1. The remaining few pages of this tractate are omitted.

VI ix. ON THE GOOD OR THE ONE

1. All existent things, every primary being and everything whatsoever that is predicated of being, exist in
virtue of the unit. For what could exist, if it were not
one thing? Separated from the unit, nothing would be
5] what it is called. For there is no army/ unless it is one;
neither is there a chorus or a flock unless it is one. Nor
is there a house or a ship that does not have unity,
since it is one house and one ship; and if the unity be
lost, the house will no longer be a house, nor the ship
a ship. Continuous magnitudes, also, if unity be not
present to them, cannot exist. For when they are di-
10] vided, insofar as their/ unity is destroyed, their existence changes. And further the bodies of plants and
animals are each one; if their unity is removed and
they are broken into a plurality, the reality which they
had would be destroyed, and they would no longer be
what they were; but they would become other things,
insofar as each is one. And health, too, exists when the
15] body is/ coordinated for unity; beauty, when the nature
of the unit holds the parts; and virtue of the soul, when
it is unified for unity and agreement. Well, then, since
the soul, by forming, molding, shaping, arranging,
brings everything to unity, must it be said, as we come
20] to soul, that soul furnishes/ unity and is itself the
unit? No, for soul gives other things to bodies and is
not what it gives, for example, shape and form. These
are different from soul, and thus, if it also gives unity,
one must consider that it gives what is different from
itself, and that it makes each thing a unit by contemplating the unit; just as by contemplating [the Idea
25] of] man/ it makes a man, grasping along with the
[Idea of] man the unity in that Idea. Each thing that
is called one, is a unit to the degree in which it possesses being. Consequently the less being, the less unity
it has; and the more being, the more unity. And of

course, soul, though different from the unit, has more
30] unity in proportion to its greater being. It really/ is a
unit, though not the unit itself, for soul is one, and
somehow the unity is its attribute; these, then, are two,
soul and [its] unity, just as body and [its] unity. That
which has intervals, like a chorus, is farthest from the
unit, continuous quantity is nearer, and soul participates
35] still more. If, because of the fact that without the unit/
soul could not exist, one should reduce soul and the
unit to the same thing, the first reply would be that
every other individual thing exists in virtue of the unit's
existence, and nevertheless the unit is different from
them. For body and unity are not the same; rather body
participates in the unit. Secondly, the soul is multiple
40] as well as unitary, even if it is not composed of parts./
For there are several powers in it, as, reasoning, desiring, perceiving, which are bound together by the unit
as by a chain. Soul, then, because it is a unit, imposes
unity on other things; but it also has unity imposed on
it by another.[1]

2. For particular beings, accordingly, reality and unity
may not be the same thing; but for existence and reality
as a whole, are not unity, being, and reality the same?
In which case one who discovered being would have
5] also discovered the unit; reality/ itself would be the
unit itself. For example, if reality were intellect, intellect would also be the unit and would be primal being
and primal unity, providing other things with existence
and, in the same measure, with unity. For what else
could the unit be except existence itself? For is it not
10] the same as being? For a man and one/ man are the
same thing. But this is like giving each thing a number;
just as you say a couple is two, so in the case of a
single thing, you say one. If, therefore, number is an
existent, obviously the unit will be also, and we would
have to discover what it is. But if number is a work

1. Bréhier notes that the Stoics identified soul and the unit; Aristotle
the intellect and the unit.

of the soul as it proceeds in counting, the unit will not
15] be found among existent things. But/ the argument
said, if anything loses unity, it will absolutely not exist.
We must see, therefore, whether in particular cases the
unit and being are the same, and whether being as a
whole is the unit. But if the being of each thing is a
plurality, and the unity cannot be a plurality, being and
unity must be different things. A man is a rational ani-
20] mal with/ many parts; these many are bound together
by a unity; therefore man and unity are distinct things
since man is divisible and unity is indivisible. And, to
be sure, being as a whole, containing all the existents
within itself is still more a plurality and different from
the unit, though it shares in the unit by participation.
25] Being possesses both life and intellect,/ for it is not a
dead thing; and therefore, being is a plurality. And if
this being is intellect, even so it is necessarily a plurality. And all the more so if it contains the Ideas. For
the Idea is not one, but rather a number, both each
singly and all together, and they are one as a cosmos
is one. In general, then, the unit is first, while the in-
30] tellect and the/ Ideas and being are not first. For each
Idea is a composite of many parts, and is therefore
posterior, for the components of any thing are prior
to it.

  That the intellect cannot be the first is evident from
the following considerations also. Intellect exists necessarily in the act of thinking; and the best intellect, that
35] which does not contemplate/ external objects, contemplates that which is prior to it, for in turning toward
itself, it turns toward its principle. Now, if it is both
the thinker and the thing thought, it will be double and
not simple. And, consequently, not the unit. If it contemplates an object other than itself, decidedly it contemplates a better and prior object. If it contemplates
40] both itself and the better object,/ even so it is second.
And it is necessary to consider the intellect to be of
such a character that it is present to the good and the

first and contemplates it, and also is present with itself
and thinks itself, and thinks itself as being all existent
objects. With such variety it is far from being the unit.
45] Accordingly the unit is not the totality of existents,/ for
it would then not be unitary; nor is it intellect, for
even in this case it would be all the things that the
intellect is. Nor is it being, for being is the same totality.
3. What, then, is the unit and what is its nature? No
wonder it is not easy to say what it is, since even in
the case of being and idea it is not easy, although our
knowledge is based on ideas. Insofar as the soul is di-
5] rected toward a formless object, it is unable to grasp/
anything because it is not determined and, as it were,
impressed by the vagueness of the object; therefore it
slips away in fear lest it possess nothing. Therefore it
is distressed in these circumstances and wishing for a
change it often descends and falls until it reaches a
sensible object where it rests as if on something solid,
10] as also sight, when weary with/ minute objects, turns
for a change to large objects. Now, when in virtue of
itself the soul wishes to see, since it sees only by being
present to its object and is unitary by being one with
its object, it does not believe it has what it was seeking,
because it [as thinking] is no different from the thing
thought. Nevertheless this is a necessary procedure for
15] one who would philosophize about the unit. Since,/
therefore, that which we seek is a unit, since we study
the principle of all things, the Good and the first, we
must not withdraw from the first objects and fall to
the last of all things; rather, we must make progress
and conduct ourselves away from sense objects, which
are last, toward those which are first. We must be re-
20] leased from all evil/ because we strive for the Good and
ascend to the principle within ourselves; and contemplating the principle and the unit we become one instead
of many. We must, therefore, become intellect, entrust
our soul to intellect and establish it there, so that the
soul may awake and receive what intellect sees. By

25] means of the intellect we must contemplate/ the unit
without any addition from sense and even without the
intellect's receiving anything from soul, but it is by intellect pure, in fact by the primary part of intellect, that
we must behold the purest object. Accordingly whenever a person who prepares for the vision of such an
object imagines that the nature of the unit involves magnitude, shape, or mass, it is not intellect which is guid-
30] ing/ his contemplation, because it is not the nature of
intellect to see such things; this activity belongs to sensation and to its concomitant, opinion. But one must
accept from the intellect the information as to what it
can do. Now intellect can see objects prior to it, its own
contents, and what issues from it. Its contents are pure
35] and simple,/ still more so are the objects prior to it,
or rather, the object that is prior to it.

Thus the unit is not the intellect, but prior to it. For
intellect is one of the existents; the unit is not a thing
but prior to each thing and is not a being. For even
being has a sort of form, the form of being, but the
unit is formless, without even intellectual form. Gen-
40] erative/ of all things, the nature of the unit is none of
them. It is neither a thing, nor a quantity, nor a quality,
nor an intellect, nor a soul. It is neither in motion, nor
standing still, neither in place nor in time; it is independent, of unique form, or rather without form since
it exists before every form, before motion, and before
45] rest./ For these concern being and make it many. Why,
then, if it is not in motion, is it not at rest? Because it
is to being that one or both of them necessarily attach,
and that which is at rest is so by participating in the
category rest, and is not identical with this category.
Consequently it would have an attribute and would no
longer remain simple. Then too, to call it a cause is
50] not to predicate/ an attribute of it but of us, because we
hold something from it, while it is self-contained. He
who speaks accurately must affirm of it neither this

nor that; he wishes merely to interpret his own feelings [1]
as he hovers around it on the outside, sometimes near
it, sometimes falling away from it because of the difficulties surrounding it.

4. The chief difficulty arises from the fact that consciousness of the unit comes neither by knowledge nor intellection, as is the case with the other intelligible objects, but by a presence which is nobler than knowledge.
The soul suffers, draws away from the unit, and is not
5] absolutely/ one, when it takes knowledge of something;
for knowledge requires speech and reason, and reason
is multiple. The soul thus passes beyond the unit and
falls into number and plurality. It is necessary, therefore, to go beyond knowledge and never to cease being
one; we must withdraw from knowledge, from the
knowable, from everything else and even from the con-
10] templation of the/ beautiful. For everything beautiful is
posterior to the unit and derives from it, just as all the
light of day comes from the sun. Therefore Plato said
it could be neither spoken nor written. But we speak
and write to direct people to it and to awaken them
from arguments to the vision, as if pointing out a road
15] to someone who wishes to behold something./ The instruction covers the road and the procedure, but the vision is the work of the one who has wished to see.

If some one does not arrive at the vision, and his soul
has no consciousness of the splendor There; if it has not
experienced or held in itself the amorous passion, as it
were, of the lover's vision when he finds rest in the
20] object of his love;/ if after he has received the true
light and all his soul is illumined by having come
nearer, still, in the ascent, he is held back by weights
which impede the vision, because he did not ascend
alone but took that which separates from it; or if he is
not yet made one, (for the unit is absent from nothing

1. Compare the anti-intellectual mysticism which for different reasons
became prominent in the post-Kantian period.

25] and/ yet from everything; consequently, although present, it is not present except to those who are prepared and able to receive it, so that they are fit and, as it were, able to grasp and touch it by reason of their similarity to it and the similarity of the power in them to that in it; whenever that power is in the same state as it was when it came from the unit, they are then 30] able to see, insofar as that object/ can be seen) if, therefore, he has not arrived, and remains outside because of these reasons, or because of lack of the propaedeutic instruction which brings faith with it; on all these counts let him accuse himself and, renouncing everything, let him try to be alone; where he fails in the arguments by reason of unbelief, let him consider the following.

* * * * *

9. In this dance we see the spring of life and the spring of intellect, the beginning of being, the cause of good, the root of soul. These do not diminish it by flowing from it, for it is not a mass. Otherwise the derivatives 5] would be corruptible. As a matter of fact, they are/ eternal because their source remains the same and is not divided among them, but remains entire. Therefore they too endure; just as light endures as long as does the sun. . . .

10. Once we have had the vision, why, then, do we not remain There? It is because we have not completely departed from here. But there will be a time when the vision will be continuous, no longer troubled by any bodily trouble. It is not that part of us which has the 5] vision which is troubled, but the other part,/ when the former loses the vision without losing the knowledge which comes in demonstration, conviction, and the reasoning of the soul. The seeing and the part which sees is not reason; it is greater than, prior to, and superior to reason, as is also the object of the vision. He who

10] sees himself when he sees,/ will see an object of this
character, or rather, by becoming simple he will be
merged with such an object and will sense it. Perhaps
we should not speak of *seeing*. The object of the vision
(since we must call these things two, the person seeing
and the object seen, for they are not both one; the statement is daring) this object the person who sees does
15] not then see, distinguish/ or imagine as two. He has
become another person; neither he nor anything of his
contributes there; becoming a part of it he is one with
it as a center is superimposed on a center. For truly they
are one when they meet, and are two only when apart.
Thus we now [1] call it different. Therefore the vision is
20] difficult to/ describe. For how can anyone explain that
it is different if, while experiencing the vision, he does
not see it as different, but as one with himself.

1. Now, that is, during the present discussion.